Women with Alcoholic Husbands

RAMONA M. ASHER

WOMEN WITH

Alcoholic

HUSBANDS

Ambivalence and the

Trap of Codependency

The University of North Carolina Press

Chapel Hill and London

This research was funded, in part, by a grant (1981–84) from
the Office of Alcohol and Other Drug Abuse, University of
Minnesota.

Library of Congress Cataloging-in-Publication Data
Asher, Ramona Marie.
   Women with alcoholic husbands : ambivalence and the trap
of codependency / Ramona M. Asher.
      p.   cm.
   Includes bibliographical references and index.
   ISBN 0-8078-2028-8 (cloth : alk. paper). —
ISBN 0-8078-4373-3 (pbk.: alk. paper)
   1. Alcoholics' wives—Psychology.   2. Co-dependence
(Psychology)   I. Title.
HV5132.A74   1992
362.29'23—dc20   91-27765
                                                          CIP

The paper in this book meets the guidelines for permanence
and durability of the Committee on Production Guidelines for
Book Longevity of the Council on Library Resources.

Manufactured in the United States of America
95   94   93   92   91   5   4   3   2   1

To

my parents, Gladyce A. and William H. Asher,

my children, Dawne and Lonny Gorrill,

and my granddaughters, Dasia and Dezerae,

for generations of love.

Contents

Preface   ix

Acknowledgments   xiii

Introduction: Outlining the Moral Career   1

Part 1
The Early Problem Phase

1   Recognizing the Ambivalence   19

Part 2
The Problem Amplification Phase

2   Sorting the Ambivalence: Acknowledging   27

3   Sorting the Ambivalence: Valuating   53

4   Sorting the Ambivalence:
Personalizing Experiences and Sentiments   86

5   Sorting the Ambivalence: Personalizing Stances   109

6   Notes on Maintaining the Ambivalence   125

Part 3

The Proximal Treatment Phase

7   Limiting the Ambivalence and Entering Treatment   137

8   Depersonalizing the Ambivalence   148

Part 4

The Post-Treatment Phase

9   Transforming the Ambivalence   169

Conclusion:

Sociological Insights, Implications, and Speculation   183

Appendix: Research Design and Methods   203

Notes   209

Bibliography   213

Index   219

Table 1. A Typology of the Moral Career of Becoming the Wife of an
Alcoholic and the Management of Definitional Ambivalence   8

Preface

The study from which this book evolved came out of curiosity about certain human experiences: How do persons deal and live with long-term serious problems? What is involved in the transformation of self-identity? And what are the dynamics in destructive/abusive relationships? For reasons largely of academic interest, familiarity, and opportunity, I decided that studying women married to alcoholics would be a fruitful avenue by which to explore these larger sociopsychological concerns. These interests then translated into related but area-specific questions: How do women who are married to alcoholics deal, on an everyday level, with their husbands' drinking? By what processes does a woman come to define her husband as alcoholic and herself as the wife of an alcoholic? And what meaning do these identifications have for her? I knew what the body of literature on women married to alcoholics said, and I knew what the alcoholism treatment industry said, but I wanted to know what the wives themselves thought and felt.

At that time I did not imagine the details nor chaos of intimate, lived experiences that I would come to see. I did not know that I would come to understand the women's experiences in terms of a "moral career." And, though a sociologist, I did not then fully apprehend the immense collective social implications of their otherwise highly personalized experiences.

Women with Alcoholic Husbands is about the lived experiences of wives from their own point of view and in their own words. I wrote this book for two reasons: first, to tell these women's stories, and second, to offer sociological insights into them. Women married to alcoholics have long been studied from an individualistic, psychological perspective; this book utilizes an interactional and cultural one. The women's experiences are cast in a social context.

The central theme of the book is not the experiences lived per se, but how a moral career is fashioned from them. *Moral career* simply means that the self is intricately involved and dramatically influenced. A moral career is comprised of strands of experiences that challenge, disrupt, and eventually change self-definitions. In this moral career the wife not only encounters challenges to definitions of her husband, she also encounters and creates new designations for herself as well: he is eventually designated an alcoholic and she a "codependent" wife of an alcoholic. This book traces a moral career and the social contingencies that shape it.

A significant contribution of this book is that it turns the table, so to speak. Rather than posing the usual question of the woman's role in her husband's alcoholism, it asks, How does this alcoholic-complicated process impact on the wife? Perhaps most important, it allows persons in alcoholic-complicated marriages and families and those who counsel them to better understand the dynamics of their lived experiences. This book takes the reader through the moral career of the wives: the early problem phase, the problem amplification phase, the proximal treatment phase, and, finally, the post-treatment phase.

This book comes out at a time when the mass acceptance and culture of codependency appear at an all-time high. It seems that one can scarcely go a week without hearing or seeing something about codependency from one source or another. Yet in both the traditional academic sector and its applied practice sector, a critical minority voice has emerged. This voice calls for a closer look at the concept of codependency and for rethinking collective thought and action toward women married to alcoholics. My work is in this second vein, and the voice with which it speaks is intimately linked to the women's actual experiences. That these experiences comprise a moral career, replete with both personal and public dimensions, is a new step in the direction of rethinking codependency.

But now I am getting ahead of the story. Few of the women in this study saw themselves as codependents until after they entered some kind of rehabilitation program. When I first met and interviewed them, they had

long been trying to understand their husbands, themselves, and their experiences—in their own terms—in the face of horrifically challenging and
contrary circumstances.

These are remarkable women with remarkable stories. Their fortitude in
coming to grips with themselves and their lives, in ultimately getting off the
well-worn paths that they neither envisioned nor desired when they were
first married, casts them as warriors of a new kind. The old ideas of the
"mad" warring wife who drives her husband to drink are replaced with
those of women fighting for survival and quality of all they hold dear.

I salute the women who participated in this research and their thoughtful, introspective responses. Many of them said they were telling their
stories in hopes that they might enlighten and help others in similar situations. Their stories go well beyond helping only other women in alcoholic-
complicated relationships, I think; their experiences provide, for all of us,
insight into personal interaction, social definition, and collective action.

Acknowledgments

The simple truth is that I could not have undertaken this research and writing without the help of others; I have received much help in the way of both material and emotional support. First, I am indebted to the women who agreed to be interviewed, not just once but three times, and to the rehabilitation agencies that helped me meet them. The women gave generously of their experiences, energy, and time, often going to great lengths to meet for second and third follow-up interviews. They openly shared their mental, emotional, and physical space with me, and I am both touched and appreciative; though I have not seen them since, they remain in my mind and my heart. Second, Dennis Brissett was instrumental as mentor and procurer of funds. He continues to give steadfast support in time and energy for scholarly and editorial critiques as well as friendship. He, more than anyone, has been with me, and for me, from the beginning of this endeavor. Others who have offered intellectual refinement along with moral support are Gary Alan Fine, Harold Finestone (now deceased), and Robert W. Gibson, as well as Luther Gerlach, Mark Snyder, and two anonymous reviewers. No doubt I have also been aided from ideas and refinements raised in numerous conversations with untold persons over the years.

Peter Cattrell, my former officemate for five years, was a tremendous source of encouragement and comradeship during those intense years of graduate school, fieldwork, and initial formulation of this project. Along these lines, Deborah Felt, Barbara Joyce, and Anita Kozan also deserve thanks.

Technical assistance in typing the manuscript was provided at different stages by Kathy Malchow and Cindy Mudrak. Coming into the home-stretch, Ginny E. Hansen supplied expert editorial assistance and, with Susan Smith, both praise and comic relief. Rebecca Stegehuis, my niece, electronically entered the final manuscript, in its entirety, with great speed, skill, and cheerfulness. My now-adult children, Dawne and Lonny Gorrill, deserve recognition and thanks for their outstanding performances and many sacrifices demanded by my studies and field research during their own busy teen years. In addition, Lonny helped with library research in the later stages of manuscript preparation.

My husband, Finn G. Jorgensen, has been a constant source of compas-sionate support and revitalization during the trials and small victories, and long workdays of analyzing, writing, and rewriting. I have felt explicit and implicit support and encouragement for my work in my academic and friendship circles, a buoyancy that has sustained me over the period of bringing this research to fruition. One of my favorite sayings—I believe attributed to R. D. Laing—is that the trouble with most people is that they have no *in*visible means of support, and in that respect I consider myself to be very fortunate indeed. Finally, I am thankful for the always pleasant and helpful assistance from my editors at the University of North Carolina Press: Paul Betz for his cordial initial, and enduring, balance of enthusiasm and objectivity, and for his editorial recommendations; Sandra Eisdorfer for managing the many details of manuscript processing and production; and Stevie Champion for diligent, crisp, and kind copyediting. Thank you to all of you!

Ramona M. Asher

Women with Alcoholic Husbands

Introduction

Outlining the Moral Career

"To have and to hold from this day forward, for better, for worse. . . ." These are the vows that join women and men in marriage. These vows can wreak havoc in hearts and minds when a marriage is laden with problems and fulfillment is missing. This book is about such experiences. It is a study of the lives of women married to alcoholic men. It is the story of how these women meet their special challenges and how they endure the often long, treacherous road to intervention and treatment of the problem.

A major challenge these women face is the problem of defining the situation, of discerning answers to the question, What's going on here? A woman married to an alcoholic has much to take into account as she creates and adjusts her view of herself, her husband, and their situation through problematic times. The process of coming to view one's husband as an alcoholic is often a drawn-out experience of emotional and social turmoil. It can include financial hardship, legal entanglements, difficulties with employment, emotional and physical deterioration, pronounced changes in social networks and activities, extramarital sexual relations, marital separation, and public intervention. This study examines two major aspects of living in an alcoholic-complicated marriage:[1] coming to define the problem as alcoholism, and constructing a life for oneself before and after such designation.

The fifty-two women married to alcoholics who took part in this study had quite common sociodemographic characteristics for the seven-county metropolitan area of the Midwest in which they lived. They ranged in age from nineteen to sixty-eight years, and a majority of them had had some college or completed college degrees. Most of the women worked full-time outside of their homes; about one-third were full-time homemakers. Although all of the women were married at the time of this study, three-fourths of them were living with their husbands and one-fourth of them were living apart from their husbands. The number of years they were married ranged from less than one to thirty-six, with an average of eleven and one-half years married and two (2.3) children. A majority of the wives were Protestant and all but two were Caucasian.

Some caution should be exercised in generalizing the findings of this study to all women married to alcoholics. First, the total universe of this group is unknown, making it impossible to obtain a representative sample of women married to alcoholics. Second, this study sample is not a random sample of the subgroup of all wives attending family programs. However, women in the sample did not differ in sociodemographic characteristics from other women in the family program clientele of the three treatment centers from which this sample was drawn. This research illuminates the social and moral experiences of the women in the study group, though it reasonably sheds light on the experiences of wives of alcoholics generally who, with their husbands, eventually seek conventional alcohol-related rehabilitation programs.

These women do not suddenly discover their husbands' alcoholism. Subjective interpretations, husband-wife negotiations of definitions, and a variety of third-party influences contribute to the process of defining troubles (Emerson and Messinger 1977). The ultimate designation is usually preceded by a long and painful process of eliminating other temporarily plausible explanations for the husband's behavior.[2] His apparently uncaring actions, for example, often lead to self-doubt and a wife may reproachingly say to herself, "Maybe if I were a better wife [mother/homemaker] he wouldn't be doing this." Many wives come to believe (partly because their husbands may tell them so) that their husband's drunkenness is a statement of contempt toward them. As one wife put it: "I feel I've been real humiliated for years and [that I] took a lot of blame, that I was a pretty dumb person. . . . So I want to get on my feet and [develop] some self-esteem."

Perhaps a wife notices changes in her husband, and without understanding the changing dynamics of their interaction, she nonetheless becomes a confused and irritable participant in it. As one woman explained: "His personality just started changing . . . through a crisis, a family crisis, and the drinking kind of scared him. I think it made him more angry, whereas before when he was drinking he was happy-go-lucky. And he was . . . completely opposite of what he normally is, and he just had a lot of anger and resentment that I never saw before. It just got to the point where we were constantly fighting. It was like the both of us not even being able to deal with life anymore . . . it got to that point."

In the midst of responding to their husbands' drinking, women find that the routine task of creating viable everyday lives for themselves can become a major struggle. One woman's poignant reflections illustrate the many strands in the web of the definitional enterprise:

My husband is an alcoholic. He has been for twenty years, so I have been to the part of my life where I didn't want it to, shall I say, worsen. After many, many threats, which of course he was calling wolf all the time, the divorce wasn't a threat; it was, . . . "I've had it!" I wasn't sure, I mean, if there was love anymore, and I'm still not sure. I'm still confused, very confused about that. But I did have papers served on him and, immediately, he came in here [the treatment center] himself after many, many years saying that he was going to and never doing anything about it. I didn't feel that I should put him here or force him to go in. I wanted him to do it on his own and he didn't, obviously.

So when the time came, I just decided on the divorce and he did it. I'm still not sure whether I'm going to cancel the divorce or not; I still have mixed feelings and this has [brought] a lot of hurt, a lot of emotional problems. They say, you know, you can forgive but you can't forget. Well, it's been a lot of things to try to forgive. They keep creeping up, constantly creeping up.

Financially, I discovered that I don't need him; he misses a tremendous amount of work. And I think, why should I have to put up with this anymore? And you're not really too sure of when love turns to pity and when it all gets up and walks out the door. I've got a lot of problems I've got to work out myself, and that's basically where I am.

Twenty years . . . I hate to throw it all away if there is the slightest chance. I'll work along with him and go to Al-Anon and meetings and these classes and see what comes and just take one day at a time, but I've got a funny feeling that it's a little late.

A variety, like these, of mental, emotional, physical, and material ups and downs together form a continuous stream of experiences that comprise a particular period or segment of these women's lives. It is a period during which a wife's views of herself, her husband, and their marriage are disrupted, evaluated, and redefined. The term *moral career* describes such a period of self-challenge and change (Goffman 1962).

Moral Career

The word *moral* in the term *moral career* refers to the significance that human conduct has for one's sense of self. Things moral intimately involve selves. A moral career can be thought of as a special career of the self. Dramatic challenges to self-definition occur in such a way that social relationships and interactions are upset or disrupted and a new label for self-definition is eventually applied to the person experiencing the moral career. This label may be applied by others, by oneself, or by both. For example, the women in this study were eventually labeled *codependent*,[3] a currently popular term for spouses and others close to alcoholics.

We will trace the strands of the moral career of the women in this study as they move from defining selves and situations as relatively normal with routine problems of living to viewing themselves as participants in alcoholic-complicated marriages—as wives of alcoholics. We will see, from their perspectives, the social situations that comprise the moral career of becoming the wife of an alcoholic. Neither these wives nor most others readily know that they are on a moral career path of becoming the wife of an alcoholic. It is an analytic concept that represents the nature of their experiences. A moral (self) career has a relative beginning and ending, and it is moral because it involves serious challenges and changes, if not personal and interpersonal crises. The social beginning of the career of becoming the wife of an alcoholic is designated as when she first defines her husband's drinking as problematic (defined retrospectively in the first interview of this study), quite aside from any physiological beginnings of a state of alcoholism.

The Definitional Enterprise

Although social psychologists tend to accept the claim that "situations defined as real are real in their consequences" (Thomas and Thomas 1928, 571), it seems all too readily assumed that people already have arrived or easily arrive at their definitions, or that they emerge self-evidently from shared meanings during interaction. However, the women in this study faced cumulative problems of defining ongoing situations in which there were competing plausible definitions, accentuated by the lack of a dominant definition and/or by rapidly changing definitions. I refer to this as a situation of *definitional ambivalence*.

The management of definitional ambivalence is the "trouble" with which a woman married to an alcoholic must first deal. A key struggle and challenge in the moral career of becoming the wife of an alcoholic is to sort out, sift through, and arrive at views of selves and situations among competing and changing definitions. Any uncertainty or vagueness in meeting this definitional challenge is not so much a matter of the wives not knowing what they think or feel but, paradoxically, a matter of keen awareness of competing plausible possibilities.

This moral career is marked by agitation in the struggle to arrive at a stable definition of the situation. This is not surprising when we consider that definitions enable us to order our lives, to make sense of things, to take actions. Much as nature abhors a vacuum, humans seem to abhor a situation without a definition. The lack of either a sensible or a shared meaning pushes us toward establishing it.[4] When we appreciate the intricate relation between thoughts (definitions) and actions (and, conversely, between indecisiveness and inaction), the practicality of defining activity is more fully apparent. Definitions help us say who we are and help us manage our social worlds; definitional ambivalence stymies us.

Ambivalence

At times almost everyone experiences being of "two minds" about something or someone. This is what social scientists call *ambivalence*. The most common understanding of ambivalence as the simultaneous presence of conflicting emotions such as liking and disliking the same object is primarily psychological, with its emphasis on feeling states. A sociological conceptualization of ambivalence has to do with contradictions around the expectations and performances of our own and others' social roles.

Within the field of sociology there are various approaches to ambivalence. Merton (1976) emphasizes the structural aspects of "sociological ambivalence" by viewing it as incompatible expectations of attitudes, beliefs, and behaviors having to do with social status. Coser (1966) elaborates on this by suggesting that sociological ambivalence emerges from contradictions arising from one's role partner. Stebbins (1967) cautions that the audience in the situation is an important link to any incompatible expectations.

What is missing from these conceptualizations of sociological ambivalence is recognition of the ever-present self-other interactions and interpretive processes necessary to take account of the contradictions and incompatibilities of role expectations and performances. I suggest that the concept *definitional ambivalence* better sensitizes us to the dynamic processes of interaction and interpretation and to situations in which contradictions and incompatibilities may arise because of a multitude of plausible competing definitions. Definitional ambivalence includes the dynamic processes of interpretive challenge and emergent action characteristic of human experience.

We might think of human life as involving routine definitional ambivalences that we handle fairly easily and disruptive definitional ambivalences that pose serious problems and require special strategies of management and resolution. It is this more extraordinary, disruptive kind of ambivalence that usually emerges in the experience of women married to alcoholics. Indeed, it is the seriousness and disruptiveness of the definitional ambivalence that weave the experiences into a moral career. These ambivalences are disruptive in isolation but especially so through accumulation, enough so that the wives begin to question selves, behaviors, and situations.

Ambivalence of definition thus is a dominant feature of the moral career of becoming the wife of an alcoholic. These women face circumstances of dramatically changing interactions that require ongoing reformulation of their views of self, husband, marriage, and "the problem." As we get into the moral career of the wives in this study, we will see that a variety of interactional and cultural factors made it difficult for them, effectively and durably, to reduce the burdens of conflicting expectations in their alcoholic-complicated situations.

Within this moral career, the women face challenges of definition in two ways. First, they must arrive at a definition, literally, for any given situation. For instance, is a husband's drinking behavior in a specific situation associated with any particular social or personal factor? Second, over time a kind of overall or pervasive definition that abides across situations is necessary in order for these wives to construct an ongoing sense of continuity in everyday life. For example, is his drinking developing into a problem? If so, does it need resolution now? And what is the nature of the problem and anticipated solution?

Thus, there is a cumulative effect built into a moral career that is characterized by definitional ambivalence. When a wife's views of herself, her husband, and her marriage undergo several changes of definition, over time, this dynamicism itself amplifies any strain she is already encountering. Shifting winds of definitional ambivalence create transitions within the moral career. Transitional phases in the career are indicated by dramatic changes in how the women view their own selves, their husbands, and their marital relationships. Thus, the line of the moral career is related, throughout, to definitional ambivalence and the management of this ambivalence. For instance, during early phases the problem might be identified as social circumstances, inadequate selves, or a poor marriage; in a later phase, it might be called the disease alcoholism. Specialized activities for managing ambivalence are also associated with phases of the moral career. For example, activities that lessen and transform the troublesomeness of definitional ambivalence appear mostly late or midway in the moral career.

Table 1 represents a generally but not necessarily sequential ordering from phase I through phase IV of the moral career. Thus, a woman might join Al-Anon or another alcohol education-support group and begin activities (resocialization and revitalization) associated with the proximal

Table 1. A Typology of the Moral Career of Becoming the Wife of an
Alcoholic and the Management of Definitional Ambivalence

Phase	Ambivalence Management Task	Typical Activities and Involvement of Self
I. Early Problems	Recognizing	Sporadic questioning
II. Problem Amplification	Sorting	Intensified questioning, confronting, self-doubting, defacing, groping
III. Proximal Treatment	Limiting, depersonalizing	Introspection, resocialization, self-assertion, revitalization
IV. Post-Treatment	Reconciling, philosophizing	Reflection, harmonization

treatment phase, but her relationship and interaction with her husband
might still be more like those of the earlier problem amplification phase.
Similarly, the process of a woman's moral career may be characterized by
interactions that indicate a back-and-forth flow among phases or even
skipping one. In other words, the diagram represents a fluid process rather
than discrete categories of time or social space. It represents the major social
strands of a moral career of becoming the wife of an alcoholic, and it should
be thought of as an interactional process (self-other) that has been parti-
tioned for analytic purposes only.

Transition from the early phase into the problem amplification phase
comes with an emerging sense that there is some sort of problem and,
conversely, thinking-feeling that there is no real problem after all, or acting
as if there is no *real* problem. The challenges of such transition are apparent

in the following revelation: "I really began to kind of feel 'schizo.' You know, is it real or isn't it? At night it would seem just intensely real; the next day it was like it never happened, and who would believe me? I mean, his mother . . . didn't give me any support at all, even in terms of being concerned about her son. 'What are you complaining about? He's taking care of you!' It's like it's not really happening. So, no, I didn't talk to anyone about it, because I didn't want anyone to really validate my craziness, I guess."

Virtually all of the women in this study eventually came to realize that their lives with their husbands involved a serious problem, even though their definitions of what that problem was varied over time. The important point is that they all struggled with the definitional shifts of "yes, there is a problem—no, there isn't really a problem." Once a problem was declared, sorting through plausible definitions of it and the emergent interactions around those definitions became the challenge. By the time these women entered a family program, when the first interview took place, definitional ambivalence was a central theme both in their reconstructions of their past marital experiences and in their presentations of their current relationships.

The three major areas of definitional ambivalence were husband, marriage, and self. These three areas exemplify intimate self and self-other involvements and comprise the particularly moral (self-challenging) aspects of the career. Along with these "personal dimensions" of the moral career were "public dimensions" in the form of the women's perceptions, from a societal standpoint, of the roles of husband, father, and wife and of marriage in American society. Religious, legal, economic, and political factors also entered as public dimensions of the moral career. Over time, the wives drew upon varying and often conflicting beliefs, values, norms, and symbols—what we can think of as *cultural resources* in the definitional enterprise. These cultural resources largely comprise the public dimensions of the moral career, but they help shape the personal dimensions as well. In my sample, public and personal dimensions came together in the definitional ambivalence of the three focal areas: husband, marriage, and self.

The women typically spoke of what "their" husband was like compared to their ideas of what "a" husband should be like, pointing to gaps between enactments and expectations of the husband's role. They talked, too, of what he was once like or what he is sometimes like. Varyingly, they saw him as a very nice, loving man and as insensitive, mean, and unruly, a Dr. Jekyl and Mr. Hyde character. They were concerned about his health or his work yet were also able to offer reasons why they need not be; they saw a certain believability in his accounts for the drinking and any accompanying problems, yet they could offer several other competing explanations. In short, the women's definitional ambivalence about their husbands revolved around competing answers to a few generic questions: What has happened to the man I married or used to know? Why is he like this? What does he want from me? What do I want from him? Restated sociologically in terms of role, Is he a good husband/father?

Many of the women intensely desired or felt obligated to preserve the marriage, whereas some seriously contemplated divorce. The wives frequently acknowledged awareness of differing ideas of what a marriage can be (intimate, utilitarian, and so forth), an awareness that sometimes appeared to undermine their formulation of reasonable expectations for their own marriages. The ambivalence of definition about their marriages can be symbolized in the plausible competing answers to generic questions such as, Is this marriage working? What are the possibilities and limitations of this relationship as it stands? And what are the chances of this relationship changing for the better? for the worse?

These women generally experience definitional ambivalence about themselves in the form of self-images and their roles as wife and mother. There are a number of competing criteria they can use when evaluating whether or not they are "okay." Or, if they think they are not, a number of criteria exist to help define the source of their "problems of self." For example, a wife experiencing marital estrangement in part because of her husband's heavy drinking might variously define her felt "disconnectedness" as due to some personality trait, to early marital adjustments, to work demands, to pregnancy, to child-rearing stress, to differences in her own and her husband's backgrounds, to routinization of a marriage over time, to gender differences, or perhaps to her husband's drinking behavior. The generic questions involved in the ambivalence of definition and meaning with regard to self are, Am I an okay person? wife? mother? What's wrong with me? Why is he treating me like this? Why is my life like this? What can I do?

What do I want? What have I become? And what is to become of me? Such disruptive involvements of and challenges to "self" are what make this definitional enterprise a moral career for women married to alcoholics. To help us understand the answers to these illustrative questions and the processes of interaction they represent, we need an appropriate theoretical framework. As such, the symbolic interaction perspective has guided the investigation and informed the analysis for this study.

Symbolic Interaction: A Guiding Perspective

Because the symbolic interaction perspective highlights the interactive, negotiated, socially constructed nature of human life, it provides an especially illuminating framework for investigating how a woman—through a process marked by problem-laden interactions, trial and error, and information seeking and discernment—comes to define her husband as alcoholic. Through it we can better understand the nuances of what meaning this new definition of him has for her own self-imagery and her relationship with him.

Paramount to the interactionist perspective formulated by Mead (1934) in his writings on "mind," "self," and "society" are the symbolic nature of human life and the assertion that the meaning of objects and events emerges within the social process. Basic assumptions of the symbolic interaction perspective include (1) that self is a social process rather than something "thing"-like, (2) that the meaning of social objects is not intrinsic but rather assigned to them, (3) that there is a processual quality to interpretation, and (4) that social actors are active participants in creating the social world to which they are responding. Blumer's (1962) eloquent restatement of Mead's ideas lays out these conceptual foundations of symbolic interaction:

> In declaring that the human being has a self, Mead had in mind chiefly that the human being can be the object of his own actions. He can act toward himself as he might act toward others. . . . Mead recognizes that the formation of action by the individual through a process of self-indication always takes place in a social context. . . .

Each individual aligns his action to the actions of others by ascertaining what they are doing or what they intend to do—that is, by getting the meaning of their acts. For Mead, this is done by the individual "taking the role" of others—either the role of a specific person or the role of a group—(Mead's "generalized other"). . . . He forms and aligns his own action on the basis of such interpretation of the acts of others. (Pp. 181–84)

Through the concept of *role-taking*—viewing ourselves (as objects) from the standpoints of others—we can better understand the significant impact that anticipation of the standpoints of others has in shaping conceptions of self, self-feelings, and actions. We can then better understand the self-other evaluative relations behind the attitudes anticipated and expressed in "I felt like I was a piece of shit to him!" The concept of role-taking provides insight into the great interactional intricacies inherent in the challenges and changes of a moral career. Thus, we can begin to see how the humiliation, turmoil, marital apathy, low self-esteem, and definitional plight expressed by these wives are intimately related to their interactions with their husbands and others close to them, as well as with their larger communities of membership.

Through interaction, then, selves become social objects and objects of acts (Mead 1934). Social objects need not be physical in structure; they can be symbolic like marriage or a persona (McCall and Simmons 1966). An alcoholic-complicated marriage is a social object in the wife's world of social objects and she acts toward it, responds to it, and creates meaning out of it on the basis of ongoing activity. Blumer (1962) tells us that "this is what is meant by interpretation or acting on the basis of symbols" (p. 182). Symbolic interpretation mediates human interaction.

Interpretation makes defining situations a complex process. Thomas and Thomas's (1928) now-famous edict, "situations defined as real are real in their consequences," is the cornerstone of the concept *definition of the situation*, resting on the observation that "the subject's view of the situation, how he regards it, may be the most important element for interpretation. For his immediate behavior is closely related to his definition of the situation, which may be in terms of objective reality or in terms of a subjective appreciation—as if it were so" (p. 571). Thomas (1937) further notes that prior to any self-directed act people examine and deliberate, and that personality and whole life policies follow from a series of such definitions.

To paraphrase Blumer (1966), self-direction does not necessarily imply excellence in constructing our acts. The important point is that acts are constructed out of what persons take into account through the things that they indicate to themselves. These include desires, feelings, goals, actions, expectations and demands of others, group norms, self-conceptions, memory, and conception of possibilities. Persons formulate lines of conduct on the basis of how they handle such matters.

Mead's claim that the meaning of an act lies in the response to it implies that in order to understand persons' actions, we must know the meaning of those actions for them.[5] The present study rests on this postulate in that it emphasizes the meanings assigned to the process of becoming and being the wife of an alcoholic from the point of view of the women experiencing it.

Another concept, *deviance medicalization*, though not part of the symbolic interaction perspective per se, contributes to our knowledge of the social atmosphere that influences experiences in this moral career. A historical shift in deviance designations of alcoholism from a moral or legal category to a medical one, or from "badness" to "sickness," has been carefully outlined by Conrad and Schneider (1980). With this "medicalization" comes a more therapeutic—rather than punitive—social response. The alcoholism rehabilitation industry, including the family programs that the women in this study attended and the treatment programs their husbands entered, exemplifies the more therapeutic approach we take today. Within the trend toward medicalization, ideas about women married to alcoholics have come to the now-popular notion of the affliction *codependency*.

Returning to our theoretical framework, the symbolic interaction perspective guides us to focus on process and interaction, on definition of the situation and interpretive meaning, and on self and performance. It allows us to move between the personal and public dimensions of a moral career, to see possible contingencies of this career as actors create and respond in their worlds of social objects. It especially allows us to apply a body of knowledge about the fluidity of the social self and social interaction to the life experiences of a group of women married to alcoholic husbands. It beckons us to see their experiences as they have seen and experienced them. It reformulates "privatized" activities as "social" activities, whether carried out in peopled interaction or internal conversations. It illumines processes of interaction that come together as strands of experience in a moral career, creating new self-imagery and social categorization: wife of an alcoholic. It invites us to see the living out of everyday lives as symbolic interaction.

A close complement to the symbolic interaction perspective is that of the sociology of knowledge. With its emphasis on the social construction of reality, this perspective provides an overarching framework for understanding the findings of this study. The sociology of knowledge concerns itself with how a body of ideas comes to be accepted as knowledge and how this knowledge is used in making sense or constructing reality out of lived experiences (Berger and Luckmann 1967). Human thought and knowing presuppose "a community of knowing," and individual experience is interdependent with "the wider community of experience and activity" (Mannheim 1936, 31–33).

Feminist scholars suggest that the generation of ideas about women and ideas that defend "the traditional status of women in society" can best be apprehended within the theoretical context of the sociology of knowledge (Anderson 1988, 44). This understanding, however, goes beyond studying the impact of socialization on gender roles; gender theorists and feminist scholars ask us "to look at the structure of consciousness—not just as it is reproduced through sex roles but specifically as it reflects the patriarchal organization of society" (Anderson 1988, 360). Any interpretations of the experiences of the women in this study, whether stemming from their private thoughts, from discussions with significant others, or from the more public arena, must be considered in this larger societal context. And it is within this larger context that we can truly comprehend a seemingly individualized moral career as comprised of strands of social experience.

My goal in this book is to typify the experiences of the women interviewed and to illustrate how their lived experiences comprise a special process of self-definition called a "moral career." The focus thus is not on particular individuals' career paths but rather on contingencies that may direct, intensify, prolong, or shorten, and so forth, individual experiences of various segments of the moral career. The interactional dynamics outlined in this career represent experiences found among all the subjects without notable differences by age, class, or race. For example, all of the women experienced and participated in a problem amplification phase before exhibiting actions that are associated with the later proximal treatment phase. By superimposing their individual biographies, I have been able to trace the moral career process that is typical of these women married to alcoholics. Major contingencies during this process are outlined, as are benchmarks of the career. As the reader will discover, the fact that these subjects are *women* vis-à-vis alcoholic husbands is perhaps the most striking influence on the moral career.

Al-Anon in Brief

The women's as well as my own comments in this book are sprinkled with the term *Al-Anon*. Al-Anon is an organization that was founded to help spouses or other relatives and friends better cope with their lives and relationships with an alcoholic. Some of the women had read Al-Anon literature or were familiar with the organization through public media, neighbors, relatives, or friends. A small number had attended one or two Al-Anon meetings before the first interview, and a few had attended periodically over time. Al-Anon literature and teachings form a major part of the family programs in which all of the women participated. Al-Anon should not be confused with Alcoholics Anonymous (AA). Whereas Al-Anon is for persons who have a close relationship with an alcoholic, AA is for the chemically dependent (alcoholic) person. Al-Anon and AA meetings are held in most communities. "The Twelve Steps" serve as the rehabilitation philosophy for both organizations, as well as for many others now fashioned after these original "step" groups.

Part I

The Early Problem Phase

Recognizing
the Ambivalence

During the first interview the women in my sample were asked to think back to their first inklings of problems associated with their husbands' drinking. They described this early period and how it differed from times when they had felt no problems involving alcohol. In this way, they designated the social beginnings of the process of becoming the wife of an alcoholic.

These beginnings comprise the early phase of this moral career and give rise to the challenge of recognizing the definitional ambivalence that is starting to emerge. Certain incidents, because of incompatibilities or contradictions of expectations, begin to be questioned. Questions about actions and attitudes evoke explanations or what Mills (1940) called *motive offerings*. A number of explanations can potentially be offered for a given situation (Scott and Lyman 1968), and the act of questioning evokes these possibilities. (This can take place solely within the mind of the questioner, as when we ask and answer our own questions about a situation or someone's behavior, or it can be actual dialogue between the questioner and the person being questioned.) The significance of a situation in which several explanations are available to account for what has occurred is that it sets the stage for the ambivalence of definition, for there can be no ambivalence if only one explanation exists.

Researchers report that it is common for family and friends to "normalize" the early-questioned behaviors of a "deviant" significant other (Yarrow et al. 1955; Goffman 1962). Behaviors are normalized in the sense that, despite their unfavorable or doubtful character, they are defined as being within a normal range of behavior. The untoward actions and actor are "brought back into the fold," so to speak. The following excerpts from the present study illustrate how this might work:

> With a group of friends, it seemed like normal behavior.

> For some reason, I just thought, well, this is the way that it is, because most of the people we were with would get pretty bombed too.

> There were things that bothered me but I didn't think that much about it. And I didn't feel I really should say anything about it because I was raised in the era that dutiful wives . . . he was the head of the household and pretty much the way he did [things] was all right. . . . I didn't like him getting drunk. I didn't like him after a certain point.

Even though these women defined their husbands' drinking as within a normative range, the first stirrings of definitional ambivalence were present. Noting that the time, setting, or amount of drinking is inappropriate is tantamount to noting contradictions and incompatibilities in their husbands' performance of social roles—particularly the roles of husband and responsible adult citizen. Normalizing these beginnings of definitional ambivalence allows social interaction and family life to proceed more smoothly than it otherwise might.

It is common in this early period of ambivalence that the wives note behavioral changes and simply draw their own inferences about their husbands' actions. In doing so they are assuming flexible attitudes that allow them to view their husbands as mostly competent role performers, as shown in these excerpts:

> Towards the end of the second year of our marriage I noticed that when he became stressed from the discipline of going to school, he would go out and drink with his buddies to release the tension. He's very smart and he's always been able to drink the night before, cram for

two hours before the test, and just ace it. In the beginning I thought it was just [the] stress factor, and then I saw a pattern that he was drinking really heavily during that time. But it was new to me, and, like I said, he catches himself; when he starts drinking heavily in a certain period he'll stop himself, and you'll think, well, it was just a little patch where he was needing a little help.

He didn't drink until he was twenty-one, so I just assumed he was going through a late adolescence when he was drinking, you know how kids drink and get drunk. . . . Since he didn't start drinking till so late, I thought he was doing just that.

Some of the women associated specific behavioral changes with their husbands' drinking and the first awareness of ambivalence. Observing, for instance, that "he always would hold his cigarette differently," or noting a "Dr. Jekyl and Mr. Hyde" or "a lot of bullshit, big talk," dramatizes early contradictory or incompatible performances of roles. The following perceived changes were typical:

[I noticed] personality changes, just from the nice guy that he is to this stupid acting person, which he wasn't. . . . He just became a different person, something I just didn't like at all. And physical changes, slow reactions, the way he walked, the way he talked— everything just changed.

Like six months after we were married, I can remember my going to work and my coming home and not having him home in time for dinner, because he would stop with the guys and have a beer, which I could always understand. I thought, that's fine; my father would stop after work and have a beer—he was working for my dad at the time, part-time, and he would always come home at six-thirty or seven, and my dad would be in the driveway at six. That was a problem right after we were married.

These kinds of observations feed into emerging definitional ambivalence about the men's role performances and are perhaps more difficult to normalize. The women then begin to experience incompatibilities and contradictions between their expectations for their husbands and their husbands' actual role performances.

Recognizing their definitional ambivalence, some of the wives in this study confronted their husbands with the discrepancies. Some women spoke up the first time they noted an untoward behavior, others after observing a pattern. It is notable that in this early phase the women tended to play down their own perceptions of situations, apparently giving more credence to those offered by their husbands. For example:

> When he would drink he didn't change much—drink a lot and never get drunk. He was up to like a twelve-pack a night, and that is when I started getting concerned. After he . . . got kind of angry, I just assumed, well, he doesn't think that it is a problem; [it] must be okay, he can handle it.

> The summer before we were married, I got really concerned because he was high on something and he denied it. And I said, "But you're staggering and your speech is slurred and you're acting real strange." And he said, "Well, that's my allergies. I get goofy in the summertime with my allergies." I said, "Well, get allergy shots." I was young and in love, and I believed him.

> I accidentally came across some bottles he had hidden. I thought, Why does he hide it? Why? It just didn't make sense to me. And I wasn't sure. . . . I mentioned something to him [about] what the bottles were doing behind the furnace. He just gave me some answer. I thought, Okay, fine, I'll let it go with that.

This practice of generally accepting the line of action (even if inaction) that their husbands present to them can be understood in the sense that we are socialized to give others the benefit of the doubt (Goffman 1967). This is particularly so in close relationships and when social power is unequal. The wives in this study conformed to these norms of interaction. Though these forms of confrontation did not lead to open conflict, patterns of ongoing open conflict were being established in some of the marriage relationships.

Conflict, especially in this phase, is not necessarily associated with drinking or directed at drinking behavior. The following comments are typical not only because they illustrate a pattern of generalized conflict but also because they characteristically highlight jealousy, which was reported by many of the wives in this study:

> We used to fight a lot, immediately. We were both young; we thought that is the way you have fun, you drink. We weren't really fighting about the alcohol; we were fighting about, oh, jealousy, things in general, but it was always when we were drinking that we would fight.

> He was jealous, very jealous, at that time. When you [I] did go out, he was very possessive, and he would get upset if I talked to another man.

The core of sociological ambivalence—incompatible or contradictory expectations for social performances—is highlighted in these illustrations of general conflict among relationship partners. We might think of a conflict situation as a generic situation of sociological ambivalence. As such, we gain a more pristine perspective on how awareness of ambivalence comes about. Whereas conflict explicitly points out ambivalence of definition, everyday interaction may implicitly suggest it.

A single memorable episode, as recounted by some of the wives, can dramatically bring incompatibilities and contradictions of expectations into the forefront. In retrospect, the troubles associated with their husbands' drinking stemmed from this first notable encounter. Demonstrating such a pattern of the mustering of ambivalence are these recollections:

> He would never go into a bar or anywhere without me. We always went together. And the first time he stayed out all night, I just couldn't believe it. Because he had never done anything like that before. He came strolling in about seven in the morning. I was just frantic.

> Right around twenty-eight years ago, I was going to go on a trip with my girlfriend. Well, he came home wiped out that night, just like telling me "hey." I was upset, because he was supposed to take me in that evening to meet my girlfriend. . . . So as long as he came home that way, of course. . . . The next morning he took me in. He had never

come home like that before, never, no, not that I remember that he had come home like that. When I think back, that's about when I first noticed. I would say that maybe that was about the start of it, of being a problem.

The excerpts of interviews presented in this chapter illustrate ways in which ambivalence initially arises for and is recognized by wives such as these. For the most part, they do not have the faintest idea that they are embarking on a very special path—a moral career of becoming the wife of an alcoholic. Recognizing ambivalence in this early phase means embracing the existence of *some* problem, but usually not *drinking* per se as *a* problem and seldom drinking as *the* problem. Designation of problem drinking and alcoholism will come later—it came anywhere from a few months to over thirty years later for the women in this study. In this early phase of the moral career, the women are just beginning to recognize and respond to discrepancies about their husbands. They are only beginning to deal with definitional ambivalence, still wondering, What's going on here? There is much ahead for them as their domestic problems and attempts to deal with them intensify in the problem amplification phase of the moral career of becoming the wife of an alcoholic.

Part 2

The Problem
Amplification Phase

Sorting the Ambivalence

Acknowledging

As untoward incidents and their unpleasant consequences increase, the character of the moral career changes. The early phase, characterized by the initial mustering and recognition of ambivalence, gradually gives way to the problem amplification phase, distinguished by expansion of problems and efforts to sort out what's "wrong" and why. There is an increasing sense that there is some problem, but drinking, at most, is seen as a consequence of problems, not as the problem itself. The wives instead focus on their husbands' and their own behaviors as well as outside stressors as possible sources of problems. In effect, they attempt to sort out the variability and viability of definitions and questions about themselves, their husbands, and their marriages, weighing the meaning of various answers to these questions.

Definitional ambivalence arises when there are contradictory or incompatible social performances or expectations. Sorting, arranging, or classifying thoughts, feelings, observations, and interactions into resource material for understanding and defining experience—sorting ambivalences of definition—is an attempt to render one's life more comprehensible. Such efforts to sort through ambivalence include the three activities of acknowledging, valuating, and personalizing. Though closely associated, these activities are separated for purposes of discussion here and in the next few chapters.

Acknowledging refers to recognizing the existence of disparate meanings of selves and situations. It especially entails noting changes in one's self, husband, or marriage in ways that challenge familiar definitions, perhaps accompanied by reality testing of ideas and perceptions. There may be reconstructions of incidents from the early phase that now serve as evidence of contrasts and changes.

During this time the women attend to cues from friends and family about whether or not these people also perceive a problem and the nature or degree of it. They may compare the present with a previous period of "no problem" or "less problem." It is a period in which a wife engages in a major dialogue that will be with her for some time to come. It is a dialogue with herself, or her husband, or others—often all of these: a dialogue of seemingly incessant queries and explanations, a dialogue of definitional ambivalences that tends to keep her wheels spinning, so to speak.

One of the best illustrations of such a dialogue comes from an interview with a woman who was being treated in a family program for her "codependency" on the basis of counselors' estimates of her husband's chemical dependency. He had not yet been officially evaluated and diagnosed as alcoholic. It is precisely this lack of official designation that spotlights the throes of definitional ambivalence. It enables us to sense the wife's typical struggle with definitional ambivalence in her quest for precise information:

> He would drink so much he would be sloppy drunk, falling down, whereas, now it's getting to the point that he. . . . One night, I talked to him and I would say, yeah, that he drank some but not that much; he appeared to be that straight. Then I found out he drank that whole quart by himself.
>
> I noticed that it's hard for me to tell if he's been drinking and if so, how much. I can see where people live in a home, and don't have outside resources, can really get hung up . . . because, well, I'm fairly active, [get] some counseling, go to work, but I'm still like swaying back and forth. When he becomes angry, see, my thing is then I've got something to say.
>
> Sometimes he is really nice and sweet, but see. . . . Before, he was so nice and sweet and loving; now, it's a feeling, the guy is just seducing

me. And once he sucks me under, he's going to start giving me all that shit again. And see, I don't want that, so *that's* a change in me. He doesn't hit, but he screams enough, embarrasses me a lot.

You go through a weekend when he drinks, I'm madder than hell, he's being just a total. . . . I guess a lot of it is that he doesn't seem to care about me and the kids; he'll be gone for a long time. And then I turn around and I say, "Am I being selfish?" I mean, if I mention [it] to him, then I'm nothing but a selfish bitch.

I wish there was something that could say *yes*, because right now it's like I'm fighting something that isn't even there—you know, *Does* he have a problem? I can't live with it, I know that, and I won't; but, what the hell can I [live with], what *am* I living? If I knew. . . . People whose husbands finally go to evaluation and treatment, they know what they're fighting, they know what direction to go [in].

I sit here and say, "Does he have a problem, or is it that my dad had a problem?" And I'm looking at my husband, and I'm thinking, this is my dad. It seems to be an awful lot like my dad. Who am I fighting, or who am I trying to help? What way do we go? He says, "My work [working shows] I'm not chemically dependent." He refuses to discuss it. He does get angry sometimes, or he laughs, makes me even more angry. So I sit there in limbo. "Yes, he is; no, he isn't." I don't know. . . .

Vacillation between "problem not-problem" has been noted in other studies of women married to alcoholics (Jackson 1954) and in research on families of mental patients (Yarrow et al. 1955; Goffman 1971). In contrast to the spouse of the woman in the excerpt above, the husbands of the other women in this study had already been officially diagnosed as alcoholic. The wives' reconstructions of what it was like to sort through the definitional ambivalence and to acknowledge a problem before it was officially designated provide the data for this analysis of the problem amplification phase.

At this phase in the process of becoming the wife of an alcoholic, "alcoholism" was not typically in the minds or vocabularies of the women. When acknowledging problems that they were experiencing with regard to their husbands, the source was often thought to be family or work-related stress. Recollections along these lines include:

I didn't realize it was the drugs or the alcohol, because he would say, "I had a hard day at work today." Since we own the shop ourselves now, I just figured that it had to do with work. And that is when I started a job and school at the same time, so I thought that that had a lot to do with it, too. I thought that it was just a lot of stress for him, that that was why he was irritable.

His wife had left him and he was having a lot of problems; I really didn't realize at the time that he was an alcoholic. I thought maybe he was drinking because of all the problems he had. If that was the case, I could help him.

We would have a couple [of] explosive situations or arguments, but not to the point where I was really worried about it. I guess I just figured that he was under new pressure, because he's always talking about finances, but . . . he's responsible, he'll pull us through. And he did, and I went back to work, and that helped. I didn't like some of the drinking episodes, but at the same time, I excused them, because maybe they just weren't so bad, or. . . .

In these and the examples that follow, there are elements of normalizing problems. Now, however, there are stronger or more frequent indications of problems even though they are not clearly defined. Normalizing problematic behaviors, though, carries definitional activity and social action only so far. As problematic behaviors increase, activities of acknowledging also increase—through awareness of problems and speculation about the sources of them.

Besides stress, the wives often viewed the company their husbands kept as the source of their problems. Here are some examples that typify this perspective:

He played [sports], and afterwards he'd really start drinking. And he hung around with four or five guys who were out smoking dope, and he didn't fit it [that stereotype] at all; he was too straight looking. And I knew it wasn't him, you know what I mean?

At that point, I hadn't really realized that he was an alcoholic. I just thought he was being a jerk. I thought maybe it was the guys he was hanging around with. Maybe it's the truck drivers at the truck stop.

As he got into sales and had an expense account, he was able to hide a lot of it from me, because we never paid for it. He was able to drink a lot on the road with customers.

The women also commonly regarded themselves as sources of marital problems. In fact, several of them made emphatic "*I* was the problem" statements. (This phenomenon of viewing self as the source of the problem will be explored further in discussions of valuating and personalizing activities in the ambivalence sorting process.) In contrast to seeing themselves as the problem, however, a few of the women squarely defined mental-psychological disorders in their husbands as the source of problems:

I had a lot of worry, concern, and frustration, but I wasn't relating it to the fact that he was an alcoholic. I was thinking he was nuts.

He's been fired off of every job he's ever had but it was never for alcoholism—it was always that he was emotionally disturbed because of the nervous breakdown and so forth. One of these times the flu or whatever was so bad that we took him in emergency to the hospital. While he was there, they examined him psychiatrically. There was never any indication of alcoholism; nothing like that was ever looked at or thought about.

But even these definitions, often supported by legitimating agents, are subject to change in the fluidity of the definitional enterprise. After all, these and all the other cases were later defined as alcoholism.

To acknowledge or even define a problem, albeit temporarily, is a notable accomplishment. It is an even further-reaching enterprise to define the problem as a problem of drinking. Many of the women in the study sample noticed a gradual buildup to problematic drinking, "gradual" meaning several months for a few, but many years for a majority. The next excerpt shows this as well as the finding that, initially, drinking episodes are seldom linked to an overall pattern of behavior:

He was out like a light on the couch and he smelled really bad of beer, and I was really angry. I said, "That does it!" I went to a park for two to three hours and I guess I was feeling sorry for myself—ready to kill him—and then I got back and he hardly knew that I was gone because he was still [passed out], and that hit me. I think I was kind of quiet that night, and the next day I really got mad and told him. Then nothing happened for a long time. But he would still go out and drink once in a while but not to that point where I noticed that much, so I kind of forgot about it because it was such a gradual [process]—it's so gradual; it really amazes me.

A second excerpt is representative of the often long and painful process of designating drinking per se as the problem:

A lot of things happened really fast—his mother came, two of his kids came to live with us, we bought our first house. I suppose my first focus on having problems was that he started going to the track and gambling, lying, borrowing money and not telling me. Later on I could see him causing fights so he could go out and drink. I didn't think about that at the time, but as I look back I see that that was kind of a pattern starting. [He'd give me] a lot of verbal abuse, tearing me down, and then he would go out, then he would get violent, put his fist through many walls and doors; that was always when he'd been drinking.

I'm relating this as I think back how it was. I didn't think about it at the time. Then I started talking more to my friends whose husbands had gone through treatment about this crazy behavior—so up and happy and then just go into a severe depression. Or he could be just totally ripping me verbally, then ten minutes later he would want to go to bed. One day he would be just crying and sobbing and wanting forgiveness and the next day he'd be back [abusing], you know. As far as him and I really talking about it, it wasn't until right before he went in; and he thought possibly that could be his problem. He knew he had a problem, he just didn't know what it was; and that's how I felt, too. I knew there was something wrong, I just couldn't put my finger on it.

Reflecting the sentiments of the majority of women in the study is this simple introspection: "I was extremely upset, angry and afraid, confused; I didn't know what was going [on], or why. I don't think too many people, or wives, really understand—maybe now they do but not back then—that this was a drinking problem. Because you realize that the drinking is a problem but you don't put it as a drinking [problem]—the drinking was causing problems, but you don't quite realize that it could be alcoholism— it just didn't occur to me."

If defining the problem as a problem of drinking is a far-reaching idea at this time in the moral career, defining the problem as alcoholic drinking or alcoholism is an even more distant notion. Indeed, the designation of alcoholism has been described elsewhere as a virtual "social accomplishment" (Schneider 1978). In this phase of the moral career, defining alcoholism is something that rarely happens without an intervening third party— the presence of which is noted for altering the formulation of troubles (Emerson and Messinger 1977). Even then and in the face of marital breakdown, the label may initially be rejected. For example, one woman reported: "A lot of serious drinking was going on. He'd stay out until five in the morning. I would abuse myself I think, emotionally, as a result of that but I'd just continue going through it. I went to a counselor from church, asked him what he thought I should do, and I remember him asking me, 'Do you think your husband is an alcoholic?' And I said, 'No.' So it was just that whole denial thing up until then."

Designating a drinking problem but stopping short of labeling it as alcoholism, a stance taken by some of the women interviewed, is illustrated by the following recollections:

> I bet it's been between ten, fifteen years [that] I would read, like maybe in *Reader's Digest*, about alcoholism symptoms, and I would say to my husband, "You'd better be careful, because you are a real good potential alcoholic." That's the way I saw it, that's the way I felt. And he said, "Oh no, because you have to make a lot of money to buy all that booze to drink; there is no way that I have all that."

> [When was it] that I really accepted that he was an alcoholic? I would say a couple of years [ago]. No, I'll have to change that; I would say that [it was] less than that that I really finally decided. I'd say maybe six to eight months [ago].

I said, "I'm not going to call you an alcoholic, but you do have a problem." My cousin had gone through treatment and stuff. I said, "If you don't want to go to AA meetings and talk, call up him and he'll talk to you."

A time lapse between designations of problematic drinking and alcoholic drinking is not at all unusual. In the next case, fifteen years passed between the time the wife first associated alcohol with her marital problems and the legitimating social designation of alcoholism, which was made when her husband entered treatment:

[It became] a serious problem, I would say, probably six years after we were married. I recognized a problem earlier; it's such a progressive type of thing that it isn't like all of a sudden it's there, and you say, hey, you know, this guy is a drunk, he's an alcoholic. And he won't even say alcoholic, he'll say he drinks too much. . . . But in terms of realizing that it was a serious problem, maybe it was when I went in for the intervention . . . maybe it was that year, or that month . . . that it was a real serious problem.

Overall, a minority of the women defined their husbands as alcoholic before entering the family program concomitant with their husbands' treatment. These women had Al-Anon or other special training or had previous treatment experiences with their husbands' alcoholism. The majority of the women in the study defined their husbands' drinking only as problematic prior to treatment, at which time the alcoholism label was designated.

One way of discerning a problem with drinking is in terms of problems that result from drinking. If drinking-related problems can be minimized or better yet eliminated, then drinking perhaps is less likely to be viewed as a primary problem, regardless of actual consumption. The following case describes such a situation: "When he got that DWI [Driving while Intoxicated] in October, his last one had been three years ago, so he had pretty much straightened up; he realized that he shouldn't drink and drive. But in the meantime he had still been drinking, he had just kind of . . . learned to stay home and do it, or to have someone else drive and do it."

The excerpt below expands on this viewpoint by illustrating that high levels of "personal dimension" relationship problems will be tolerated, even skirted, when they do not spill over into the "public dimension." Whereas the flow of problems into the public dimension will accelerate alcoholism designations, conversely, containing the problems within the personal dimension of marital relationships or partners can inhibit such designations:

> There had always been a drinking problem, but it would be after bowling, or fishing trips, or, you know, there wasn't a regular pattern. If he drank, he got drunk; if he stopped at the bar, I knew he wouldn't be home. But it wasn't as often; it was, maybe, once a week. It got to be three and four times a week and the hours were later and later.
>
> It actually goes back to when we were first married. He was working the night shift and he got off at eight in the morning and I had already left for work. He was going to the bar at eight o'clock. I would catch him in lies and find out much later that he'd been drinking. There wasn't a lot of trust. I associated it with, He can't stand to be home, he wants to go out and have fun. I didn't recognize it as a problem with drinking. His friends would always get after me that I was a party pooper.
>
> When he was out and I was home, I'd be very frustrated, angry, meet him at the door—typical. I would fight, I would argue, I'd be angry. After I got into Al-Anon . . . they teach [you] to let go of it with love— I couldn't do that; my escape was just to completely withdraw. And he just came and went as he pleased, and I never said a word. We didn't say anything but "Hi." I don't know that I specifically knew that it was a *drinking* problem, but I knew there was a *marriage* problem.

Characteristically, in this case incompatibilities and contradictions had existed between the wife and husband for an extended period of time. These competing attitudes, beliefs, and performances constitute definitional ambivalence; the plausibility of these competing definitions fuels its flames.

Plausibility implies that a definition cannot easily be dismissed. It must be entertained and responded to. As long as the wives view a definition as plausible, they take it into account in internal conversations and in interactions with others. The existence of several competing plausible definitions requires eventual sorting of the definitional ambivalence. Acknowledging the existence and plausibility of disparate definitions of selves and situations, in attempts to explain problems, appears to sharpen and heighten awareness of the definitional ambivalence. In other words, *the problem of "having problems" crystallizes*, not the specific problem itself. With heightened acknowledgment of definitional ambivalence, it is not unusual to begin to heed cues from others regarding the viability of one definition over others. To get indications from others regarding the degree and the nature of concerns in our lives is simply to enter into the normal everyday activity of the social construction of reality (Berger and Luckmann 1967). But this everyday activity takes on special weight when the situation at hand presents a problem to at least one of the actors: "Interaction is disrupted, identities are threatened, meanings are unclear, situations seem disorderly, people have intentions that run counter to others' wishes, seemingly inexplicable events take place, people do not know what is happening to them, and the list could be extended almost indefinitely" (Stokes and Hewitt 1976, 842).

Within such contexts problematic experiences undergo a qualitative shift in definition from what Schwartz (1976) calls normal trouble to special trouble. And this is when persons often actively seek out others and more information. In this transition to defining problems as more serious, or even in the discernment of them initially, it is fairly common for the wives of alcoholics to devise strategies to check out the emerging definitional ambivalence. The following comments represent the colorful threads comprising this strand of experience in the moral career:

He evidently had the stuff hidden—he had to have. [He] would go into the basement quite often, so I figured something was down there. I looked and could never find it.

He was in the bathroom shaving. I walked out to the kitchen, and the back door was open. I went out to close it, and here's a bottle sitting outside by the back door. I watched when he left and he took the bottle with him.

I started probably a typical behavior of looking, getting a few clues, looking and finding hidden bottles. I was trying to determine, too, a definition of what is "heavy drinking," and so I would monitor the

quantity. Well, I took a few months, tried to get a little more information, and I did discuss it with a close friend. I had to prove it to myself,
you know; I just couldn't believe it right away. I had to make certain in
my mind that it was a problem.

Then it took me some time to get up the nerve to approach him, but
of course I became tearful. I think it was about six times, in the seven-
to eight-month period, that I confronted him and tried to talk to him
about it. Unless I could present the evidence, he would totally deny it
and start getting angry and try and turn it back on me, which I
recognized right away—he was trying to put it back on me.

Well, I made up my mind that the pattern was going to go on, and I
had gone to a one-day seminar trying to find out more about the
disease. I looked up a lot of medical books. Toward the end, one way I
recognized it—I think he was being very careful of controlling it and
supposedly not drinking and I really couldn't see any physical signs—
and then I thought, aha, the way lately I would be doing something—
just taking a shower or wash[ing] my hair in the bathroom and he'd
say, "Oh, here you are." Make sure where I was and sneak off and do
it—take a drink. A light bulb went off in my head and I thought, ah!
The next time he does that I'm gonna just sneak out and see what really
comes out, which was crazy behavior on my part . . . but I guess before
the intervention I really would start feeling the beginnings of a problem, and in that way discovered various items again.

Interestingly, the last case was one of the shortest in problem duration
(eight months) and was the least overtly chaotic case in the study. Notice, in
seeking information and testing reality, the wife's autonomy of perception
and action, how she trusts her own observations and follows through by
acting on them—attributes notably missing in most of the other cases, at
least in this phase of the moral career. This woman was different from most
of the others in that she had entered her marriage as a long-term careerwoman with an advanced college degree; her prestigious supervisory position required self-autonomy, executive leadership, and management qualities. She went on to confront her husband about his drinking and need for
treatment by arranging an intervention with his colleagues and family. I
have no doubt that her long-standing professional status and authority

helped her diminish the length and, relatively speaking, the intensity of the problem amplification phase. For all practical purposes, in fact, her case might well be viewed as a "negative case"—one producing serious, difficult problems but not really a moral career in the sense of disrupting and altering her self-identity—compared to the rest of the women in the study.

Information on alcoholism may be offered to wives by others; it comes from a variety of sources, often a friend or a relative of the wife. For instance, as one woman explained: "Our church Bible studies had a three-week session, and that really brought . . . a lot of things to light . . . that I did not realize. And this one very good friend gave me this Al-Anon book, [a] little over a year ago, that I've been using." Another woman's experience illustrates how family members might become involved: "Before we got married even [there were problems with alcohol]; we had been living together. And his brother is an alcoholic; he gave me information on alcoholism. But my husband . . . resented the fact that I was reading about alcoholism, because he didn't think that he had the problem yet. I knew that he had a problem drinking, but I didn't know it was as bad [as it was] until that last four or five months, [when] I accepted the fact that he was an alcoholic."

Testing for the "reality" of a drinking problem may also result in attempts by others to attenuate designations of problematic drinking. When this happens, incompatibilities and contradictions in expectations and performances are minimized, normalized, or avoided by the others, and perhaps by self. This occurred in the following case:

I probably knew when I married him, but I didn't know. But I remember saying to my mother, and I was crying, "Mom, I don't know if I should marry him because he drinks too much." And Mom sat down and talked and said, "Don't worry, it'll work out if you love him," which was really wrong advice, but she didn't know that. And, then, I knew he drank, but it was all for the boys and he would get smashed a few times. . . . I didn't always like it, but . . . I almost thought it was normal. Everyone around me was drinking, and his family is alcoholic; my friends all drink, and I guess I just figured he wasn't hurting me yet. At times he did, but . . . it was just from being drunk, and every wife probably goes through that [at] one time or another. . . . And . . . very slowly [it] got worse, and I didn't even know it. . . .

We can better understand the glossing over of problems on the part of both this woman and her mother by realizing the subtle social pressures to do so. In order to maintain social interactional order, actors must repair disruptive interactions that occur. Such "remedial interchanges" (Goffman 1971) and compensating definitions of the situation are examples of what Stokes and Hewitt (1976) call "aligning actions." Aligning actions are "forms of conduct, mainly verbal, in which individuals simultaneously effect alignment . . . they sustain the flow of joint actions by bringing individual acts into line with one another in problematic circumstances, and they sustain a relationship (but not necessarily an exact correspondence) between ongoing conduct and culture in the face of recognized failure of conduct to live up to cultural definitions and requirements" (p. 844). Thus, by minimizing incompatible expectations and performances, this woman and her mother repaired disruptive interactions and relations.

In contrast to the preceding diminishing and remedial pattern, a heightened sense of definitional ambivalence may emerge during reality testing with friends or relatives. For example, one woman stated: "There's a few friends at work . . . I probably said more to them, you know. They were to the point where [they said], 'Well, why don't you [leave him], the son of a bitch, he sounds like he's no good.' And then I'd think, Am I making him worse than he is or is he really that bad?" Another woman observed: "I was pretty much the Lone Ranger until just the past few months. The only person I confided to was my mother, and she wasn't really too helpful to me. I think that she stirred up a lot of the feeling that I had, 'Oh, that's so terrible,' you know, this 'rotten person,' 'this creep,' . . . and all that, instead of having enough insight to be able to steer me on to a program of some sort."

Information seeking and reality testing may also result in getting information that seems off the mark, often diverting further efforts temporarily. On initial exposure to information on alcoholic-complicated marriages, several women noted that the images presented did not fit with their own current (though precarious) images of themselves, their husbands, or their marriages. In the refashioning of selves taking place in this phase of the moral career, changing definitions of self or significant other do not yet point to official alcohol-related labels. The following reports are representative of such information seeking and noncorrespondence of observations:

I thought I wanted to learn a little bit about alcoholism [at] one of the lectures; but after hearing it, I thought, Oh, that didn't fit my husband. The people who were lecturing—she's the alcoholic, and just from some of the things that she said about her life . . . of course didn't fit my husband, how could it? [It] never really occurred to me at that time. She did sprees and drinking by the bottles—that didn't fit my husband. I thought, He can't be an alcoholic—he doesn't go on weekend sprees; he's able to hold down a job and lead a rather productive life.

I recall either reading something or hearing something about alcoholism, and I looked in the telephone book and I called AA. I asked some questions, and . . . it didn't hit [me] that he sounds like he is an alcoholic.

My stereotyped image of an alcoholic was a skid-row bum. He was the one that would not have a job. And my husband had a good job, he had the education, he was a very intelligent man. He didn't fit any of the images of an alcoholic.

These examples of information seeking and reality testing illustrate ways in which the wives of alcoholics attempt to sort out a situation of definitional ambivalence. These strategies are closely related to interactions with others and their offerings of designations of the problem. Affirmations from others are an important contingency in the definitional enterprise and are taken into account in the sorting task.

Actors use both verbal "expressions given" and nonverbal "expressions given-off" to infer things about others (Goffman 1967). We also take these cues into account to see ourselves through the eyes of others (Mead 1934). This is what sociologists refer to as "taking the role of the other" or simply, *role-taking*. We can view ourselves from the standpoint of close significant others or, from the standpoint of our larger community or society, a *generalized other*. These are the ways through which the social self emerges and changes throughout life. The image a person holds of his or her "self" is always in the context of self-to-other. In a moral career—a process that gets its very name from the fact that self is especially at stake—the significance of self-other contexts for self-imagery and definitions is especially keen.

The cues that wives of alcoholics receive from others are critical in their changing views of themselves, their husbands, and their marriages. For some of the women interviewed, cues from family or friends supported their emergent acknowledging of problems and targeted certain definitions over others. Such a framework of social support in close significant other relationships is typified by the following examples:

> I think my friend was more conscious that he was an alcoholic than I was, and especially in the last year or two. The reason that she became so conscious of it was listening to her brother, who had put himself in treatment, and knowing us so well, she said, "It's alcohol, he's an alcoholic."

> When his sister came in, I would say, "Say, he wasn't right, going out last night, was he?" "No, he wasn't; he shouldn't have done that, he's got responsibilities to you." And it was just kind of reinforcing telling me that it was happening . . . because it is such a gradual thing. You wonder sometimes—[he] just went out with the guys, just went out to have a good time—but she reinforced me, and then when she brought home the books, that was the real [clincher].

> I guess it was about three years ago, when I was contemplating leaving the situation, [people were helpful] particularly a brother. I'd call him and he'd talk hours with me, and he kept telling me that my husband was an alcoholic and unless he does something about it there's no hope, [saying], "I'm worried about you, Sis," and was really encouraging me to get out of the relationship.

> Usually it was older women that had lived with an alcoholic for a number of years—I would discuss it with them. And I found them very helpful in seeing that I wasn't the only one. One [person] stands out in my mind, and I just adored her. . . . She told me, "You know, don't even bother to have him admitted, because unless they want to do it themselves it's not going to work." And she looked at me and said, "If you aren't the pattern of me, I don't know who is," and she

suggested that I get out while I was still young. Well, this was several years ago, and I'm still in there.

During the acknowledgment period, such social support of perceptions and designations is important and self-enhancing, but apparently for some it is not yet strong enough to significantly alter the ambivalent and moral features of this definitional enterprise. For others, cues from family or friends may actually diffuse the definitional enterprise. In such cases there is usually some negation of problematic drinking, or an otherwise dissipating action of some kind. The following excerpts illustrate this:

I talked to his mother. I said, "I'm concerned about him." I really was ashamed—I didn't want to talk to my parents, I didn't want to talk to my friends. And his mother said, "Well, what are you complaining about? He's bringing his money home, he takes care of the family, doesn't he?" So there went . . . any hope of hope, you know.

I talked to one of his friends that he was doing it with quite often, and I expressed my concern—how much he was doing [it] and how it was affecting us. His friend would just say, "Well, it's just a phase, he'll get over it, I'll talk to him," and that type of thing.

They would say to me, "You have got such a good husband," because my husband worked every single day. If my husband came in at three in the morning, my husband was on the job at six-thirty A.M. They never said, "Maybe there is a problem." To this day, with this treatment, it was not accepted by either parents. I couldn't talk to my parents about it because their reaction was, "You tell him not to go to the bar, tell him to get home; make plans, have company." He never showed up, he never stayed with the plans. His parents said, "He was married too young, had a child too young. He hadn't outgrown his flings with the fellows. That's why, after all, you can't blame him for drinking." I did not know. I was too afraid to seek [help], and I was very, very unaware that there was anything such as this disease.

Husbands are also a significant source of cues that negate or dissipate designations of a drinking problem. (Many of the husbands later acknowledge their difficulties with alcohol, usually when other definitions are no longer successfully negotiated; even such admissions may maintain ambivalence, however, as discussed later.) It is difficult for wives to surmount the powerful impact that their husbands' negations of drinking problems create. Representative of negating comments and influence from husbands are the following three excerpts:

He would say, "I don't have a drinking problem, I have an infidelity problem," and I believed that, you know. I thought, Oh cripe, it's women. As I read further, they would rather admit to that than the booze.

I just thought it was a lot for one person to drink in a night, and I couldn't understand, he never got drunk. He just said, "I'm not drunk, so I don't think that I have a problem."

He went out of his way to not tell me. He would lie, or he would just stay away till he had sobered up enough and come home and act like nothing had happened. Toward the end, he would go to any lengths to get that next drink. He would look me right in the eye and say, "I haven't been drinking." I mean, here is a bottle sitting right here and he [would say], "Well, I haven't been drinking. What's the matter with you?" He always thought his drinking was no problem until the very end. He would say to me that we had a roof over our heads, a nice home, food on the table, and what more did I want? I should see what the poor people were dealing with. And as long as he provided these things, things were okay. So he just felt that his drinking was no problem. At times he would say he probably spent too much time away from home.

At the very end he was saying that he knew he was a hard-core alcoholic, but he loved being one and he was never going to do anything about it. It was probably within the last year. It was very heartbreaking for me to hear him say he was an alcoholic but loved being one, because I thought when this came—when you heard them say this—this was acceptance of it [and treatment would come], but it isn't done in that way.

The last excerpt is especially instructive, representing shifts in definitions offered by the husband spanning twenty years of marriage. Initially, negation of drinking problems and then performance of the husband-father role of provider are utilized in negotiating an acceptable definition of the drinking situation. Much later, a definitional shift in self-image includes the label of alcoholic. Surprised as wives may be that their husbands do not always seek help once they admit to being alcoholic, self-admission of alcoholism has been suggested as a potential means for justifying further drinking (Roman and Trice 1968). In the preceding example, the husband's defense of his drinking on the basis of being alcoholic represents a definitional shift from primary or situational deviance (when behavior is explained in terms of socially approved roles) to secondary deviance, when deviant behavior or its associated role are used to attack, defend, or adjust to social responses to the deviant person (Lemert 1951). Other research has suggested that taking on the "alcoholic role" crystallizes the problems with alcohol and increases the gulf between significant others and the drinker (Roman and Trice 1968; Bacon 1973). So, while crystallization of the problem would seem to relieve definitional ambivalence, the "gulf" alludes to a heightened awareness of contradictions and incompatibilities in role expectations and performances.

Sometimes the cues expressed by the husband include distortions of information relevant to defining problematic or alcoholic drinking. Deception by the husband about his drinking is common in a substantial number of these cases, not just as problems emerge but, notably, in the beginning as well: "When I met him, I didn't know he was an alcoholic, but about three months after we had been going together pretty heavily, he told me. He said he wasn't drinking, then, but later on he admitted that he had been drinking, and using drugs, the whole time, but he would abstain when we had a date. When he was with me it was not a problem, because he didn't drink when he was around me, not at all. In fact, he led me to believe that he had not been drinking for over two years."

In addition to cues from significant others, the women took into account their perceptions from the standpoint of the larger community, or generalized other. Of special interest are standpoints originating or referring to the normative order of social institutions such as the legal justice system and the occupational sector. Problems arise when norms about behaviors in question and the sanction for them are inconsistent or ambiguous

(Rubington 1973). The samples below represent a range of responses that at one point can implicitly support attitudes and behaviors that at another point may warrant treatment or punishment. The plausibilities implied by this cultural inconsistency add to the complexity of the wives' tasks in sorting and acknowledging ambivalence. The first examples involve the occupational sector, wherein the use of alcohol may be variously approved or disapproved of socially:

> Drinking was with business contacts. Well, for a long time, of course, I was involved, and—as a good wife—you don't rise high in the business world unless you have a wife who is willing to play the game, and I was a very dutiful wife.

> He was sent home from work. They told him that he would go home and go into treatment, "otherwise you're fired."

Contradictions in the letter of the law and carrying out the law also add to definitional ambivalence from the public dimension of social control:

> A third one [DWI citation] that he got, [he] paid the judge off and got that off the books. That one was just a breeze, you know—paid five hundred dollars and off he would go. Well, that isn't a situation that makes me very happy; too bad that that was the way it was.

> It [the accident] was all taken care of by this lawyer. I was very, very bitter, very resentful of the bar owner, and really wanted to know—even from the police—why my husband didn't get a ticket. Why he wasn't tagged, why he wasn't fined; he was under the influence.

These examples remind us that, within the normative order of social life, a certain negotiable level of deviance can be tolerated, beyond which some form of informal or formal negative sanctioning will occur. Time, place, visibility, and consequences of actions are some of the contingencies. In this study visibility of the husbands' drinking-related behaviors emerged as an important element in the definitional enterprise, underscoring the significance of self-performance and audience. The wives, as "audience," observed changes about their husbands, along both personal and public lines, as part of continuing activities of acknowledgment.

Virtually all of the women noted changes over time. They noted changes in themselves, their husbands, and their marriage relationships. From the women's point of view, most of the changes in themselves were associated with the changing interactions with their husbands, changes that illustrate the activities of sorting ambivalence by valuating and personalizing, discussed in the next three chapters. Here, the focus is on changes the women observed in their husbands. Three typical types of change are general changes, changes in behavior while drinking, and changes in the activity of drinking itself.

The general behavioral changes are not specifically tied to incidents of drinking, but to overall changes in patterns, attitudes, or overt behavior. For example, the wives in this study reported:

> During the courtship I met his friends, who seemed like very nice people, and he acted very extroverted and very caring and very sensitive. [But] soon after the marriage I discovered that he was introverted, he wasn't caring, he wasn't that and [was] really selfishly demanding. It's been worse and worse and worse; for the last ten years he hasn't allowed anybody in the house.

> I just felt like after the children started coming, we drifted apart; he spent more time away on his days off, drinking. . . . I'm not saying the behavior was so bad then, but . . . I often felt . . . that the more kids [we had], as each one came along, things began to fall apart more and more and more. Slowly but surely, as he had to be out doing banking or whatever, he would be gone for a long time, and he would come home and you would know that he had had a few. And I just got so I resented him going off on his days off, because I just knew that he was going to come home, and be—I call it "snooted up." . . . The last few years, I'd say the last five years or so, just really got hard.

> It seems like . . . he is getting more paranoid dealing with people. They are either the prince charming or the jerk: either a blankety-blank and "he did me wrong, I'm never going to deal with him again," or "he's just the best guy in the world." And he's not always being rational and perceiving some of the things that happened to create either one of these concepts.

In contrast to the general changes above, many of the women noticed changes in their husbands' behaviors specifically during their drinking episodes. These changes ranged from subtleties in gait, speech, or eye contact to what the wives regarded as more social, public, or shared observations. Such behavioral changes included the following:

> If he drank too much, he was always more or less a clown. . . . It isn't so bad, you can tolerate them when they are a little silly or something, but he started getting mean, argumentative, and belligerent—obnoxious, you know. And that wasn't like him; he was a very kind, gentle man. [We have] no conversations anymore. We used to communicate a lot—[now, there's] no communication at all.

> He had taken his things and moved back to his house, and he had started seeing old friends. I had heard from the fellows that he would fly into a rage and throw furniture and smash chairs. He's [a] crazy, fanatic perfectionist about housekeeping, [so] that's very, very unlike him to do things like that.

> He would start to not remember things he had done. If he fell asleep at any point when he was drinking, he could wake up and talk to you, talk on the phone, go to the bathroom, and he would not remember it. Then I knew it was getting serious.

One final example of changes when drinking gives us an especially sharpened view of the process of change and contingent shifts in definitions of selves and situations:

> My husband had a pattern. Most of the time he didn't come home from work for an hour or two, or three or so . . . he would come home late, and usually he was drinking. This one night he came home and we had gone ahead and eaten, and he had had quite a bit to drink. I didn't say anything, but he could tell by the look on my face how upset I was. That's usually the way he was. If he saw I was upset, he got very defensive, and he would try to pick a fight, I guess, to put the blame on me. What we had to eat was on the back burner, on warm, and he took it and threw it against the wall, and then he proceeded to yell and scream and tip over the lamps in the living room. He started punching

holes in the living room wall, and about that time, I thought, Oh my God! He had never done anything like that before, scared me half to death, so I called the police. . . . The police came, and one of them took my husband into the bedroom and one talked to me and suggested that it sounded like he had a drinking problem and that I should check into Al-Anon and talk to the head of the chemical dependency division of [the] county . . . talk to them about getting some help, and I did. That's when I first started with Al-Anon.

One woman noted behavioral changes when her husband was not drinking, a period, Wiseman (1981) suggests, of heightened self-awareness and performance challenges that has been under-studied. The wife's insights on this phenomenon, which Wiseman calls "sober comportment," were as follows: "At first it [his excessive drinking] didn't appear to me because I wasn't seeing him all the time, but now I realize from friends that he was drinking quite steadily during that time [on the days we lived apart]—he was just drying out when he was with me—and that is probably why he was such a jerk on the three days I would see him. He was impossible; people that were used to dealing with me in the business couldn't stand him, and I used to feel real bad about that, you know. I tried to make excuses: 'I'm really sorry, [he] is really stressed right now.'"

Besides general changes in behavior and behavioral changes while drinking, the wives reported a third type of change—that in the drinking act itself. In other words, they described a difference in the *way* their husbands drank. The comments below typify these observations:

It wasn't a problem when I first met him. When I first met him, he wasn't using anything—no drinking, did no drugs. [He] was straight for a year, and then. . . .

For a while we would go out to dinner, for an evening with his parents—just get together and see people. But then he got to the point where *he* would go. He didn't want to take me into bars with him anymore because he knew I would nag him that he was drinking too much.

In the beginning he would drink like twice a week, three times a week; he would pick up a pint, come home, and drink it after supper, or after the kids would go to bed. He would never drink when the kids were around. But then he got to the point where he would buy a pint and drink it, and beer, around the kids.

He's at the chronic stage, he's at the bottom now; everything revolves around his drinking. He drinks quite a bit at home now—it is cheaper—and he goes to the places where he can bring his bottle in; he very rarely goes to a place where he has to buy the liquor over the bar because of the cost. He carries his bottle in the car with him . . . he has me drive whenever we go anyplace so he can take his glass with him. He mows the lawn, he has his glass. When I close my eyes and think of my husband, I see [him] doing everything one-handed, with the other hand on this big tumbler of his booze. In this last year, this was the turning point. He brought his bottle into work with him—he works third shift, so he thought he could get away with it. [But] people reported him.

Some of the women noted changes between past and present drinking activities. Over time, a multitude of drinking-related interactions were woven into overall images of selves and the marriage relationship. The following excerpts illustrate these past-present comparisons, as well as the endurance and shifting character of definitional ambivalence:

We've been married for thirty-one years. His drinking has always been related to business. When he was on the road all week, I'm sure that he was in a situation where he probably drank every night, but I wasn't aware of it, and the children and I were home. So it was not really a family problem, and I don't think it really was a problem for him either until probably these last fifteen years. When he was home, why it became much more obvious to us, and we were aware of the fact that there were quite a few nights that we were alone, and we'd expected him. His drinking has never been a problem on weekends, on days he's home.

I would go out, entertain customers with him, and we would have customers at home—entertaining was a big way of life. However, as I felt he was drinking more and the kids were getting older and what have you, I began rebelling and would not join him if he had been drinking, until it came to the point that he no longer asked me to join him. He just went out on his own and drank.

When we were first married, I loved him very much; I thought nothing would work without [him] around. I didn't drive; I was very, very dependent on him. And in the middle stage I got so that I realized that I couldn't depend on him, so then I started, more or less, taking over, controlling the things that had to be done, paying for [things], making sure that we had a roof over our heads. . . . And now [at] the end, we're kind of going our own ways. . . . I try to ignore him, pretend like he's not there—maybe he'll go away.

The first three years we were married he went to school full-time and he worked full-time, so therefore he really didn't have any free time. When he got out of school, then that was when he started the drinking, really. He did a lot of stopping and staying late. Where[as] the last few years, although he was drinking a lot more and he was drinking straight brandy, he was drinking at home and he wasn't doing as much staying in a bar. So, how do you want to look at it? Well, I would say that it's been more of a problem lately, even though he's been home drinking, because he's been less able to function, as far as even talking to the kids; I mean they [have] just stayed away from him.

At this point, two further contingencies regarding definitional ambivalence and related social experiences deserve mention. The first is simply the opposite of active information seeking, reality testing, responding to cues from others, and so forth. A substantial number of the women interviewed chose not to talk to anyone about their changing lives and problems, or chose to speak only to one person or only after years of silence (usually out of feelings of shame, embarrassment, or individualism).

The second contingency is that families having a history of alcoholic drinkers or treatment, surprisingly, passed very little concrete, constructive information on to their female relatives, the subjects of this study. Family members who had become knowledgeable from their own earlier alcoholic-complicated situations often did not convey or relate their experiences to the ongoing problems confronting these wives. Close others could have provided valuable insights, but apparently they were reluctant to intercede or apply labels in these situations.

Cultural and interactional factors such as individualism, traditional roles, and learned passive behavioral styles may account, in part, for this second contingency. Still, in light of excessive drinking's known potential for problems, it seems remarkable that relatives would maintain such a position. Perhaps because it is often regarded as a "disease," alcoholism may have been seen by family members as something that has to "run its course" instead of being acted against. Recent trends in public education and intervention practices, however, may lead to changes in patterns of family feedback in years to come. In any event, such "hands-off" situations can only reverberate with the challenges of definitional ambivalence for the women in this moral career. The following excerpt from an interview illustrates this familial noninterference and/or quasi-helping pattern:

[Before we were married] he would go out on the weekends and go to a party, and he would usually get loaded. See, his parents are Baptists, so he couldn't go home—I would have to haul him home with me. One time he got loaded so bad on vodka and beer that I had to drive the car home. We were on the highway, and he was pulling my hands off the steering wheel, and he was pounding on [the dashboard]. He made me stop the car, and he got out and threw up and sat down on the ground. I dragged him back in and finally got him home and threw him out of the car.

I went stamping in the house and Mother asked me where he was, and I said, "Well, he's outside. I didn't stay out there." I had my engagement ring on, threw that across the room, and she said, "Well, you can't leave him out there." It was November, so we up and yelled at him to come in. He came in and he threw up all over my mother's carpet [and] pottied inside his pants. We just left him between the kitchen and the living room and went to bed.

After the last two or three years, she told me then that she always felt that he had a problem, even before we were married, and she was wondering. My father was an alcoholic; they were divorced and he's dead now—that was a love-hate relationship. I used to beg my mother to divorce him.

[Author: "She had never said anything to you before that about your fiancée?"]

[Respondent: "No. Oh, I suppose I seemed content."]

The efforts of wives to discern and acknowledge information about what is going on help them to realize that their problems are now more serious than routine, and to grasp the tremendous definitional ambivalence that comes with that realization. Characteristic of this stage in the problem amplification phase, however, there is still precious little that cuts through the incompatible and contradictory attitudes, beliefs, and behaviors of definitional ambivalence. In their attempts to sort through this definitional haze, the women also valuate and personalize the ambivalence.

Sorting the Ambivalence

Valuating

To valuate is to appraise; valuational activities are part of the attempts to sort through and manage definitional ambivalence. They involve partitioning things into "good" and "bad," assessing positive and negative aspects of selves and situations. Despite their troubled marriages, the women interviewed for this study were able to name positive attributes when asked what they most liked, admired, or respected about their husbands. These positive valuations involved a variety of characteristics such as their husbands' role performances as provider, father, and husband, as well as special talents, intelligence, personality, and so forth. To illustrate:

He supported us all through this period. He did provide for us.

I've seen him at his job and what he can do, and I respect his knowledge and the way he can carry out his job performance. I really admire that in him.

He's really smart—I like his head. I like his personality; he's really a nice guy. Um, I don't know, I'm in love with the guy.

He's just a good person; he just is. I don't think too much of him has been spoiled yet.

However, many of the women did not make clearly positive statements about their husbands, speaking rather in qualifying terms and modifying positive valuations. Consider the following responses and the definitional ambivalences implied by them:

He's really basically a good man. He would not hurt anyone on purpose. He wouldn't deny anyone anything—he has denied us of himself, but not of any "thing." He's a hardworking man and that's a catch-22 right there, because I always felt his work came before his family. We had long discussions regarding that. There is still a certain resentment of that.

In spite of the fact that he is so sick, emotionally or alcoholically or however you want to view him, eventually the man always picks himself off the floor and will try to get a job and try to hold it. And [he] always gives me all his paychecks. I handle the money—of course, he doesn't want to be bothered with it, another shift of responsibility. I think he is basically kind, basically generous, and I think he is intelligent, and I think he is very sentimental. I think that he is very thin-skinned, and I think that he is totally unable to handle feelings; he runs from them like he's running from hell.

By comparing the preceding excerpted interviews with those that follow, we can deepen our awareness of moral career as process. The first excerpts symbolized positive views wives held of their husbands—regardless of any concomitant negative views. Next were representations of wives' qualified-positive or mixed-valuation images of their husbands. The excerpts that follow are illustrative of a further breakdown in positive imagery to the point of considering it as "only potential" or as "long gone." Together, these highlight a process of moral career in which a majority of the wives' views of their husbands underwent a qualitative shift in definition. His "self" was redefined as predominantly negative rather than primarily positive or as both positive and negative, while often the very foundations of formerly perceived positive attributes were questioned:

What I felt I've always loved about him, I question right now, if it's true. I've always thought of him as being a loving, kind, helpful person who would do anything for anybody, [who was] thoughtful and [would] stand behind me, help me. He really helped me along through school, and in a whole lot of ways, and yet there were times that I felt he was pulling me down and stuff. Right now, I question it all, because I don't know. . . .

I would probably have to go back to the first years that we were married—the fact that my husband had a good sense of humor. He was the laughter in our house. But that's all been lost for so many years.

When I could see him in a good light, I guess I liked his sensitivity. He's thoughtful, he helps, . . . he's very good in many ways. But the drinking had taken over all of those behavior traits, and I couldn't see the good things anymore. And I guess it wasn't until after he had been gone awhile . . . that you kind of forget the bad things and remember the good things.

These examples illustrate the weight of negative valuations as they emerge and endure over time. At this point in the moral career, countering or even balancing unpleasant and painful negative valuations with positive ones seems to exacerbate the definitional challenges such women face.

Interestingly, Al-Anon may provide a contingency for a mixed positive-negative conception of the husband. One feature of Al-Anon is that it helps transform problematic and contradictory attitudes and beliefs of "he's this *but* he's also that" into less conflictual ones of "he's this *and* he's that." Consider the comments of a woman whose husband had had previous treatment and attended Alcoholics Anonymous but who had persisted in sporadic drinking, mixed with periods of sobriety, for several years. She had been a member of Al-Anon for four years and exemplified the person who engages in the kind of combined positive-negative valuating that is replete with definitional ambivalence:

I used to try to lower him so bad—this was before Al-Anon. Now what I do is, I'll say . . . what I think is wrong about him, like, . . . "You lie so bad and you're such a liar, and how can you even respect yourself for lying?" And then I'll say, "And yet I love you so much because you can be so good; you're such a good person and yet you're such a creep." That is exactly what I say to him. Before, it would be all bad; I wouldn't . . . allow myself to see any good at all . . . before Al-Anon. Now I will tell him the good along with the bad.

This brief survey of what the women in this study found most positive about their husbands exposes several contradictions that contribute to definitional ambivalence. When we review their negative valuations of their husbands, the contradictions and incompatibilities and the attendant definitional challenges become even more apparent. Except for one woman, who found it difficult to "dwell on . . . what I don't like about him," the wives readily responded to the question, "What do you most dislike or disrespect about your husband?" The examples used here are drawn from the same excerpts as the positive valuations were, which underscores the contradictory definitions the women held of their husbands and their marriages.

Several women pinpointed drinking per se as what they most disliked about their husbands. Others targeted behaviors that they associated with the drinking, such as temper or altered mood. Examples of these stances appear in the following comments: "Really, the only thing I can think of that I don't like is his drinking," "He's mean when he gets drunk," and "I hate him when he's drinking. It's like living with Dr. Jekyll and Mr. Hyde. I have a stranger in my house and I don't want him there: 'don't touch me; don't come near me; I might throw up; I might kill you, just don't—leave me alone.'"

An emergent and growing distrust accompanied the wives' increasing awareness of discrepancies. Duplicity became an important and disliked attribute in their changing views of their husbands, as the following two excerpts highlight: "I think he's been basically dishonest—during this summer, the last three years—about his drinking; he's been very dishonest to me," and "Obviously, infidelity would have to be high on the list! He can't communicate. When he feels faults or he feels that you are pressing on him or picking on him, he cannot communicate and he'll use 'distruth' . . . he just can't be honest."

Other women pointed out negative behaviors that related more closely to their expectations of their spouses' roles, emphasizing responsibilities of the husband-father or family man. The following excerpts illustrate negative valuations referring to inadequate role performance:

I dislike his drinking, obviously, and what it did to him as far as his moods [were concerned]. Sometimes he is too tight with his money. His parenting—he could be very concerned and fun with the kids, but it was like when he was in the mood. He left a lot up to me.

If just bothers me that . . . he'd rather go to the track or he'd rather go golfing than pay the bills. It was just always up in the air whether or not we'd make ends meet. We always usually did, but sometimes it got very hairy getting behind and stuff.

He had an affair when he was drinking, and I have never cheated on him. What happened is that he had the affair and I didn't know about it. . . . He went into treatment [and] the day he came out, he told me that he had had it because he was feeling guilty about it. . . . That hurt, because what that did was, he couldn't handle the guilt, and so he took it from himself and gave it to me and said, "I'm done with that. I've been carrying [it] around . . . for five years now, and I want to get rid of it, so here, baby, it's yours." And that really did have a large part in destroying what was there or maybe being able to build and work on that.

I don't respect him, because, for his "hurt little boy," he still is a child to me. . . . I think he still expects me to take care of him when he is feeling bad. He's still using it now in the divorce. He can't accept the fact that it's over, and so he's coming at me with this hurt little boy, and I just want him to be a man. I want him to stand on his own two feet, to be responsible for himself and for his actions and say, "Hey, this is the way it is. I am responsible for this too"—take his part and go on.

Some of the women implied an "essential" negativity about their husbands. It is as though the husband had crossed an invisible line—the other side of which, from the wife's perspective, was nearly inconceivable and certainly incompatible with her values:

I guess I have terrible disrespect for anything that is addiction. I disrespect somebody who just is always afraid and has every opportunity to go to therapists, psychiatrists, and get help, and he won't. I don't understand that.

I disrespect the way he used me, sexually. This is a very big hang-up for me.

I think that the characteristic that I dislike the most is that we are not able to communicate. We are not able to just sit and talk or discuss anything. I dislike the fact that my children, our family, our home . . . don't seem to be important to him.

In these comments there is an implicit distancing of the women's sense of self from their husbands. It is as though the "self" implied by their close association or collaboration with such a negatively valued husband was more than these wives could bear.

The women saw themselves also changing, through acts of omission or commission, into a type of person they did not like. This was so despite a ripeness for self-righteousness, considering many of their husbands' undesirable behaviors. On entering the family program, a substantial number of the wives said they wanted to feel better about themselves, like themselves more, and get their selves "together." These feelings of low esteem or inadequacy related to changes that they observed and felt in themselves over time, and that emerged mostly through interaction with their husbands.

Even relatively stable or long-enduring characteristics of the women were sometimes renegotiated and reinterpreted through interaction into a changed negative valuation, as illustrated by the following excerpts:

He wanted somebody that would sit around and drink and laugh it up and just do all sorts of crazy things, and I wasn't into that. He began to put me down for that, and so then I began to think, Oh, I'm really boring and just a stick-in-the-mud.

I think now that it just shows how much I didn't care for myself for taking all that. . . . So I must have been awfully, awfully low to have allowed myself to live in that situation.

I always felt that I was inferior to him because he had the college degree. I had worked part-time, in between having babies, to help support him to go to school. . . . One night he was drunk and we were with another couple, and, in front of them, he told me that he's the one that went to school—"What have *you* done?"—and it stuck with me.

Most of the women's self-images changed for the worse, often in association with their venting of anger. Notably, even though these wives felt justified about their anger, they conveyed a marked discomfort with expressing it:

> Occasionally, [he was] a little bit verbally abusive, but he's always been a kind and gentle person. If anything, I would be more that way in the last couple of years. As I say, I really felt angry. I yelled at him. I just plain screeched . . . so I preferred not to see him [when he was drinking].

> There were a couple of times that he would ask me to bring him his food in the bedroom in bed, and I would take it to him. He would get mad about the way that it was arranged on the plate or something and throw my good china up against the wall and break it, and I would be so angry I would leave it three days, four days even, until he sobered up and cleaned it up. I wouldn't clean it up. I did in the beginning—I would clean up his mess—but I'm talking about when I changed from Miss Nicy Nice to Miss Horrible Mean.

> I would stuff a lot and I wouldn't feel, but then I would try to control it and stop it. I became a real naggy, picky person: "Why can't you stop?"—always digging at him, probably pushing him out the door again.

This discomfort with negatively valuated changes in oneself can best be understood as something much more than subjective individual phenomena. Denzin (1984) suggests, as have others (Hochschild 1979; Kemper 1981; Scheff 1979), that "the self-justifying features of emotionality vary by ideology . . . certainly by sex. . . . In short, many of the feelings people feel and the reasons they give for their feelings are social, structural, cultural, and relational in origin" (p. 53).

Women in these circumstances experience discomfort with their angry outbursts because they are incompatible with traditional definitions of ladylike behavior. Such changes are disruptive to self-imagery. If self-control is a natural attitude taken toward self (Denzin 1984), then a violation of this has severe implications for self, producing feelings such as helplessness, betrayal, self-violation, and emotional vulnerability (Meisenhelder 1979). Emotional outbursts that are about "the moral and personal destruction of the other as a person" (Denzin 1984, 84) are also morally destructive to self. Thus, angry outbursts, resentful attitudes, and such become interactional contingencies for self-imagery in the moral career. Increased dislike of the husband may, at least initially, foster increased dislike for self.

The intensity of self-change and self-anger at times implies a feeling of "What have I come to?" This is poignantly demonstrated in the following excerpts:

I hated him when he was drinking. I hated myself for the same reason, because we both got upset and said some awfully mean things. I reacted to how he reacted. That's what I hate about it: I reacted to his drinking, got so angry and said things. I remember once, this wasn't long ago, getting so upset at him that my emotions lost control [and] that he told me to get the gun out. I didn't point it at him, but close enough so that he would get the message, and I didn't have my hand near the trigger or nothing. I just stood there holding it, not near him, but I couldn't do it, and afterwards I just walked out and cried.

After that one beating, I was afraid to tell him how I felt. When I got real brave I would [say], "Don't you think it is time you slow down?" But I've never really told him that I really dislike it, that I really hated the drinking every day. I really hated happening to find those bottles. One thing I detested more than anything is when he'd . . . walk out of the house . . . to a bar and have to take three beers with him to get two miles. I thought it was sick. I never accepted it. It always made me angry inside. It was [like], Why can't I just speak out and say something? and, So what if he left because he got mad because he couldn't handle my telling him he drank too much? Yet I couldn't do it.

In these examples we see the wives in a catch-22, not only disliking themselves for getting angry at their husbands but also disliking themselves for not expressing their anger. Either way, they view their selves as changing for the worse. One young woman compared a seemingly positive self-image and a projected negative one to meet the challenges of defining self:

I'm only twenty-three years old, and I have my whole life ahead of me and I don't want to throw it away. I saw a lady at an Al-Anon meeting [who] was probably in her fifties, and she had terrible bags under her eyes and she started crying and saying that she had lived with this all of her life. I had told . . . all of them that I was at the point where I didn't know if I wanted to divorce or stick through this, and she said, "Oh, don't do it. Look at me, look at me. You know, you're going to end up just like me." So I thought, I am not going to be like that.

There is a close relationship between negative self-valuations and blaming oneself for the husband's excessive drinking or the continuation of problems. The excerpts below illustrate how feelings of inadequacy and self-blame work together in interpretive processes:

I think he's very, very manipulative, and I've tried very hard to end this relationship. There have been several points where I've been in much better emotional shape than I am right now and was on my way to turning it off. And back he comes into my life with promises and pledges of undying love, and they can't get carried out. I don't know if I hate him or if I hate myself, but I am bowing to this relationship.

When he'd call and say he was on his way home, or he was going to have a couple and he would be leaving in about a half hour, and he wouldn't come, I'd feel angry, and I would also feel hurt, especially when this got to be more and more [often]. I began to feel like, I'm nothing for him to come home to, and also I guess a lot of those times is when he would get intimate, and I guess I began to feel that . . . I didn't want this, just at these times. I began to feel angry and used and mixed up. And then I began to take the blame too, because things began to slip at home, housewise. I wasn't very organized, or he didn't think I was very organized, and I kind of . . . actually went down hill, and so this would always be thrown up in my face. . . . I began to think, Well, no wonder he's not coming home. And then I gained weight, and if I didn't keep myself up, I thought, what am I keeping myself for anyway? So I began to take the blame, and yet I would be angry . . . really lost, really confused and lost.

Among the substantial number of woman in the study who blamed themselves for their husbands' drinking or for their marital problems, the underlying theme was that something was wrong with them or with what they were doing. As they saw themselves from what they thought must surely be their husbands' point of view, they believed that something was very wrong with themselves. Their husbands' continued drinking, anger, avoidance, uncaring, and the like only reinforced this interpretation. In this phase of the moral career, wives are often convinced that they themselves created the problem, and that they are responsible for problems staying or going away. Exemplifying this point is a woman who, even after four years of Al-Anon meetings and literature, was still embroiled in this definitional struggle: "I've always said, 'Why don't you tell me what you don't like about me so I can change that?' . . . because it takes two to be married. He goes, 'You're working your program,' and he tells the pastor that 'she's okay.' But I can't be okay . . . well, that's why I get caught—maybe I am okay, but I keep thinking that I can't be if . . . he's treating me like this." The women may blame themselves for problems based on a variety of personal or interactional shortcomings, especially those involving personal attractiveness and strength, and financial and household management.

These negative valuations go hand-in-hand with interactional and interpretive processes and changing self-imagery. Virtually all of the women in this study viewed themselves as changing in some ways that they did not like in response to their husbands' alcohol-related behaviors. Cooley's (1902) concept of the looking-glass self describes how one's view of one's self is filtered through one's interpretation of others' views: "A self idea . . . seems to have three principal elements: the imagination of our appearance to the other person; the imagination of his judgment of that appearance; and some sort of self-feeling, such as pride or mortification. . . . The thing that moves us to pride or shame is . . . an imputed sentiment. . . . This is evident from the fact that the character and weight of that other, in whose mind we see ourselves, makes all the difference with our feeling. . . . We always imagine, and in imagining share the judgments of the other mind" (p. 152). Accordingly, these negative valuations reflect the wives' self-sentiments based on their perceptions of how their husbands and others viewed them. Explicit marital conflict highlights this process of negative self-imagery even more.

Generally, the women's accounts of conflict with their husbands revealed three major types: relatively low-key overt conflict, substantial verbalized conflict, and intense overt conflict including physical violence. A couple might move among these types of overt conflict within or across situations. It is important to note that virtually all of the wives reported rather intense subjective conflict, regardless of the objective level expressed.

Denzin (1984, 169) argues that "emotionality and the self are at the core of violence." What I want to emphasize is that this critical involvement of self or significant other is an intricate and influential contingency in the moral career of becoming the wife of an alcoholic. It is precisely such deep involvement of the self that makes it an inherently *moral* process.

Along lines similar to those I have drawn in conceptualizing definitional ambivalence, Bateson (1972, 182) has suggested that family interactions involving violent conflict are not constructed on the premise that "this is violence," but rather on the basis of the question, Is this violence real? In other words, should it be taken as something else? what was the intentionality of it? and so forth. The plausible answers constructed are exponential to the number of questions raised, highlighting an interactional situation of definitional ambivalence. Perhaps the most complex definitional ambivalence enters in the case of "paradoxical violence." In this type of violence, more than one interactional meaning is communicated at once—for example: "All the messages here are untrue," "I don't want to harm you," and, finally, "I want to harm you" (Bateson 1972, 184).

The inherent contradictions in the above set of messages aptly suggest a host of incompatible, yet separately perhaps plausible, attitudes, beliefs, and behaviors in a situation of violence. A situation of violence portends a certain immediacy, calling up all sorts of questions about the "real" selves of both the "perpetrator" and the "victim." It is reasonable to think of situations characterized as violent, as well as definitionally ambivalent, as accelerating interpretive efforts.

A minority of the women in this study initiated or contributed to acts of physical violence, though most were carried out by the husbands. The lack of physical violence, however, does not indicate that the problems are less severe. Subjective appraisals of conflict may be far more active or intense than outward expressions of it. Consider, for example, this appraisal: "There never has been any physical abuse, and there never have been any verbal tongue lashings. . . . I think it's taken a more subtle form of abuse. There has been abuse in staying out all night and not knowing where he is. That's abuse in my eyes. Or his not wanting to communicate or do any family things with me or with my daughter. To me, that's a form of abuse."

To view one's own self or significant other as abusive or violent almost always involves changes in self-imagery. We can infer that this involves the breaking down and shifting of images, perhaps from relatively supportive partner to dangerous adversary, even if a loved one. The following excerpt demonstrates ways in which the women verbally negotiated conceptions of self or husband as abusive:

> [He's] very seldom combative . . . there have been a couple of incidents [where] we've actually gotten into fights. He's never abused me physically. We kind of push and shove a little bit and get into really loud shouting matches, but those aren't routine either or anything that he does whenever he gets real drunk. . . . If he gets real drunk, it's more of a pattern to just fall asleep, pass out. And physically abusive, no— yes in that . . . a couple [of] times we've had fights, and he caught me by my arm, my wrist, and squeezed, and that hurt a lot—but he never hit me or anything like that.

Increasingly looming definitions of self or husband as abusive or violent are represented by these reflections:

> In the past he was very verbally abusive, very, but he was never really physically. . . . I mean he pulled my hair once, and once he picked me up, and he was so angry, he ran down the stairs with me and threw me on the couch, but he never hit me. . . . I really was kind of afraid of my own temper, too. My thing was, there is no contest between strength as far as male and female [are concerned], and if he was to strike or hurt me, then I would have to kill him, not maim him. Sometimes I would get really scared of that. But he never did; maybe it was some kind of check system within him. Maybe there was some fear of me, too. I don't know, but I was very fearful of that next step, what it might go

over to. He'd pick up a telephone or a table and throw it or something. He never hit me or the kids.

He's been physically [abusive] against the kids, a bit. I have a real hard time with this, because I am going through some counseling. They call it *battering*; however, that sounds like a strong word for it, I guess. He has a push down, shove down—not really literally beating them, but push and shove and things like that, which can be just as physically bad. Verbal is the biggest thing he uses; he screams a lot.

[He was] not physically [abusive] with me, but he would start putting [his] fists through walls. . . . He's *not* a violent person, so that was just . . . terrifying to see. . . . I've never seen that side of him before. It . . . didn't seem like *him*.

Physical violence may be part of the present experience while at the same time symbolically portending violence in the future. Anticipated violence foreshadows changed views of selves. Consider the role of anticipatory or symbolic violence in the accounts below:

I came home . . . we had this dog, and he had beaten the dog up, and it had fecal material and blood all over the apartment. I said, "Where is the dog?" And he said, "He's downstairs." He was hanging from the telephone pole, [by] the choke/chain . . . he was almost dead. I got the dog off the telephone pole, had to clean that whole mess up. After that . . . I was just afraid of it, although he's never laid a finger on me. He had to handle that incident at [treatment]. It scared him that he lost his temper, and then I lost the baby a week after that . . . I'm having to work that out.

He's always been sarcastic, very critical, and very authoritative; as the drinking got worse, that got worse too. There were a couple of situations where . . . I couldn't take it anymore and I slapped his face. I got it back and was told . . . "Hey, you slapped my face and I'm going to slap yours back." Well, it would be ten times harder when I got it, and I would feel, well, he's right, I did slap him, but [we] didn't take into account at all . . . why I slapped him. The things that he said to me didn't seem to be that bad. . . . I couldn't say that that was as bad as him getting a slap across the face . . . but it kept me from doing that. I was definitely afraid that . . . he would whack me.

He got all mad at me because I took the liberty to go to his friend and talk to him about his drinking. So we got into a big fight and he beat me up. Then this friend came over and took him to detox. I let him come back, and he did stay straight for about six weeks. Then I'd start finding bottles. When it would get to be bad times, I'd find vodka around and then we would have to have a fight about it. Then it would be back to beer. I didn't want to get beaten up in front of my kids again. I spent eight years scared to death that if he got drunk enough, he'd do it again.

As these excerpts illustrate, episodes of violence not only call forth definitional challenges in ongoing situations. They also symbolize potentialities of the future: what has happened once could happen again. In constructing ongoing actions and definitions, the wives take such a threat into account. The symbolic nature of the violence brings it into a past-future framework, whereby what was could be again. The wives' views of themselves and their husbands expand from actual to possible repetitions of spousal interaction, including physical violence. Definitional ambivalence heightens because these newly expanded views and anticipated images may be quite contradictory to and incompatible with existing ones in terms of marital and familial expectations. Questions of self-imagery suggest, What has—and will—become of me, him, us? Subtle facets of violence emerge as the anticipation of violence enters the silent negotiations of spousal interaction and as motive offerings are built around it.

Another stance taken by the wives of alcoholics involves more specific definitional shifts. They no longer view their husbands as men merely capable of violence but, in fact, as violent-selved men. At the same time, they may change their views of themselves from blameworthy, or helpless tolerators of violence, to assertive rejectors of violence. Representative of these contingencies in the moral career are the following excerpts:

I feel that he's been verbally abusive from day one. He has a hot temper. In the beginning there was that physical abuse, and I said that if he ever did it again, I would leave. And then he had a whole period of many years, until four to six weeks ago he did it again. The next morning he woke up realizing that he could have killed me and was apologetic and crying, and so I thought, fine, we'll get help. It was like I forgot about it, and then as the days rolled on, he minimized it, and then we had one more incident where he came home and didn't hurt me as bad—it was more verbal abuse—and I just packed my things and went to a shelter. He hasn't relayed to his counselor the things that I have relayed to her about the incidents—like he sees it in a completely different light, like it is more of a little roughing up. . . . It was a *beating* as far as I was concerned.

He never corrected the children. He never [gave] any discipline. He never showed feelings. But when he was drinking, he'd come home and he was going to houseclean. He was going to take care of all of it. So his thing would be to go and take care of it with the children. Our oldest child received the most physical [abuse]. Many times he would just punch her like she was a man, in the middle of the night. He would be very abusive verbally. His thing was, at one o'clock in the morning, . . . to pull the kids out of bed and they were to go sit down on the chair until three in the morning and get a tongue-lashing and a few kicks or whatever he felt they had coming at this time.

I didn't know how to stop it, and I didn't know what was happening in my life and for them. Into senior high my children have had physical abuse. I was so ashamed. I covered it up. I didn't want the children to tell anyone. I had mentioned it to his mother once, and she said that she could never believe that her kind, gentle son could be a violent person.

I thought something was so wrong with me that I really thought that I was losing my mind. I just couldn't share it with anyone, and I felt that I was to blame and I was deserving of this. It was more verbal abuse to me. The physical abusiveness was maybe three or four times. [After I went to counseling] this stopped because every time he was abusive, I would call the police and have the police come out. I feel that he then knew where he stood with this.

These examples illustrate the sometimes lengthy and processual nature of definitional ambivalence, challenges, and shifts. A significant change in these women's moral careers was that their self-imagery no longer included an ongoing, victimized, physically battered self. We must remember, however, that this stance often is taken only after many years of abuse. In this study it emerged only with the aid of a counselor's intervention prior to the introduction of alcoholic and spousal rehabilitation programs that are a part of the later proximal treatment phase of the moral career.

A final illustration of violent conflict shows ways in which the dynamics of interaction (and violent acts) and definitions of selves are intricately woven into the social fabric of lived and constructed experience. Notice how the ongoing negotiations of interactional episodes and changing self-imagery coalesce in the moral career process:

> I tried everything: be very nice and try to talk, yell and scream, not say anything, get physically violent. I really got into this thing with physical violence really bad. That's why I went to a psychologist for my physical violence . . . I had gone after him with knives. I would take the first punch and then he would slap me to settle me down. I can understand how people can kill when they are enraged, . . . he pushes me now because I have gotten a pretty good handle on my violence. He'll get me, he'll take the first slap or the first punch, and then I am out of it. It just happened again, and I ended up getting my hand all cut up cause I hit him with a vase.
>
> On Sunday when I talked to him he said that I worked my program [Al-Anon] so well, and it made him angry that he could see me working my program and being happy with myself now, and he couldn't do that. See, I had gotten to the point where I could handle my violence, so it made him angry that he didn't have that control over me, and I could control myself. . . . He knows what it takes to get me there now, where before it wouldn't take anything. . . . He would slap me and boom—just like that!—I'm crazy. It happens maybe twice a year, and it was just . . . a month or two ago, he picked me up and threw me against the wall. He never hit me first before, ever, until I controlled [my violence].

As this scenario demonstrates, and as a symbolic interactionist interpretation suggests, "To bring the other into an emotional act is to call out in one's self an emotional attitude toward the other and then to build up a line of emotional activity regarding that attitude" (Denzin 1984, 59). The violence that one feels and expresses is present not only within oneself but also in the actions taken against oneself by one's adversary. Both persons call up in themselves a violent attitude toward the other and build up emotional activity toward violence. A sort of metaviolence emerges in this two-way interaction of role-taking and looking-glass selves.

Generalized situations of conflict, such as these marriages, provide settings in which special stances toward the adversarial partner may emerge. Many women begin to assess a futility in their conflict-talk episodes with their actively drinking husbands. The wives in this study described these as no-win situations:

> There were times that I would look at him and think, Why am I arguing with him? He's too drunk. And other times, where he was in a good mood and I was not paying attention to how much he was drinking, he seemed perfectly all right and I would start arguing with him. It wouldn't dawn on me until later why he was saying all those stupid things to me, because he had been drinking and I just didn't realize it. And I would go crazy and pull my hair out [trying to maintain a logical discussion]—"What the hell's wrong with you?," you know—but a lot of times I would just walk away.

> If I didn't talk to him right away he knew that I was mad—"Now you are not going to talk to me all night." He started that thing. And if you did talk, you were still mad, [and] then you would start an argument, so you were better off not saying anything. Either way it was not good, really.

Many of the women adjusted to these no-win situations by socially withdrawing from their husbands. Variations on this theme are depicted in the following accounts:

> I've learned there is no point in talking to him when he's been drinking. And he's basically a very neat person, whom I love. When he's sober, he's such a delightful person that somehow all my good intentions would go down the drain . . . my reaction was withdrawal.

Oh, I guess [I] just try not to say anything to rock the boat; keep things to myself.

Eventually I realized it didn't do any good to be angry about it, because we would just get into an argument, and I ended up feeling the worst and taking the blame.

What are some of the social contingencies on the emergence of withdrawal as an interactional strategy? What types of interactions contribute to the construction of a no-win situation? The answers to these questions can further explicate the ways in which marital conflict is lived out in the everyday experiences of women in the process of becoming (still mostly unwittingly) wives of alcoholics.

The verbal comeback is an evocative ploy in verbal negotiations. Symbolically this device is part of a defensive or self-preserving act. Many of the women in the study, however, noted that overall they were unsuccessful in negotiating a positive self-image through comeback strategies and eventually resorted to some form of interactional avoidance or withdrawal. Definitional ambivalence is an inherent part of the verbal comeback interactional style, as shown in these recollections:

He had a reason for everything. If I would say something, he would counter it with another reason that would make sense. Like when I said, "Where did you get the beer?," [he would counter], "Well, Ben bought the beer." [Or if I said], "You've had enough, Frank," [he'd answer], "What do you mean, can't anybody be happy around here? I haven't had that much to drink; I've only had about two or three. Somebody has to liven it up around here; you've been so grouchy."

If I came back with something, he would say something else. He was always one step ahead of me, and it was kind of like I kept myself in this "kick-me game." You know, if I said something, I would get back . . . more, and the verbal abuse was increasingly [worse].

Sidetracking to another topic—that is, distancing interaction from the original issue and the selves at stake in it—is another interactional style that emerges during confrontation. The following excerpt is an exemplar of sidetracking and the accompanying no-win sentiment, as well as a vivid portrayal of definitional ambivalence:

He would always get off onto another issue. It was always: "Oh, you're just like your mother," or "You're getting your period," or "You've been working too hard," or "You're tired; you're not getting enough rest," or "Who have you been talking to?" It would always be something that would not be related to his drinking, and then we would end up getting into an argument over something else and he would walk away, and the original issue wasn't resolved. And I wasn't even aware of the fact that, hey, we just got off of this . . . until the next time, and the same thing would happen again. I began feeling that I'm crazy. . . . I would be so totally confused when we would have an argument over the drinking. I had worked very hard to not be like my mother—my mother is a very controlling person—and so that's all he would have to do was call me "Phyllis." I would get angry with him for doing that to me, and then we would get into that issue, when what we were really talking about was his drinking.

Or he would say, "Well, be specific: when did that happen, what time? . . . What day, what time? . . . tell me exactly what it was." If I was feeling angry or hurt by something that he said, he would want to know exactly what words he used and when he said it, and all I knew [was] that I was hurting. I was feeling a certain way because of something, but I would have to give him all the details or the data or it wasn't valid, and so I would be racking my brain trying to figure [it] out . . . Oh my God, I've got to get all this information for him; otherwise, he's not going to accept that it really happened, and did it really happen? Is he right? . . . Am I overreacting? I mean, he would have me convinced that I was overreacting because I was tired, or because I did this and I did that.

Closely related to such sidetracking is an interactional style that turns the discussion around to focus undesirably on the person who initially raised the disagreeable subject. This "turnaround" style is illustrated by the excerpt below, in which the wife accepts blame for her response to the husband's upsetting behavior:

He would come home, and of course I would be really upset and probably cry and stomp around there for a while. . . . I don't know how he did this, but he would turn it around and he would make me feel bad—about him being out drinking. And I would. I would feel bad. He'd make *me* feel bad about the things that I had said to him when he came home. . . . He'd say, "Well, I didn't do anything wrong; all I did was stop in and have a few beers. Wasn't hurting anybody." So then I would feel bad.

A final interactional style in conflicts is a "no-talk stance," bringing us full circle from the dynamics of changing views of self and significant other and the negotiated order of the relationship, to a kind of nonverbalized conflict that eventually diffuses to a generalized silence. These comments highlight the no-talk stance:

[I was] very bitter, hateful. I'm speaking now in the last year even. I didn't . . . care for him at all anymore. There was a period of about six months where, when he did come up that driveway, I did get nervous because I knew he was coming home. I was just wishing that he wouldn't come home. It wasn't until I joined Al-Anon that I really got those feelings. I'd be angry and he would ignore me, or he was usually so tired that he would fall asleep listening to me. The next day, he'd act as though nothing had even happened. He wouldn't talk, but because there was no argument—I had cooled off by morning—I didn't say anything, and we just didn't talk . . . [there] was just silence.

Another no-talk situation relates to emergent implicit rules of interaction. Consider how interpretation of such rules is lived out in everyday experience:

One of the rules was I could do anything I wanted to if I would let him drink—[it was] never discussed, but that's the way it was. I could spend any kind of money I wanted to . . . if we could pay the bills. He just didn't care as long as he could drink. So I never had to talk to him about anything, nor did he want me to. I think that's how everything happened for us. We established these rigid patterns and they were rules for us. . . . I think maybe there would be some sort of feedback like, "Well, *I* don't give a shit about that," meaning: "I don't want to *hear* about it; that's your problem. Just let me drink, and do whatever you want."

When verbal confrontation is part of the negotiated order of living together, an interesting phenomenon sometimes occurs. Confrontive questions and the act of questioning itself emphasize institutional form (marriage) over its substantive content (relationship). In Stone's (1962) words, interaction has shifted from the level of "interpersonal relationship" to the "structural" level. As interpersonal dimensions deteriorate in quality, there is an increased emphasis on the structural aspects of the marriage. As the shared, meaningful content of the relationship is lost, the wives may begin to focus on the form of the relationship in order to salvage it from complete disintegration. It is as though *not* to question the husband about his drinking behavior implies a disavowal of the marital partnership and the expectations that it entails. This can be seen as a last-ditch attempt by wives to reinstate, albeit symbolically, marital role expectations and to validate existence of the marital union, at least at the formal structural level. The following excerpt illustrates this phenomenon, along with retrospective reinterpretations of it:

> I tried to say, "Why did you do this?" . . . I realize now that it was idiocy to argue with a drunk—that's what I was doing. "Tell me why." I had to have an answer. I never got it, never got it. In the beginning I felt worried when he wouldn't come home. Then I would feel the anger: where the hell is he? "Where were you? What were you doing? Who were you with?" And I never got any answers. He seemed to enjoy not telling me because I would just get so upset, and that gave him an excuse to say, "Quit nagging; you're jumping on me as soon as I walk in the door, and I didn't even do anything. So what if I stayed out all night? I didn't do anything wrong. I didn't hurt anybody." So it's a hard thing to learn not to do; that's what they say—detaching yourself because you want to know why.

The wives' demanding questions are attempts to exact more socially appropriate behavior in the face of their husbands' flagrant nonperformance of the roles of spouse and father. The women acknowledge inadequacies of the interpersonal relationship and forfeit negotiations on that level in favor of adherence to role obligations at the marriage-as-institution level. The implication here is that *any* answer is more important than *the* answer. For without enough role adherence to warrant a viable response to questioned behavior, not only the obligation to answer is negated, but also the right of questioning. The wives' insistence on "understanding" or "knowing" thus can be seen as a strategy to keep their marriages and their selves "together," if not wholly intact. When seen in light of the severe implications for self-other and relationship definitions, the adamant questioning by the wives, instead of being symptomatic of their "crazy behavior," is a social, valuational, and self-survival effort of the first order.

These interactional styles represent ways in which wives of alcoholics interpreted and negotiated conflict in their relationships with their husbands. They demonstrate how conflict is lived out in daily experience and how it is related to the definitional challenges of this moral career. The kinds of things the women in this study reported fighting about with their husbands are not different from conflicts that arise in any marital relationship, most especially ones under stress. What is different is that drinking becomes a noted variable in arguments regarding problems and may eventually become a sort of filter through which entire scenarios and biographies are viewed.

The issues of conflict presented next are those articulated by the wives as drinking-related, chosen to demonstrate nuances of interaction perceived as alcoholic-complicated. They highlight contradictions and incompatibilities in role expectations and negotiations of self or significant other that are notable in definitional ambivalence and a moral career. The women identified dissension involving socializing, finances, family roles, sexual relationship, and personal attributes.

In the area of *socializing*, these conflicts were cited:

> I ordered coke. Well, he got very, very angry . . . to the point where I walked out of the place, because he started kind of yelling at me that I was not having a drink with him.

> If we started out both sober, we had no problems. If he came home and had been drinking, and then wanted me to go out, it was disaster,

and I just retrenched. I just refused, I wouldn't do it. So consequently our social life has narrowed tremendously. We have a lot fewer friends, and he has a lot fewer friends. . . . I blame it on his drinking.

The effect of one husband's drinking on the family's *finances* was related as follows:

We both made good money. . . . It really hurts to see what other people have who don't make as much as we do. Right now I'm living off of my salary. If I didn't have the back bills, we could make it very comfortably, me and the kids. So where was all of his check going? It certainly wasn't helping. He'd go off on a binge, and he could play pool and lose a hundred dollars on the Dallas game. I'd get brave— why should I worry about it?—and I'd go spend. That only made it worse, but it helped me at the time.

Examples of imputations concerning *family roles* include these excerpts from study interviews:

He went as far as to have everything I owned packed and thrown in the living room because our house was still a hangout. I wanted it [to be] our house, our family . . . not the hangout where anyone could come any time of the day. And that's how it was the first month, and it was driving me crazy. So I'm the one who had to tell them. He just couldn't see it.

We worked—got out at twelve [midnight] and hurried over to the bar, and closed it up at one A.M., and then of course there were friends—went over there and finished partying out. And the next morning I would have to get up with my little one, and he could lay there and sleep. I had to get the one off to school, and the baby, I could see how it was interfering with that. . . . I would be holding the baby in my arms trying to feed her and fall asleep and wake up with a nipple in her ear . . . and something had to be done. That's when I went back on days and told my husband, "You want second shift? Fine. I can't handle it. We've got children." I guess that's when we started to go to our own "woods" or whatever.

Regarding conflicts in *sexual relationships* arising from the husbands' drinking, several women made these observations:

Other women came into [the picture] and I would say things about it, and the more I said the more he drank.

My sex life really stunk bad for the past few months, probably because I can't stand sex with somebody that stinks of beer or alcohol.

I never had a chance to diagnose why, but I never had an orgasm with him, ever, and it was just an unpleasant experience. I don't know if it was because he was drunk on the first night and I was drunk, but I think that it had really . . . planted something in between my ears. . . . I was angry. There was not a trust. There was not a good feeling. It was all totally destroyed right away.

I was made to do things that . . . you know . . . I got to where *I'd* have a few drinks myself, because I knew what nighttime would bring for me when he drank. He's got a tremendous sex drive, and I didn't, and just a lot of kinky. . . . To this day, it humiliates me so bad that I went along with things like that. I would hurt physically sometimes. . . . I had a few physical problems from sexual abuse. . . . After, if he noticed I was sick or upset for any length of time, then he would be nice. . . . He is basically a good person, it's just that the drinking . . .

Denzin (1984, 177) distinguishes interacting *with* another—stepwise lines of action mutually and reciprocally fitted—and interaction *at* another—objectizing and directing negative feelings toward the other. In the account immediately above, the woman felt used and objectized—sexually interacted "at." In the account below, prior to gaining self-esteem, the woman acted sexually "at" her husband and through the process of role-taking objectized herself as well. Having once gained self-esteem, she fashioned a new social self and sometimes withheld her newly vested self from sexual interaction "with" him. A new positive view of self raises the stakes, rendering certain kinds of self-involvement a moral insult:

I guess the biggest weapon I had was sex, and it just got straightened out. There was a point where I had no physical feelings. It was like hurry up and get it done. Through Al-Anon, my whole life has changed. I used to hate my guts. I hated myself so bad, and now I can look in the mirror and say, "I'm okay." My whole outlook on life has changed, and . . . I guess it has changed the sex, too. . . . It's got to the point where it's okay, but it's still my weapon, and it's not just a weapon towards the drinking, it's his behavior. If he doesn't pick me up [from work] two nights in a row, the first night . . . I'll say, "It's okay, you know, you're human; you can make a mistake." But the second night, forget it: I just don't feel like making love. There's such . . . there's a difference. There's sex and there is making love . . . and my weapon was that, because it no longer [felt okay to share sex if he behaved unlovingly in other areas], and yet, it's stupid [to withhold sex], because that doesn't help either. But I guess it's easier than yelling and screaming.

Finally, over the course of the drinking, tension over *personal attributes* became extremely problematic:

It got to the point [where] I said I didn't know him anymore: he wasn't the same man I had married. He was so nasty all the time. You couldn't say a word without [him] yelling at you, and it was always my fault for everything, never his fault; he was perfect.

I completely let him manipulate me: if I wasn't such a bitch, he wouldn't do that; if I was a humble, loving lady and told him when things hurt me, he would never do that. He's always said that if you come to me nicely, . . . and I feel that I have done both of those [things]. That was his excuse to have another drink or smoke another joint, you know, but I bought into it.

At that time I'm still not thinking drinking was the problem, so that issue actually was not there. We did a lot of fighting and therefore he would take off and go out drinking. It was always with the idea that he was going to find someone else who would love him and take care of him . . . [that] type of thing.

The issues identified above—socializing, finances, family roles, sexual relationship, and personal attributes—highlight two important aspects of conflict in these alcoholic-complicated relationships. First, *role* was a central feature of the negotiated order of conflict. This was so whether it was the enactment, negotiation, improvisation, imputation, or distancing of role that was at issue. In other words, issues of conflict mainly revolved around whether or not one or both partners were fulfilling roles according to the expectations of the other. Social expectations are not just an individual matter, however. Cultural pluralism allows for many combinations of attitudes, beliefs, and behaviors to be activated, with at least some segment of cultural support for the stances taken. Many expectations exist as possibilities within the cultural milieu, even contradictory ones. In taking a stance in interaction, an individual draws on these cultural resources. Thus, contradictions and incompatibilities of sociological and definitional ambivalence play out at two levels—the interactional and the cultural. This double-pronged aspect of ambivalence lends a subtle complexity to issues of role-related conflict, presented here as a mode of conflict that was prevalent among the subjects of this study and their husbands.

Second, the process of problem interpretation, illuminated through issues of conflict, was marked by an increasing association of drinking with the presence of problems. As time went on, drinking was more frequently suggested as a causative agent or consequence of problems rather than merely an incidental, unrelated thing. As this association intensified, there was a qualitative shift in definition that transformed drinking into an integral part of "the problem" in the marriage. Once drinking per se became a viable object of questions, negotiations, defenses, or disavowals, it was "placed" in interaction and was difficult to avoid. Even if the wives did not yet view drinking as the problem, they did know that they did not like it or what happened when their husbands drank. Explanations for and about drinking started to come into the picture more often as behaviors were questioned, giving rise to *motive talk*.

In motive talk, the ambivalence-sorting activities of acknowledging and valuating merge. Because motives arise out of the questioning of untoward conduct (Mills 1940), both the social demand for and offering of motives address the selves being negotiated in the interaction. Information, explanation, and selves are being sought and offered, accepted or rejected. Thus, *motive accounts* (offerings) are linguistic devices to achieve, maintain, and mend social relationships, and the giving and receiving of motive accounts emerge with valuative inquiry (Scott and Lyman 1968).

People may be questioned about their reasons for actions if their actions are viewed as atypical, as out of line with desired goals, as against normative conceptions, or as improbable under the circumstances (Hewitt 1984). The concept of *vocabularies of motive* suggests that motive talk is situation-specific and is meaningful within different social groups (Mills 1940). As such, people discern situations according to the particular vocabulary of motives deemed appropriate for the situation. Mills (1940) relates vocabularies of acceptable motives to the cultural-level generalized other in that the generalized other serves, through role-taking, as a mechanism for social control. Thus, successfully avowed and accepted motives take normative expectations into account, anticipating "situational consequences of questioned conduct" and satisfying "the questions of an act or program whether it be the others' or the actor's" (pp. 905, 907).

The preceding points suggest that motive talk links self, other, and definitions of situations and that it is a central feature of social interaction. These points also suggest that vocabularies of motive have a structural plausibility within social groups. Consider the social category of marital spouses. Acceptable motives in this context would ordinarily refer to some aspect of the partners' roles and the marriage relationship that has been buttressed by cultural expectations of sex roles, family life, and so forth, providing a wide range of possibilities. Notice, for example, the variety and plausibility of motives offered in the following reflection:

> He does a lot of physical work on his job . . . he would be exhausted, and he had a lot of stress. He had often said that if he came home after work he would be physically abusive to me and the children and [because] he didn't like doing these things . . . he would go to the bar to relax. Also, he didn't want to hear things about the kids bickering, the tattling. I was a rotten cook . . . too fat . . . a messy housekeeper, even though I had everything in its place because I knew how he liked things—[he] said there was really nothing to come home for. He liked being with the guys, to play cards, shoot the breeze with the guys. He found companionship there. These were all of the reasons he said he enjoyed being at the bar.

These motive offerings refer to contradictions or incompatibilities regarding role expectations and performances. The implication of alternatives

(Mills 1940) behind the motive offerings or questioning suggests the definitional ambivalence of a motive talk situation.

Another noteworthy feature of motive talk is that shifts in vocabularies of motives signify differential alignment of oneself with social groups (Mills 1940). One wife in the study, for example, stated that her husband did not offer motives for his drinking behavior until he was designated as a member of the social category *alcoholic*: "He didn't really give any reasons before he found out that he was an alcoholic, and then when he would get drunk, [he would say], 'Oh, I just felt like it.' He craved it, or he felt like drinking; he wanted to get drunk." An interesting change often occurs in motive offerings as drinking behavior or the public and personal consequences associated with it become more disruptive or visible. The normative social structures and processes that ordinarily encompass drinking activities and the vocabularies of motive surrounding any use of alcohol now become inadequate to contain and explain increasingly problematic drinking patterns.

When the negotiability of explanations for drinking based outside of the family, such as social expectations or occupational stress, begins to diminish, explanations shift to the now more negotiable base of family relationships. The negotiability factor is important here. Increased marital conflict and the wives' negative self-other valuating and self-blaming (characteristic of the problem amplification phase) invite renegotiations of situations and selves. Like plausibility, negotiability implies plurality—and definitional ambivalence. Together, the wives' ripeness for self-culpability and the decreasing viability of motives based in the public dimension produce a fertile ground for new vocabularies of motive in the personal dimension of family relationships. Typifying these shifts from explanations based outside of the marriage to ones based within the marriage, as problems with drinking escalate, are these excerpts:

At first it would be a stop with the guys, have a quick one and relax. The last few months, when things were really getting hairy at home, he said, "Well, there are no smiling faces at home; at least I see smiling faces in the bar." He would say this when he had had a few, too: "You're not the woman I married," pertaining to my weight, or "Nobody appreciates anything around here." You know, that type of thing.

I thought he was doing it on purpose, and after about a year, I had considered divorcing him and he had said, "When we have a child and everything, I'll settle down." It was always some reason why. . . . We were married four years and we had my daughter. Then . . . he didn't change. Then all of a sudden the excuses were because of me: I was bitchy or this or that, and it was my fault.

These excerpts suggest that shifts in vocabularies of motive may also stem from association with a group that is resisted—through disavowing one's membership in it or through exposing weak or undesirable flaws in the group or its members—which, in turn, increases the negotiability of self-protective motive offerings.

The promotion of self through specialized explanations may portray attitudes toward the questioned act in such a way as to "account" for it on the basis of excusing or justifying behavior (Scott and Lyman 1968). The outcome of building such an account, whether it is accepted by others or not, influences the definition of self that can be claimed and imputed by self and others. *Excuse accounts* imply that the behavior in question is undesirable but mitigate responsibility for it on the basis of accidents, biological drives, scapegoating, or the like. *Justification accounts*, in contrast, accept responsibility for the act but deny that it is wrong, relying on linguistic techniques of neutralization (Scott and Lyman 1968; Sykes and Matza 1957). This woman's recollection of her husband's reasons for drinking illustrates typical excuse accounts, based on bodily feelings and accidental circumst.•1ces: "You name it; he was either celebrating because he was happy, or he was drinking because he was depressed, or he was drinking because there was nothing else to do—that pretty well sums it all up." The next explanation characterizes a justification account, purporting self-fulfillment and denial of a victim. "He said this for a long time: 'Where do you think that you met me?' Because I met him in a bar. And it was like this was his defense, that 'I am the way that I am' and 'I drink because I want to drink.'"

Within a vocabulary of motives a person might hit upon an explanation of particular social strength and flexibility. In other words, a motive offering may be useful (accepted) *across* situations within a social group like a marriage. Consider the following example: "I guess he didn't change. I would cook supper, and he wouldn't eat it, and it was because I didn't understand. And then when I started yelling, it was because I didn't understand; his reaction was the same to me." What is not known and is worthy of further inquiry is whether motive consistency enhances the avower's stance or whether motive consistency, which is negatively interpreted by the questioner as a "nonsituational" response, undermines the avower's stance.

A motive offering is generally accepted if it answers the question about a challenged behavior. These comments are representative of complete acceptance of an excuse account:

> Well, first of all he was in sales, and [he said], "Don't you know you have to entertain people when you're in sales? That's how business is done, and the customers expect it." And he couldn't make a living unless he did it this way. I didn't know anything about business and let him manage his business his way—[he'd say], "You manage your stuff and don't tell me how to run my life." And I'd believe that. I believed that that was how business was conducted. And I believed that if he couldn't do that that he would no longer be able to make a living. He had me convinced.

Less than complete acceptance of a motive offering, although it maintains the social relationship, is illustrated in the excerpt below. In this example, the woman was less successful in negotiating her views of herself, her husband, and their marriage than he was. At the same time, however, at least subjectively for her, his motive offerings began to break down:

> I could see where I wasn't keeping myself up; the house wasn't all that organized, and yet it was livable. . . . I'd try to say, "Well, there are two little kids running around here; why don't you help me?" And as far as the smiling faces [were concerned], well, heck, when he came home snooted up, everybody walked on eggs, or stayed out of his way, or we ended up arguing. So . . . I felt like he had just complaints; but [I thought], hey, buddy, take a look at yourself, too. But I couldn't rebuttal that, really couldn't."

A further breakdown in the acceptability of motive offerings, typically on the basis of unreasonableness or illegitimacy (Scott and Lyman 1968), is illustrated in the following rejection: "Well, I can understand his fear of being in a group situation or I can understand his fear of a job interview, but I think there would be other ways [than drinking] of learning coping skills. I can empathize with his need but not with the means." A second example also shows a breakdown in the wife's acceptance of her husband's motive offerings: "Well, I guess I got hooked on that for a little while . . . but then finally I wised up and said, 'There are a whole lot of businessmen that don't do business in bars, and you don't have to drink to put a deal together.' And so I just rejected it."

Wives' rejections of their husbands' motives for drinking signify an important line of development in the moral career. These mark, however strongly or timidly, a foothold in facing the challenge of sorting the ambivalence in this phase of the career. Certain definitions, images, and appraisals of self, husband, and relationship are being laid to rest and others are emerging as more plausible. The self-validation this involves for the women is evident in these comments:

He would go to doctor after doctor. The doctors "didn't understand" him—they were blaming all his problems and illnesses on his alcohol. They wouldn't give him "the right medical attention" so therefore he had to drink to kill the pain . . . otherwise, he was dying . . . and the alcohol was the only thing that would get him through the day. . . . If the doctors paid more attention to his medical needs, then he wouldn't have to drink. I knew better, because when he wasn't drinking he was perfectly fine.

Another common development in the interactional process of motive talk is that, especially with time, one or both of the spouses default on the custom of giving and accepting (or negotiating) motives as an "organizing principle" of social interaction (Hewitt 1984). It may simply not be worth the hassle anymore. In such a case, the account is avoided because of an overriding need to circumvent disruption of interaction (Scott and Lyman 1968). It is as though it is no longer reasonable to reason: "Any little thing that went wrong around the house, anything, it was like walking on a land mine—you know, one little step. . . . I used to tell him, 'Gee, you don't have to find excuses, just go and drink. I don't even care anymore, just go.' After awhile he didn't give excuses, because I didn't care to hear any and he knew that I didn't."

A special type of motive talk that warns another person of forthcoming questionable conduct and includes an explanation for it in advance is called a *disclaimer* (Hewitt and Stokes 1975). A disclaimer is used to ward off negative reactions and to define the coming conduct as not being a challenge to an identity. For instance, the disclaimer "now don't get mad, but . . ." signifies that untoward conduct is impending and implies that there is a special allowable reason for it. In the case of an alcoholic husband, it ostensibly diminishes the wives' rights or obligations to challenge his behavior or the self implied by it: "A couple of times it was while we were on vacation that he would start drinking [breaking sobriety], for no reason; he just decided that he could drink. He says, 'Now, don't get mad, I bought a bottle for us,' and . . . I say, 'Oh no,' and then he says, 'Oh, this is just while we are here; when we get home, I'll quit.'"

The valuating activities of appraising selves, conflicts, and motives highlight the wives' attempts to establish and define situations and selves during the problem amplification phase. These efforts have the capacity to expand and constrict selves and can now be recast as two sides of the same (interactional) coin: (1) "the efforts made by a particular individual to make a role in a situation and, at the same time, to put forth a self that the other present will regard favorably," and (2) "the effects of one individual's acts on the other's capacity to make a role and preserve a valued conception of self" (Hewitt 1984, 171; see also Weinstein and Deutschberger 1963).

The second of these two aspects of interaction refers to casting another (an alter) into a particular role, or *altercasting* (Weinstein and Deutschberger 1963). Generally, altercasting involves defensive interaction—either being, or putting someone else, on the defensive. One can create an issue and draw the other person into defending a position they do not want to defend, thereby associating the other with the negative features and implicitly validating the created issue of conflict as worthy of negotiation. Such features of altercasting are prevalent in the comeback, sidetracking, and turnaround styles of interaction and are common to couples in alcoholic-complicated marriages. Many of the wives feel that their husbands' alter-casting—the husbands "imputing" a role of a particular kind to their wives (such as "nag") and acting toward them on the basis of that imputation—places powerful constraints, as Hewitt (1984, 171) suggests, on their (the wives) conduct. This in part reveals the intricacies of conflict and defini-tional ambivalence, and the wives' struggles to assess and valuate them in the moral career of becoming the wife of an alcoholic.

The concept of altercasting also sheds light on the women's emergent self-blaming and negative self-imagery: "repeated altercasting of one person by others in a particular way will affect self-conception. . . . Effects of altercasting may be especially severe in instances in which the victim is given a reason to doubt an existing self-conception" (Hewitt 1988, 178). Needless to say, self-presentations and attitudes taken toward self—the other side of the coin—shape the women's imagery, too. Their own negative self-images combined with negative imagery about them promoted (altercasted) by their husbands can strike devastating blows to their "selves," especially when the wives are consciously engaged in valuating or appraising them-selves. It is precisely such challenges to self that comprise the moral sub-stance of this career of becoming the wife of an alcoholic. Typically, per-sonalizing their experiences was an important way of dealing with the definitional challenges they faced.

Sorting the Ambivalence

Personalizing Experiences
and Sentiments

To personalize means to adjust life situations and experiences to distinctive features of one's own, imbuing them with individual character. In this study, personalizing refers to ways in which the wives of alcoholics individuate their lived and symbolic experiences. The women's self-individuation of problematic experiences rests especially on their felt emotions and personal responses. Personalizing is a way of marking experience as one's own, a way of both comprehending and creating self in the interactional milieu. These few words by one woman capture the general tenor of personalizing lived experiences: "I took it very personally . . . that he didn't care enough about me; he would rather be out drinking than be home with me."

Although all people routinely personalize experiences, the personalizing I speak of here is marked by extremes in much the same way that definitional ambivalence can be routine or disruptive. The wives' personalizing is tied up with their disruptive and moral experiences, their perceived self-culpability, and interpretations and feelings that their lives and family relationships are very different from those of "normal" persons and situations. Thus, a significant aspect of personalizing is to construct views of selves and situations within an "aura of uniqueness." In acting toward a situation or the selves within it on the basis of uniqueness, three threads of personalizing activities come together: secrecy, social isolation, and a philosophy of individualism. The combined effect of these factors influences many of the women to view their own selves, their husbands, and their marital situations as unusual, incomparable, and singular in experience.

This aura of uniqueness is related to secrecy in different ways.[1] Some women in this study revealed their "differentness" by keeping things secret so their lives would appear "normal" to others. Some of the wives seemed to view their lives as so unusual that secrecy manifested itself in severe social isolation. In both instances, there was a sense of uniqueness of selves and situations; in one it was masked and protected *in* public performances, whereas in the other it was masked and protected, as much as possible, *from* public performances. In conceiving selves and relationships as something "special and out of the ordinary," the women both responded to and helped create a sense of unusualness. Protective stances were effected by keeping things secret, by isolating self from others, and by employing individualist ideology, as the following excerpts from interviews illustrate:

I think that at that time I didn't want anyone to know about it. I was trying to hide it, and I wanted to make everybody think that we had a really good marriage.

One of my big things: I always try to handle it myself. . . . Very, very close friends knew a few things, but . . . most everything I kept to myself.

I thought no one knew that my husband drank, and I thought that I had done such a [good] job of keeping it within our four walls that it was closed to the world, and it was such a well-hidden secret. I hated the nice weather—to open the windows and to have him come home and let the neighbors hear. So it would be one hundred degrees [Fahrenheit], and my windows and my shades were down.

[I told them] just a couple of weeks ago—and they have been friends since I have been an adult, and one I knew has been through this. . . . I was out with them and I did tell them, and it just opened up a whole new world; they're just right there behind me.

Within the shroud of uniqueness, varying levels of awareness are implied by activities promoting secrecy. Glaser and Strauss (1967) have conceptualized situational variations of the interactants' levels of awareness as *awareness contexts*. They define an awareness context as role-associated and as "the total combination of what each interactant knows about the identity of the other and his own identity in the eyes of the other" (p. 670). In an *open context*, actors know the identities of others in the situation and their own identity in the others' eyes. A *closed context* means that one actor is unaware of the identities of the others or of one's own identity imputed by the others. In a *pretense context*, actors pretend not to be aware of each others' identities even though they are aware, and in a *suspicion context*, actors suspect that the others' identities are not what they appear to be.

When awareness contexts are closed, action can either be directed toward keeping them closed or opening them up. In suspicion and pretense contexts, which abound in alcoholic-complicated relationships, not only identities but also overall definitions of the situation are at stake. Socially created, maintained, and at times transformed, awareness contexts have a direct bearing on the definitional ambivalence and ambivalence-managing challenges to wives of alcoholics. Indeed, this moral career commonly involves qualitative shifts in awareness contexts, from suspicion to open contexts. The following reflection nicely typifies the kinds of changes that may occur in awareness contexts during this process:

I suppose this sounds stupid. . . . In the beginning he would come home late when he was drinking, and I would pretend to be asleep and pay no attention to him. And the next morning he would get up and go to work, and I would be either sleeping or pretending I was sleeping. . . . [I] didn't talk to him, so I really ignored him at those times. He would not come home early because he didn't like the kids to see him that way, ever, drunk. I have a neighbor whose husband also drank. She and I sometimes discussed it, but she is the only one that I believe that I talked to about it. If the children were aware—looking back, of course, they were much more aware than I was aware of at the time—I stupidly thought I was shielding them from it. It really wasn't until the other night when I told the youngest one that Dad was going in treatment, and that I was going to leave him if he didn't continue with treatment and stay sober, and he said, "We should have done that a long time ago, Mom." I also told the oldest one, and he said, "I don't know why you put up this long," and this really came as a shock to me.

This disclosure reveals a common pattern of the pretense context, in which actors pretend not to be aware even though they are. Each family member—husband, wife, and both children—maintains this pretense in interaction with the others. The strong role association of awareness contexts is brought out in the fact that the alcoholic husband-father in this case began to come home drunk only after the two sons had grown up and moved out of the house—apparently when the pretense was no longer required. People maintain pretenses to keep up appearances, to keep interaction flowing smoothly, and to avoid disrupting or rebuking the selves being performed or imputed in the interaction. We want to help the ones we love to put their best foot forward, and we want to do so ourselves. Sometimes we simply may not know how, or do not dare, to confront another's performance and self-imagery and our own that is tied to it. Pretense is an attempt to protect the selves of the husbands and wives, meanwhile undermining them by maintaining situations of self-questioning definitional ambivalence.

The women in this study funneled attitudes, beliefs, and behaviors through a filter of uniqueness, personalizing these into individuated interpretations and responsive acts. The plurality, plausibility, and contradictory aspects of definitional ambivalence afford great latitude and dynamism in fashioning personalized problem designations. It is only later, often much later, when the overriding official designation "alcoholic" is made, that the ambivalence of the definitional enterprise diminishes. Virtually all of the women sensed a certain uniqueness about their situations. All of them personalized this uniqueness to fit their experiences and constructed their experiences to fit the uniqueness. Many of them were secretive about their problematic lives.

Some of them were secretive because they viewed themselves as the cause of the problem. Ironically, women who view themselves as influential enough to cause dramatic or excessive (drinking) problems in their husbands do not consider themselves as otherwise particularly influential. Instead, many feel low self-esteem and even victimization. Insight into their sense of uniqueness and secrecy is gained with the realization of how these attitudes link with critical definitions of self.

Cooley's (1902) concept of the looking-glass self reminds us that persons' views of themselves are always mirroring what they believe others think of them. Wives view themselves as the cause of marital or drinking problems in part because they see themselves as the problem, from their husbands' point of view. In this way, the husband's and others' actions and interactions with the wife mirror ideas of self-image to her. The following interview excerpts embody such self-imaging and self-feelings of the wives:

> A lot of the fights that we had were about all of the things that I did not do. This whole marriage has been an effort on my part to be more acceptable to him, to . . . try and keep the house to meet his expectations, to try and get my daughter shaped up to meet his expectations, and to be this wonderful, loving, giving wife, who also brings home over fifty percent of the income and is never tired or . . .

> I felt pretty much that I was to blame for my husband's drinking. His parents [and] my parents seemed to be blaming me. It was my home—me—the fact that we were married so young and had a family. I was depressed. No friends, no neighbors, nothing. I was a closet person and never shared this with anyone, because my husband drank because of me—I didn't know what I had done wrong to destroy this person, but I had. He drank because of me, being married to me, the children.

Through reflected self-images, such women see themselves not only as culpable but also as actually causing the everyday problems they are experiencing in their marriages. This negative self-imagery may be used as the basis for social isolation, secrecy, and the sense that one's own situation and self are very different or unique from others.

The theme of the husband not caring, evidenced to the wife by his actions, was a prevalent one as the women in this study personalized their experiences. For example:

I didn't feel I caused his drinking really at any point. I thought maybe there was something lacking in me, that I couldn't persuade him to change. I figured if he loved me he would change for me, if he really cared.

He never said anything. But I thought if he enjoyed my company and thought a lot of me . . . then he should be here with me. But he's not here with me; he's out in the bar drinking with all those people. Therefore, I must not be as good of a person as he would like to have. So, therefore, it's my fault.

Two other excerpts reveal ways in which the women might act on their interpretations of responsibility for problems:

Hey, listen, I went from one shrink to another for fourteen years. He would do some crazy thing and accuse me of being crazy, and I would go off and see another shrink.

I was really worried. I remember praying for . . . I guess the ability to bind it up more inside myself. I think whatever sense of self-worth I had was sort of tied up in him. And if there was something seriously wrong with him, it meant that I was nothing. . . . I'm not sure if that's all of it, but I think that that's a part of it.

Feeling responsible for either causing or holding the solution to problems, as in the cases above, is not the only way to personalize sentiments and experiences. The wives of alcoholics act on a variety of emotions thought to be a part of their unique situations; felt sentiments personalize experiences. Feeling an emotion refers to the workings of emotionality, which has been described as "a circular process that begins and ends with the transactions and actions of the self in the social situation interacting with self and others" (Denzin 1984, 58). Emotions given out from the self always refer back to the self of the giver—not necessarily harmoniously, as demonstrated earlier in the wives' negative feelings and imagery about their angry outbursts.

Embarrassment was felt by virtually every woman in this study. The several faces of embarrassment are not the major interest here; rather, of concern are the subtleties and social significance of embarrassment and its implications for relationships. For example, Goffman (1956) eloquently observes the integral role of embarrassment in social interaction:

> By showing embarrassment when he can be neither of two people, the individual leaves open the possibility that in the future he may effectively be either. His role in the current interaction may be sacrificed, and even the encounter itself, but he demonstrates that, while he cannot present a sustainable and coherent self on this occasion, he is at least disturbed by the fact and may prove worthy at another time. To this extent, embarrassment is not an irrational impulse breaking through socially prescribed behavior but part of this orderly behavior itself. Flusterings are an extreme example of that important class of acts which are usually quite spontaneous and yet no less required and obligatory than ones self-consciously performed (p. 111).

Goffman's (1967) concepts of *face/facework* highlight the implications of embarrassment for relationships. He notes that in many social relationships—for instance, marriage—members come to share a face, so that in the presence of third parties an improper act on the part of one member becomes a source of acute embarrassment to the other member. The following interview excerpts illustrate the reciprocal performances and self-imaging in public presentations of a shared face:

> I wanted to go to a Christmas party that work was giving, but I didn't because he was going to go with me. Because I felt that if he did drink more than I would want him to drink, he would make an ass out of me. I would have to go to work, and . . . face all these people. I guess in a sense, he is me, and I'm me to him.

> It embarrasses me that he's missing work, because I feel that you are responsible for your job. [If] you don't bring in money, you don't have a place to sleep, you don't have food to eat. And if he couldn't handle that responsibility, why should I have to have people talking about me? Because I was responsible for my job, . . . but I couldn't report to work for him. It's got back to me: "Why does she stay married to that drunk?" And . . . it's really embarrassing, yes . . .

When he would chase other [women], . . . it was like telling everybody that [I] was a bad sex partner or wasn't loving, or "[She] doesn't
care for him, so he's got to get it someplace else." That was one thing.

In such ways a couple shares performances of selves, whether consciously or
not, as what Goffman (1967) calls a "dramaturgical team." Care must be
taken to keep up appearances in the presence of others so that the selves that
have been built up are not destroyed. The following accounts given by the
wives suggest that the lack of this kind of "circumspection" on the part of
their husbands was devastating to both of their social selves in the women's
eyes, as well as in their anticipation of the responses of others:

He used to embarrass me all the time in bars. He used to break
glasses and start yelling at me, saying, "I hope you feel happy now." He
would try and pick fights with people. He would sit there and stare at
somebody and give them dirty looks. He usually . . . made a pretty
good fool out of himself in bars.

I would call in sick for him. Or somebody would call and he was
drunk and I would say he was sleeping. I would say almost anything
[rather] than to have to tell somebody "the lush is laying on the couch
passed out again."

My own circle of friends don't drink and that always concerned me,
that they'd find out. Somehow this would degrade me and lower me in
their eyes.

Maintaining self-control by acting in character with the role supposedly
being performed is important for teammates, though it is often not done in
these relationships. Gross and Stone (1964) also point to the importance of
control over self and situation; for example, loss of poise, through lack of
control over the body, can give rise to embarrassment: "It embarrassed me
when he would get up and stagger across the room, or his tongue was so
thick he couldn't talk."

Embarrassment contributes to social isolation and secrecy, feeding into
personalized uniqueness. Emotionality overall is intimately linked to changing definitions of selves and situation. Hence, "as emotionality unfolds, it

assumes new forms, new meanings and new interpretations. With these new forms and meanings come new displays and interpretations of self" (Denzin 1984, 271). Consider the changes of emotion and selves that are implicit in the following reflections:

> I felt like I was smarter, like I was the mother and he was the son, like, you know, I was taking hold of everything, [like saying] "Can't you grow up?" and . . . "Act your age." So, I guess that's about all that I really felt, and a lot of confusion.

> [In] what way did I grow up [by being in this marriage]? In every way—emotionally—because I had to. I couldn't lean on him anymore; he had to lean on me. He needed me more than I needed him.

> I felt lonely . . . used . . . unimportant. I didn't even really feel like a person. I didn't feel married to him. I felt that he wasn't the same person that I married. I cried every night just about: Where is he? Why doesn't he call? I felt a lot of hurt. I felt a lot of things.

Along with embarrassment, anger—whether mild or raging—was part of the emotionality for virtually all of the women in the study. Confronted with husbands who normalized, minimized, or denied their consumption or the consequences of alcohol, these wives often experience mounting anger. The excerpt that follows characterizes one way in which anger emerges in such situations. Disavowal of the wife's self by the husband becomes so acute that she can no longer endure it. Notice, too, the contingent path of the moral career when the wife partially joins in his disavowal of her:

> He would say he just likes to go out every once in a while with the guys, and it's not any big deal, and I should start doing things with my friends more; so he would deny the problem. He would violate my feelings. And the more he violated my feelings . . . the more I started repressing them, until [I got to the point where] I didn't know how I felt. If I were to say, "I'm feeling angry and I'm feeling hurt and I'm feeling rejected because you stayed out all night and didn't come home until nine in the morning the next day, from work the previous day; I had no idea where you were," . . . then he would say, "I don't

understand why you feel that way." And by violating my feelings, I mean he's trying to get me to deny my feelings and not accept them, and so your feelings aren't okay.

That this woman's feelings were undermined by her husband and dis-avowed, in part, by both of them is not unlike Hochschild's (1983) findings in her study of the management of emotions in the public marketplace. She found that women experience emotional situations that repeatedly subordi-nate them to men sexually, intellectually, economically, and politically. These negative experiences produce suppressed hostile emotions that can be expressed toward self in a number of debasing, alienating ways. If this happens in the course of everyday interactions in the public sphere, just think how such mechanisms for women's emotionality may be even more encompassing and devastating in the personal sphere. In close relationships there is even more intimate access to the building up or tearing down of selves.

It is not surprising, then, that some wives of alcoholics become so enraged that their imagery of self is fractured into a part that imagines great acts of revenge and one that cannot carry them out. While some of the women descriptively appeared to fit an "emotionally divided self"—"a self turned against itself, disembodied, characterized by self-loathing and re-sentment" (Denzin 1984, 282)—the emptiness and disconnectedness of such a state do not aptly describe the majority of the women in this study, who had an intensified, knowing grasp of themselves, their husbands, and their marital relationships. In fact, I would reassert here one of my original premises: it is not a matter of not knowing (or feeling) self and situations that challenges these wives; on the contrary, it is a matter of intense awareness of selves and situations, sharpened by dramatic definitional shifts, contradictions, and plausibilities. The difficulties lie not in what they are not connected to, but in the objects and possibilities before them that they are intimately and morally connected to. In other words, the diffi-culties lie in definitional ambivalence. It is not in the loss of self-definition but in the undermining, repeated challenges to self-definition and self-performance that we can understand these women's experiences of emo-tionality and anger. Consider the following excerpts from the present study:

He would stand there with that kind of smirk on his face, like "Ah, I'll show you, I'm the boss." I would just get so mad I would slap him, and then I knew better, because he would get me by the hair. He brought out my temper, my anger, and I just wanted to strike out and hurt him like he's been hurting me mentally. And that's the only way I knew how to hurt him, because anything that I said wouldn't hurt him; he could care less.

I have strong resentments. He went out without me. Alcohol started replacing sex, and I just felt like I was playing second role to alcohol. I knew that he was buying [gifts for me], either because he was drinking or because he had this horrible remorse, guilt, and he couldn't understand why I really didn't enjoy those gifts that I got. I've been angry for the children—probably that has been the greatest. I've got lots of resentments.

[I felt] anger, horrendous rage, pure hatred. I'd slap him, I . . . just hated him . . . this drunk person . . . I mean . . . it wasn't [him] but this "person" I hated—[who] acted stupid, said stupid things. . . . I was being denied this nice intelligent person that I married, denied a friend, companion, husband, father for the kids. He was just gone, in all those ways, and I just resented it. I got into total despair. I didn't know what I was going to do. I just couldn't live my life this way anymore, and I didn't see any way out.

I used to always tell him, "Everything that you do when you're drinking [takes] feelings away from me, and someday they're not going to be there." I wished he were dead, and a lot of times I thought I could give him a push and it would be all over. . . . That's terrible, but, you know, when you go through. . . . I had a lot of humiliation. He exploited me sexually a lot—pulled my top down or something in front of people. I mean, if I was a different person I probably could have stuck a knife right in him.

In the above illustrations of anger and resentment, the wife either attempts to communicate herself to her husband or holds a view of self that, in her eyes, is not being acknowledged by him. His contradictory or incompatible expectations of her create an interpretive definitional struggle. It is the struggle, I think, of an often eroded or impoverished self fighting for viability against a dehumanizing resistance, cocreated by her ongoing diminished self-definitional enterprise and others' imputations.

Whether the self-views of these women were impoverished, as Leonard (1983) would suggest, simply by having grown up female in a patriarchal society, or by socialization in problematic families, or for other reasons, is beyond the scope of this study. The problematic characteristics of their alcoholic-complicated marriages, in any case, were enough to chip away further at positive definitions of self—a process that exacerbates definitional ambivalence and the challenges of sorting the ambivalence. After all, these women are enmeshed in a *moral* career, distinguishable because it is marked by repeated and deeply disruptive challenges to and changes in definitions of self. In a very real sense they are enmeshed in a struggle for moral (self) survival.

Observations made by Goffman (1971) in a study of mental illness, and their implications for family organization, shed light on the challenges to definitions faced by a family dealing with any serious trouble, such as the excessive use of alcohol. They address the milieu that may contribute to impoverished or eroded selves as well. Goffman emphasizes that merely unpleasant home life is not the issue, but rather, meaningful existence is at stake:

> The individual's failure to encode through deeds and expressive cues, a *workable* definition of himself, one which closely enmeshed others can accord him through the regard they show his person, is to block and trip up and threaten them in almost every movement they make. The selves which had been the reciprocals of his are undermined. . . . A deep bewilderment results. Confirmations that everything is as it should be cease to flow from his presentations. . . . the family and its household prove to be vulnerable in the extreme. . . . If the family offender elects not to heed the warning, there is then really nothing effective that can be done to him. . . . Households, then, can hardly be operated at all if the good will of the residents cannot be relied upon. Interestingly, it is right at the moment of punishment and

threat, right when the offender presumably has additional reasons for antagonism, that the family is most clearly dependent on his self-submission to family authority (pp. 366–68).

Development of the moral career is ferreted out from the subjective realm of experience into a relatively objective tracing by noting the overt stances taken by persons facing such problems (Goffman 1962, 168). One stance that I believe to be a major contingency in these women's moral careers involves behaviors that may well be associated with what I earlier referred to as impoverished or eroded self-imagery. Two "sensitizing concepts" (Blumer 1969) suggest that a good many of the women, despite their best intentions, do not, for perhaps long periods of time, effectively carry out the positive selves and situational changes that they imagine and speak of as desirable throughout the problem amplification phase.

The first of these sensitizing concepts is *deficient negotiated-self*, which I suggest be construed as a relatively consistent inability or unwillingness to negotiate desired positive outcomes, images, and feelings for and toward self. This study suggests that the overall self-imagery of the women is somewhat impoverished, but full research and analysis of this proposition are beyond the scope of the present inquiry. The idea of a cultural heritage of impoverished selfhood for females is raised by many scholars of women's experiences and issues. Here I am attempting to establish the *performance* of a deficient negotiated-self, not to analyze its origin.[2]

The second sensitizing concept, *stultifying interaction*, addresses the situational contexts often associated with such (deficient) self performances. By stultifying, I mean interaction that renders a certain futileness and ineffectiveness of self-negotiation and communication. Together, these two concepts signify certain attitudes, beliefs, or behaviors that direct the path of the moral career in ways similarly outlined by other researchers: "Willingness to accept or endure another's problem behavior or to seek further remedies or responses are critical contingencies in the development of a trouble in an ongoing relationship" (Emerson and Messinger 1977, 126).

What are some of the ways in which deficient negotiated-selves and stultifying interactions coalesce in the everyday lived experiences of women married to alcoholics? The numerous illustrations in this study of the wife making a declarative or questioning remark about her husband's drinking, followed by his countering, denying, or ignoring her statement or the implications of it, resulting in her feeling disavowed, exemplify a deficient negotiated-self and stultifying interaction. Her self-intentionality is both belittled and thwarted; the self she wants to negotiate is unsuccessful in coming across or being accepted. (In this way deficient negotiated-self is a concept referring to performance and interaction, not to an individual.) This is so in that communication—the sending, receiving, understanding, and acknowledging of messages, agreement aside—is effectively blocked.

Lack of communication shuts out the possibility of mutual discussions of issues and emergent shared meanings, notably with regard to problem solving. Both stultifying interaction and deficient negotiations of self are symbolized in this woman's account: "I just became weary of fights and arguments and violence, and I guess I just never talked about it because it would be denied. I would have to listen to how crazy, how no-good I was, and I just didn't want to hear it again." A pattern of inability or unwilling-ness to negotiate desired positive outcomes, images, and feelings for and toward self, as well as the situational contexts that give rise to it, are depicted in her comments.

In a similar vein but illustrating further implications about self negotia-tion and performance and the self-other relationship is this observation: "After a while I got kind of numb, [feeling], well, it doesn't matter any-more. . . . And he'd come home and I wouldn't scold him or anything, . . . and then he didn't really know quite how to react to that. . . . But I thought, every time he stayed out drinking—and this has probably been . . . five, no ten years ago—I cared less every time he would stay out drinking. It was like he was killing that love in me for him." It is not farfetched to imagine this wife waiting for the last bit of love to be extinguished—the unspoken but implicit point being that something (big) will happen when the love *is* all gone. It is as though she relies on this evidence of the gradual destruction of the relationship to define and justify emotions and actions, present and future—unable or unwilling to act on behalf of herself without it—choos-ing not to, even if unwittingly, or being unable to negotiate satisfying self-images, outcomes, or feelings for herself at this time. Her views of her husband's behavior as "not good" make possible a satisfying view of herself as "better" in contrast. However, it is unlikely that a woman in the process of relinquishing love and relationship from her life could positively and fully embrace a righteous self across situations and time. Rather, the self that she negotiates in ongoing interactions is more likely to be self-undermining and limiting; it is more likely to be a deficient negotiated-self.

As amply demonstrated in this study, the wives of alcoholics frequently doubt their own observations and interpretations about selves and situations—especially in the face of denials and counters from their husbands. Many fail to adhere to their own interpretations when confronted with those of their husbands. The pronounced definitional ambivalence of this problem amplification phase and the challenge of sorting out the ambivalence may also diminish the confidence with which the women view their interpretive skills. Recognition of certain behaviors (like the unexplained absence of the husband for many hours, a noticeably deteriorating relationship, an emerging pattern of coming home late and drunk, or any number of similarly related observations) is often not taken as sufficient evidence or validation of problems (and related emotionality). It is as though it is not "bad enough" that the husband is not a full social and marital partner whom they can count on; it is as though more inadequacy on his part or justification of the wives' feelings is required. For some of the women in my sample, verifying his presence at a bar apparently gave final validity to their perceptions, interpretations, and feelings about the problem:

> I had a nasty habit of checking up on him. If I was at my mother's, [on the way home, I'd say], "Well, we'll drive by the bars and see if he's there."

> What I used to do is get in the car and drive around from bar to bar. I found myself driving, looking for him. . . . And I had to take [my daughter]—how foolish, but you do do irrational things at times. And she said, "Mom, why are you always looking for him?" And I thought, Well, what am I going to do if I find him? And that was it . . . [I stopped].

In these cases interaction is still stultified; the wives are still unhappy with the selves and the outcomes negotiated (either by acts of commission or omission), but they can now better justify their feelings.

Another version of apparently looking further for validation of interpretations and feelings is illustrated in the following account, which depends on increments of problematic behavior to justify an angry response to it:

> I would not be able to sleep until he came in. I would be pissed, because I knew that he was out drinking and I knew that he was going to be drunk, but I would go to bed . . . watch the clock, and I would almost hope that he would really be late, if it was midnight. I could feel a lot more pissed off at him if he came home at two or one o'clock in the morning than if he came home an hour late. And yet, he's going to come in the same way; he's going to come in drunk at eleven, or he's going to come in drunk at one. . . . But again, . . . I would have a reason to really be upset with him.

Consider the implications of another woman's story and the definitional power she granted her husband's denial of drinking, regardless of her own observations. Her own interpretations were clear enough for her to confront him, but they were only fully validated when confirmed later by another. This account demonstrates the wife's inability or unwillingness to negotiate a positive image/feeling/outcome for herself in this encounter, symbolized by her quasi-disavowal of her own observations and self: "[After treatment] alcohol was used. Once I caught him this summer . . . I saw him drinking and I confronted him and he denied it. Later I found out that he *had* [been drinking]."

The wives of alcoholics often fall short of carrying through on the implications or logical extensions of their observations. The actions they take toward definitions of situations and selves are often characterized by a sort of "start-up and halt" stance, which is typified in this recollection:

> I confronted him the summer before we married [when he was supposedly maintaining sobriety after treatment]. I said, "Hey, when you use this stuff [cough syrup], you get high." And he denied that he gets high. And I said, "You're gonna take that cough syrup and in twenty minutes you will not be able to drive this car. And that will prove it to you that you get high when you use [it]." And sure enough, he couldn't drive. He was all over the road. . . . And then it was never

talked about after that. I felt, well, now he knows that I know he's using [it]. And . . . he continued to use [it] after that.

This woman exercised a degree of self-assertion, but it was more as a defense against a definition that insulted her intelligent self. Successful (mutual) communication of the problematic situation of impaired driving, or of definitions of selves and the overall situation—given the husband's failure to maintain post-treatment sobriety—are neither confronted nor negotiated. It is as though "now he knows that I know" becomes the end of the means rather than a means to a problem-solving end. We might look at this stance as a self-protective claim of intelligence for self. Although positive in the short term, an ongoing problem in marital interaction, left unresolved, can only feed into deficient negotiations of self in the long run.

One final interview excerpt illustrates an apparent extreme of deficient negotiated-self, but as it unfolds nuances of interactional and cultural factors emerge and impart a better understanding of this seemingly idiosyncratic style of interaction. Notice, too, the definitional ambivalence inherent in the varyingly mixed and changing definitions of selves and situations:

I know I'm going to get more dependent on him in the future if we have children. That scares the heck out of me. I have just lost my own identity. While I'm at school and while I'm at work I think about him all the time. I call him up and ask him how he's feeling, how's he doing. I'm so wrapped up in his life, and mine seems so menial.

That's one of his main complaints. That I got real dependent on him. He thought he married Helen Reddy. That's kind of the image I gave him—the kind I had of myself. That's what came out in counseling.

I guess when I love somebody, I put all my feeling into them and I don't take care of me anymore; I take care of them. The more vulnerable I get and open up, then I get scared and—I do the song and dance around him so he won't reject me. Which ultimately turns into rejection anyway. I don't know. I didn't know it when it was happening—and if I did I blocked it and said, No, that's not really what's happening here; I really am my [own] person. And then a couple [of] months down [the road, I was] looking back and seeing it.

I don't like it much more than he doesn't like it. I think it was a combination of me putting [myself] there and some of his macho stuff, too. As much as he is a liberated man and I am liberated, I think we both have our macho images . . .—the femininity and the subservience. Like when we got married he says, "You don't have to work now. You can stay home. It wouldn't bother me," which is telling me that's the old way and that was kind of a cue.

What does he mean by this? I remember [thinking] that; that stands out in my mind. I just continued [working]. I said, "Hell no, I'm not going to stay home. This is my life. I need [to work]—there's no way I could stay home." Now if I had a child, I'd want that.

In this case, there are mixed messages—or definitions. They emanate from the wife herself and from her husband, as well as from their interactions and cultural sources. Here we can see some of the threads that come together in creating a deficient negotiated-self and definitional ambivalence.

The sensitizing concepts of deficient negotiated-self and stultifying interaction alert us to significant aspects of definitional ambivalence and challenges in the moral career. These concepts link interpersonal and institutional processes and can be used to examine interactions and self-performances within situations as well as those built up over time.

This digression from the initial discussion of anger nonetheless centers on emotionality, providing a deeper understanding of the quintessential relations between the women's definitions of selves and situations and their self-feelings or sentiments as these act upon one another to shape the moral career of becoming the wife of an alcoholic. The acting woman herself, of course, is at the heart of this interaction of interpretations and feeling, even if not consciously, for "emotionality, in all its forms, is a choice. . . . To be or not to be emotional, to lend a bit of self-feeling to one's actions or to withhold feeling, to be overcome by emotion or to hold it in check, these are choices the person has and makes in everyday life. . . . In these choices . . . individuals shape and determine how they will see themselves and how they will be seen by others" (Denzin 1984, 277).

Along with embarrassment and anger, feelings of rejection, fear, and stress contribute to the women's personalized sentiments. (Interestingly, feelings of guilt are more prominent later in the moral career.)[3] Rejection represents the women's claims of hurt, rejection, loneliness, and depression. Such self-feelings mirror the women's views of themselves and especially their belief about how their husbands view them. Consider these self-expressions and the personalizing of sentiments and experiences that they imply:

> [I've felt] a lot of rejection. Simply because he wouldn't share with me his feelings, and when he was using [alcohol] there just was not sex. I'd never ever been turned down from sex before, and it blew my mind. I'm doing better now since we've had the marriage counseling— granted it does affect me, but I'm better for that.

> We moved and he was given a sales territory. He was gone a lot and I was in a real vulnerable spot, and at that time I think his drinking really . . . took off. He sort of had me where he wanted me, real powerless. . . . I didn't have any support system at all.

> I was rushed to the hospital for emergency surgery, this one time. Nobody came to see me, and I was so depressed, I was crying. My mom called up the next day, and I said, "Gee, nobody was down here; you could have come down, you know." And she said, "Well, Gary was down there." I said, "No, he wasn't." Well, we found out he went out drinking with his buddies and got loaded. And he goes home and goes to sleep, never shows up at the hospital, nothing. We didn't find this out until later—the fact that . . . you can leave a loved one in the hospital alone and in pain and think about yourself, go out and get drunk.

> I used to have . . . real intense feelings of loneliness, that I am one [alone] and not a part of a couple [even though I am married]. It hurt like hell. I mean, I would just be overcome with it, just, maybe washing dishes or taking a shower.

In contrast to these lived experiences of rejection, the women's feelings of fear involve not only immediate situations but also future events. The fear nearly always involves anticipations that are dreaded in some way. Fearful events in the present emerge as double interactional effects because they are symbolic of frightful events that might also occur in the future. Besides the fear of physical violence, various other fears recalled by the women in my sample are typical during this phase of the moral career:

> Well, [I've experienced] a lot of fear. Of what it would do to him and what could happen, you know, being in the profession that he was in. It scared the shit out of me [that an innocent person could be hurt if he drank on the job].

> I was kind of leery to tell him when anything went wrong in the house. Oh, I don't really exactly say the kids . . . if you had to bring [up] a sore subject, it might go okay, but when he drank the next time it would all come back. So I got to the point where I really hated to complain or ask about anything or tell him that anything [had broken] or needed repairs or . . .

> Maybe all through our married life was the fear of always becoming pregnant—another child to be alone with, to raise alone, to take care of alone.

The wives cited fear for the husband's life and job performance, fear of negative or angry responses from him, fear of added responsibilities for the women, and, overall, fear of financial, physical, or emotional ruin. One account contrasts "special" excessive drinking with "usual" excessive drinking and evokes changes and challenges in feelings and definitions of self:

> One time he came walking home to me, a couple of miles from where he had crashed his car into a tree. And it looked like he had been knifed [he was so bloody], and he was just drunk out of his mind. And I was sound asleep at home. It was just a frightening experience that I will never forget. . . . But when he just drank . . . normally . . . if I felt like he was really losing it, like he was really getting wasted, and nobody else was, then sometimes I would feel embarrassed or sometimes I would feel hurt or I would feel . . . I don't know. I would have a lot of self-doubt, I guess, about . . . did I make a mistake? I guess I've thought about that all along, you know—in staying involved with him and marrying him.

Notice the definitional ambivalence and challenge in this woman's view of herself in relation to his behavior and their marriage: is she wise? is she stupid? is she capable of making a viable problem-solving decision about this?

One instance of guilt-related fear is the thought that the wife's own actions, especially during this problem amplification phase, may have a negative effect on her children—both in the present and the future. One woman reported:

> [You're afraid of] the neglect that was there with the rest of the family—and that happens, you know. You're putting so much energy and so much time [into anxiety about the drinking]. You're scared and you're worried and you're confused, and . . . all that is going through your mind all day long is what happened the night before. What is going on? How are you going to deal with this? . . . You're washing dishes and you're crying, fixing dinner and you're crying. . . . The kids come in and you snap at them. . . . They come in and they talk to you, and you pretend that you're hearing them, and they get done talking to you and . . . you haven't heard anything that they've said. I . . . felt like I really neglected them . . . because I was so concerned.

Emotional tension and stress, represented by physical sensations and nervousness, serve as gauges for self-evaluation as these women valuate and personalize their experiences and feelings. Stress comes out in an array of expressions:

> Well, I really don't know if I can blame it on him—I don't suppose it's helped at all. I have high blood pressure and [have taken] medication now for about fifteen years. I find myself sometimes very, very nervous. I'm sure I've got a nervous stomach: it burns and eats away at me, every now and then. I used to cry a lot. I don't sleep well. I go in stages where I dream a lot of terrible dreams; I imagine it's emotional. I don't know whether to blame it on him or not.

> Mental health, anxiety, the relationship . . . there were strains on that. Financially, [it] just bugged the hell out of me to see that much money go for beer. I was working so hard for the dollars, and that's always pissed me off.

It [the fear] was mostly emotional; I walk on eggs. He reminded me a lot of my dad, and I began to fear for my girls, because my dad touched me improperly when I was in that developing stage. And I began to feel afraid that he just might do something that dumb. . . . [I was] emotionally upset about a lot of things I feared.

Self-definitions and high levels of stress play back on each other, magnifying both the experiences of stress and lowered images of self. The stress is personalized into images of inadequate selves:

I really believed at that time the things that I was feeling, that I was mentally not all right. I was too afraid to see a doctor or to share with anyone my feelings, until they . . . got to a point where they just overwhelmed me. I worked my depression out on the couch, crying. When it was putting me out of commission, then that was when I did seek professional help [from] the doctor for my anxieties, and at that time . . . he'd give me something to deal with it.

I would sit there and listen to him coming at me with the verbal abuse, and I would feel like my head was going to explode, and it was like I couldn't handle [it] anymore. And there was like all this pressure would build up in me, and I couldn't say anything back to him, and so I just felt like I was [trapped and losing it].

The stresses of alcoholic-complicated relationships on the processes of self-imaging and self-performance are many and great. For some of the wives in this study, repeated interactional cycles of building up and tearing down of selves, through multiple alcoholism treatments and sobriety-breaking periods, exacerbated these stresses. Such on-again, off-again drinking brought one husband to treatment for the sixth time and apparently depleted his wife's resources: "I realize that if I don't get help right now . . . I could really get myself into a position where I might not be able to pull myself back out again. I'm better now as time goes on, but if he were to start drinking again, today . . . I don't know what I would do. I just don't think that I could handle it."

At this juncture, a few general observations about emotionality bear restating. Foremost, emotionality is embedded in social interaction. Persons designate feelings by seeing themselves from the standpoint of others, and they act toward the (changing) selves anticipated by their own and others' designations. Through emotionality, definitions of self expand, diminish, support, challenge, reveal, and conceal. Still unwittingly embarked on a moral career of becoming the wife of an alcoholic, the women in this study apprehend their variable and contradictory emotionality and lived experiences by personalizing them as specially unique, often veiling them in secrecy or social isolation. What cannot be stably or approvingly defined can be designated a special case. And adopting a stance of uniqueness toward problems may be a temporary strategy, notably in this problem amplification phase, for comprehending the otherwise seemingly incomprehensible.

Sorting the Ambivalence

Personalizing Stances

Overt stands taken by wives in response to their husbands' drinking further illustrate ways in which the women personalize their experiences. These responsive acts are not only ways of personalizing experiences, but also ways of comprehending and creating selves in ongoing ambivalent interaction. In this study, the wives tended to assume one of two contrasting stances: placative and confrontive. In taking a placative stance toward their husbands the women sought to appease them somehow, or to make concessions with regard to problems and solutions. The wives described placating behavior as an initial attempt to satisfy the husband and hopefully decrease problematic drinking and any underlying problems they perceived.

Reflecting back on such actions, however, the women spoke of intimidation or victimization as having been a part of their placating stances. The following example typifies this pattern: "I for years thought that a lot of his problems I could really [help resolve]—if I did differently, then he'd do differently. I could be more supportive. I could work harder. I could do all sorts of things. . . . I could love him more. I could show that love more and try all those things. Then I realized it wasn't working. . . . I felt shut out of his life and I . . . was really resentful of that . . . [it] hurt bad."

Such intimidation hinders free-flowing ease of self-expression in the one place where persons most expect it, the home. The household is no longer a stable organization of persons against the world: "The home, where wounds were meant to be licked, becomes precisely where they are in-flicted. Boundaries are broken. The family is turned inside out" (Goffman 1971, 381). Importantly, because self is an emergent reflexive process, a self in performance (in intimidating situations) is also a self in discovery and creation. Domestic and marital upheaval, in the eyes of the wives, is sym-bolic of low respect and worth that they perceive coming from their husbands toward them—and by imagination or by action, many rebel against this low status through confrontation.

Actually, there appears to be a curvilinear pattern of confrontation-resistance: a lower level in the early phase of the moral career, working up to a peak at some point in the problem amplification phase, then decreas-ing, often in that phase as well. The initial period of lower confrontation is more apt to be of a placating and problem-solving orientation, whereas low confrontation in the later period appears to be more of a withdrawal-avoidance type. The following interview excerpts represent these general movements, although it is important to keep in mind that intensities of confrontation vary considerably with individual couples' situations. Need-less to say, definitional ambivalence during this entire phase of problem amplification is pronounced; changing overt stances symbolize changing views of selves and situations:

I guess I've been through all of those [feelings and behaviors] at one time or another. I think I would switch: I used the humor bit there for a while and just kind of tried to laugh it off, and I tried to accept it. I thought that being the good wife . . . I had to accept him as he was . . . which is fine, and I thought that that meant accepting his drinking, which I know now that I don't have to do.

Well, first I thought that I could help him. If I'm really nice and really good little Miss Susie Housewife, then he won't want to drink, because he would be so afraid of hurting me that he won't do it. So I was fragile, and I played the role very well. And I would get up in the morning and give him aspirins for his headaches, call into work for him, and do almost anything he wanted me to, but then . . .

I saw that that wasn't working, and so I went to the complete opposite with the anger and the yelling and the screaming. Because I got to the point where [I thought], I don't have to put up with this and I'm tired of being nice. I think it was more a gradual thing; he would say, "I don't have any clean socks," and I would say, "You know where the washing machine is," you know, maybe once a week. But it got so that every time he would complain about something, I was getting where I was more and more saying, "Hey, you are just as capable of handling and taking care of yourself as I am of taking care of you," until it got to where everything he would say . . . I would have a comeback for everything.

A few of the wives maintained a confrontive stance throughout. The excerpt below illustrates one woman's notably more assertive and matter-of-fact approach compared to the commonly used indirect, reproaching stance:

> [I did] not argue: I had tried to talk to him. He would argue and I would . . . say, "Well, I just want you to know how I feel." There have been lots of occasions where I have just said straight out, "I don't like your drinking and I won't go with you." I always confronted it. . . . I never just sat back and said, "Yes, honey."
>
> He's put me in a lot of embarrassing positions, and I had held my head high and just carried on, like nothing was going on. . . . We would go to a restaurant, and he'd sit and throw his food around and say, "Hey, woman, come here," and stuff like that, to me. And I would not say much, and I would finally say, "I want to go; I'm leaving. Are you coming?" And if he wouldn't come, I would go. I wouldn't sit there and beg him to go.

The stances of a few women were influenced by their participation in Al-Anon for a period of time (up to four years) before their husbands entered a treatment program and they entered the corresponding family program (included in this study). The following excerpt demonstrates some of the changes in self-definition brought about in part by resocialization in Al-Anon, as well as the impact of role expectations on self-definition and performance: "There is a huge difference. I'm real free now to go and do what I want to do. See, it was my job to be there—to be mad at him when he came home drunk. I don't know why I thought I had to do that. It was my job to sit there and wait for him so I could blow up. I don't know what I thought would happen if I wasn't there watching the clock. And, of course, now I don't do that. I would never call friends and say, 'Let's go out.' I just didn't know how to do it."

To many of the women in the study, the role of wife most often meant to be the keeper of the hearth and family. Later, especially with the aid of Al-Anon, it changes to be first the keeper of oneself so that other obligations can be met. The next excerpt shows a definitional process, albeit a wavering struggle, to incorporate the disease concept of alcoholism into views of husband, self, and situation—also a part of resocialization in Al-Anon and family treatment programs. Even as the designation of him as alcoholic crystallizes more and more as disease-related, the definitional ambivalence of who and what she is, in relation to her husband and his alcoholism, prevails:

> Well, the last two times, I was very angry. I just figured, I can't live like this; I can treat myself better than this. He would come home and I would hold him and love him, because he's sick. He was so sick that I had to put my hand down his throat so he could [vomit], but I would do all these things for him. This was after Al-Anon and stuff; this was anywhere from two to four years when he would come home drunk. It was no longer anger in me, except the last two times.

This example illustrates the challenges to definitions of selves and situations brought about by events in this moral career—in terms of role expectations, designations of responsibility, definitions of situations, and self-feelings. The emotionality and self-imagery the wife experiences may, as in this case, contradict designations from other sources. Thus, challenges to self and definitions may continue and even be amplified when outside help (Al-Anon) is rallied.

As noted earlier, many of the women in the study dealt with feelings of uniqueness and embarrassment by isolating themselves socially. The thread of embarrassment personalized into a stance of social isolation is a strong one in the fabric of the moral career. Now we will examine additional aspects of social isolation in the experience of these women. Consider the intricate process of the changing social relationships, definitions of selves, and situations implicit in these examples of changing stances:

I was extremely active up until I met him, and we were active up until we got married. I used to bowl, take ceramics, go swimming. He said, "Go ahead and do them. You do whatever you think is right." . . . I had tried it a couple of times and came home, and we were fighting all night long, arguing about it. And he had said, "I've just called the police and I was just so worried sick; you said that you would be home at nine, and it's nine-fifteen." . . . I got to the point where I had told myself . . . that it's not worth it: withdraw. And I did—from people, everything.

On his days off, he'd be gone, and by the time that he came home, he was in no shape to do anything. On Sundays he usually just wanted to lay around and watch TV and read his newspaper. And at first I thought, well, that's okay, he's out working all week. But it got to be, if you would ask him to have company over . . . he wasn't in the mood, or we couldn't afford it, or I didn't have things together. And we couldn't just do things on the spur of the moment, so I really began to feel that our social life was down to zero, just absolute zero. Because I got tired of worrying about taking the kids to a show or finding fun for them. Why couldn't he? Or why couldn't he join us?

I have dropped out of things . . .: [my professional association], church group, bridge. Because if I didn't come home and my husband knew it, he would not come home. And so therefore I have felt that I needed to be home. Or if he did come home and I was not there, he would most likely drink. And so I just felt that I had to be home too, so he didn't drink. So I feel as though I have given up a lot—stupidly probably, but that is what I have done. And I would very much like to start doing something that I used to enjoy doing on my own.

We see in these personalized stances a blend of interactional and cultural factors taken into account by the wives as they view themselves from the standpoints of their husbands and societal norms. Vis-à-vis their husbands, the women exhibit relatively lower social power—that is, "the capacity of an individual . . . to modify the conduct of other individuals . . . in the manner which [she] he desires and to prevent [her] his own conduct being modified in the manner in which [she] he does not" (Tawney 1931, 211). This lower power is consistent with the overall social power of women in our culture, and the women's personalization of experiences must be viewed within these larger public circumstances.

Within imaginative activity lies a key to understanding the paradoxical interplay of freedom and constraint exhibited in the social actions of these women. They, as we all, are limited in the making and taking of roles by what we imagine the possibilities to be. The constraints the women speak of (in the above and other excerpts) align with traditional norms and values for the female roles of wife and mother. If we juxtapose this complex of traditional role expectations and the socialization recounted in the following excerpt, we get a firmer grasp of the extraordinary constraints under which some of the women imaged themselves and their lives:

> In my opinion, . . . I was raised in a home where my father was an alcoholic and my mother was the enabler or controller or whatever you want to call it. And my role model therefore was a person who is doing [this] still, you know—she raised me to do what she does. I don't hold it against her; she did the best she could with what she had. But yes, I believe that I was given a certain set way of doing things, and that frightens me because I'm doing that to my daughter. I think parents do that: you raise your children with your beliefs and . . . to react as you react. I remember one time my mom really got mad because he went to the bathroom in a closet. I remember them arguing sometimes when he would come home. I suppose I thought it . . . went on in every house . . . I guess I never really gave it . . . a whole lot of [thought]. I must have thought it was normal.

In this case, the daughter—now herself in a moral career of becoming the wife of an alcoholic—could only imagine modifying her mother's type of self-involvement in the same situation (she said that her mother could have hired someone to clean up the closet instead of getting mad at having to do it herself). Neither mother nor daughter imagined that the mother was not responsible for cleaning up the husband-father's improvised closet urinal.

In what ways do imagination, freedom, and constraint help us understand this? The impacts of imagination, freedom, and constraint commingle in the concept of *reification*. To *reify* means to take an attitude toward a social object as if it is an existing, natural reality rather than a humanly produced, socially created, and variable one. As Berger and Luckmann (1967) set forth:

> The reified world is, by definition, a dehumanized world. Persons experience it as "a strange facticity" over which they have no control rather than as of their own activity. Even while apprehending the world in reified terms, man continues to produce it. That is, man is capable paradoxically of producing a reality that denies him. . . . Through reification, the world of institutions appears to merge with the world of nature. It becomes necessity and fate, and is lived through as such, happily or unhappily as the case may be. Roles may be reified in the same manner as institutions. . . . The paradigmatic formula for this kind of reification is the statement "I have no choice in the matter, I have to act this way because of my position." . . . This means that the reification of roles narrows the subjective distance that the individual may establish between himself and his role-playing. (Pp. 90–91)

The symbolic interaction perspective emphasizes "realities" as "constructions," as humanly created and maintained through social interaction and interpretive activity—reminding us that

> however familiar a situation is, it is worth remembering, it must nonetheless be kept alive and in motion by its members. . . . We are, of course, strongly influenced by those around us, by the language they speak and the world of social objects they build for us, by their approval and disapproval, by the situations they created and by their presentations of self. But we occasionally surprise ourselves, not to mention others, by acting in ways that suggest our disregard of others' approval, our disbelief of their presentations of self, or our willingness to do things we have never done before. (Hewitt 1984, 179)

The capacity and act of imagining options and taking action toward them brings a freshness that can transform the routine into the unexpected, the old into the new, the restricting into the liberating. On the one hand, women like those in this study often act toward their alcohol-related problems as if the problems are a given and not subject to release; on the other hand, they are also searching for a key that can unlock their problematic, restricted lives, thinking of this key as some undiscovered "truth" rather than "construct." Each of these stances constrains their selves and their lives. The paradoxical relation of freedom and constraint and the possibility of imaginative release are such that

> the very routine and stable everyday reality that we create maintains itself to a great extent because we believe in it and continue to remake it in our acts . . . partly on the basis of our belief that things can be no other way. . . . In part . . . because we need to have some sense of an orderly social world in order to act . . . people derive their conceptions of themselves and of what they can and should do from their sense of the structure of group activities. . . . As organisms, we possess considerable power to transcend the limitations of our environment, of the world others have created for us. Yet we spend our time recreating those worlds, believing that the patterns of interaction in which we engage, the role structures of our groups, and the situations in which we act are natural and unalterable features of the world. (Hewitt 1984, 179–80)

The "catch" is that individuals, alone or collectively, must be able to imagine selves and situations from new perspectives. Persons need to be able to take the role of different referent others and imagine themselves outside of their own world of experiences as they exist. Going back to Mills's (1959) "sociological imagination," this calls for changes not only of personal spheres but also of public (societal) ones. Meanwhile, through observations of the self-eroding features of alcoholic-complicated relationships and traditional norms and values in the socialization of females, and through understanding the impact of reification on freedom and constraint, it can be seen that the "personal troubles" of these women coincide with "public issues" of reified social (structure) roles.

I suggest that the personalized stances taken by the women in this study, overall, indicate their active involvement in creative survival within their

alcoholic-complicated marriages. Wiseman (1975) has drawn a similar conclusion in a study of Finnish women married to alcoholics, observing that a
substantial minority of these wives fashion satisfying autonomous lives for
themselves. The present work, however, focuses more on creative coping
than on life pleasure or autonomy—both of which were sparse in the
experiences of the women I interviewed.

In a different twist on the stance of social isolation, some of the women
manipulated their spheres of social involvement to create pockets of com-
fortable social activity for themselves. One way they did this was to isolate,
or perhaps insulate, themselves from social interaction with their husbands.
They accomplished this strategy in two ways: by staying away from their
husbands as much as possible around the home, and by going out without
them. The following illustration of avoidance in the home to avert confrontation reaches into the household and family management, as well as
emotional, spheres:

> I had to handle all the things with the kids, all the problems . . .
> anything that came up . . . because I didn't know how he would react
> to it. At one time he might react real, you know, violently, . . . very
> strongly, to a minor situation. The next time he might not. So there-
> fore I couldn't take the chance. He was becoming a little bit more
> physically, you know—I mean, he would hit the kids for something
> that I didn't feel was right. And so we were constantly getting involved
> in [issues like], "Hey, that wasn't fair." And I felt sorry for the kids, and
> yet I was torn. . . . Do I support him? He's my husband; he's the father
> of these kids. I don't agree with what he's doing. I don't agree with his
> discipline. It's too strong for the offense. . . . I was kind of torn
> between them. I didn't want the kids to think that I was siding with
> them, and I didn't want him to think that I was siding with the kids,
> and I was in the middle of it. And so, what I did [was], I handled
> everything and didn't let him know what was going on unless it was
> absolutely necessary.

Somewhat surprisingly, "wives of alcoholics" have been conventionally
characterized as having "controlling" personalities. Yet, again, interactional
and cultural factors are revealed to be strong influences on the supposed
controlling in this example.

Another strategy for avoiding social interaction with the husband in the home came down to outright ignoring him. For example: "I would find myself kind of [escaping], hide. . . . He would follow me around the house; I would go [from] room to room. His mouth would be going constantly. And, of course, everything that I said back . . . it would be like beating my head against a brick wall. Towards the end, I don't think I hardly talked to him."

In staying away from the husband by going out without him, some women were able to release tension, garner social support from friends, or focus on other things for a while. These kinds of activities nurture the self and also enter into definitions of self. Sometimes the outside social involvement was notably people-oriented: "Friends became . . . they were someone that I could turn to. I couldn't turn to my husband. I couldn't talk to my husband."

The next example illustrates how some women turned to others for support and emotional release, as well as suggests the support of Al-Anon in this past-present comparison of self: "Oh, at work, I think [everyone was aware of it]—there wasn't one person in that building that probably didn't know what a creep he was because of his booze. And, of course, it was all him and not me, you know, at that time. . . . I was really a wreck . . . I would go in the bathroom and I'd sit and bawl. This was before Al-Anon and stuff. . . . After Al-Anon, I didn't have the need."

Several of the women turned to physical and creative activities outside the home. Consider the following samples:

> When I look back, I think I've gotten into a lot of different hobbies . . . to kind of keep me busy so that I wouldn't have to think about this. I think it was kind of an escape for me.

> About a year ago I enrolled in . . . like a health club. . . . [I] usually exercise three times a week. It's a tremendous relief for stress and anxiety . . . between work and between relationship problems. Towards the end, things got real stressful for me: besides being gone and working out, relieving tension, it was also not being there, and so it was staying away from him besides. I could go in there tense and come out feeling just great . . . totally relaxed. [I went] more frequently and

[stayed] longer periods of time just because I didn't want to [be around him]. I was avoiding him, you know.

I would go run or go and play or seek out happy people. I would get involved with my music. I would read. I worked for years—and work would help me with that, too. I could escape into that.

Nearly two-thirds of the women in this study worked outside of the home, and for many of them work was a release or an escape. The women emphasized the nurturant self-involvement of their work, typified by these excerpts:

If it hadn't been for my job, I would have been completely loco by now. My job was my only form of escape.

When I got my job, I started meeting people and realizing that these people do listen to me, and I can have fun, too. I don't have to sit home all the time. He didn't like it one bit that I could go out and meet friends. . . . He was always telling me I didn't have any friends, I couldn't have any friends because I was so rotten. So I showed him that I could make friends and that I, too, could go out.

Well, let's put it this way: what I have when I go to work, I do not have at home. I'm beginning to feel confident at work; I do not at home. I can feel good about myself at work, and I do not feel that way at home. I can touch other people at work . . . pat them on the back and say "Hi" and feel good. And even a man can come up and touch me. I don't feel it at home; I can't. When he touches me, it's for, you know, [sex]—at least that's what I see in my mind. I look forward to going to work. I don't look forward to going home.

Domestic work, too, sometimes took on new meaning for the women as they personalized it to fit their situations: "Clean: that's one thing that I do. My house is not a . . . spotless place, but when I get really, really uptight—I mean, it can be two in the morning and I'm cleaning everything." One woman reorganized her entire day around household work: "My thing is that my work [is] my escape, so I have gotten to a point where instead of getting all the things done right away . . . I find myself working until maybe ten at night. I drag my work out so that I never finish to have any time to sit and watch TV or whatever."

A few women consciously turned to religious activities to cope with the mounting problems they felt in their marriages and with their husbands' drinking. Such activities symbolized renewed self-worth and respect for these women, as the following excerpts demonstrate:

[I've been active in the] last two years. I just believe now that, to know that no matter what you say or do, you always have that love and that guidance, and all you have to do is have the faith—that's a good reassurance. I guess it makes sense to me, because I notice I always was looking for something and never finding it and always saying, "Why do I keep getting in these jams?" Well, it wasn't anybody but my putting myself in there, you know. But I guess now I have a . . . good way to look at it.

[For] about three years I've been involved with a Christian group. Also, I think one thing that's been a good out for me: I've been teaching religious "ed" for the last eight years, and I think that helped to make a lot of changes in my life and how I view things. I suppose, really, the church group is what I've kind of turned to.

I was born and raised a Catholic, and someone introduced me to this new salvation—accepting the Lord and turning over a new leaf— about seven years ago. That became almost the most important thing in my whole life. And that's another thing that always bugged him . . . but it was my sanity, too; it kept me from having a nervous breakdown or whatever. I did real well with it, and now I am learning more how to be less fanatical about it and make it practical.

Religion, work, outside social involvement, exercise, and hobbies are all ways in which some of these women personalize their problematic experiences and create new stances for themselves—stances that afford some distancing or relief from their husbands or their problems. The women who choose these strategies of problem management engage in social interactions with others and have the benefit of anticipating and seeing others' responses to them. To feel a part of a group or a community outside of the homebound, private sphere of daily life affords them another, usually positive and often contrasting, view of self.

Mere activity, although appearing to help, may not be enough, for "false-self presentations" (Goffman 1959), without embracing roles and performances, can also be erosive:

> I don't know: when you're married to an alcoholic, the problems are so undefinable. It's like lives of quiet desperation. I knew something was wrong. I couldn't put my finger on it. I wanted to give an appearance of being happy, of being able to handle everything. . . . So I would work, and I had a house, and I did all these things and looked functional; that was important to me. But I also did everything with a smile, you know. I thought, I've got to look happy; if I convince people that I'm happy, maybe I am happy then, and [so I tried to] just kind of block out all the pain. . . . It presented an image. And [it allowed me to] ignore what was going on, because I couldn't describe it, I couldn't define it, I couldn't do anything about it. And then I could always drink and by five o'clock it would all go away.

With this example we come full circle back to "uniqueness." In instances like the above, however, subjective experiences of uniqueness are masked and socially transformed into a semblance of normalcy and even well-being. We see in this, and in the other examples of personalized activities, an interesting variety of creative stances in dealing with the personal and public dimensions of the moral career.

One final personalizing activity, suggested in the last excerpt, involves the women's own drinking behavior as a response to their husbands' drinking. The women's use of alcohol is presented here only insofar as they personalized their use or its meaning, incorporating it into their definitions of self or situations. For many of the women, alcohol became a strong (social) object in their world of experience, variously symbolizing problems in their lives or temporary relief from these problems. They acted toward alcohol, for instance, by dumping it down the sink and by directing action away from it, such as planning nondrinking activities.

Of special interest here are the ways in which the women's use of alcohol changed in relation to interactions with their husbands. Two major processes emerged from the interviews: (1) during the marriage the wives' drinking simply decreased, or (2) during the marriage the wives' drinking increased, then later decreased. None of the women suggested that their drinking was on the increase in the period covered by the three interviews. A few women thought that their use of alcohol had remained about the same, usually very low, most of their adult lives. Many of them reported late adolescent partying before marriage that, for some, extended into the early years of the marriage. The women who reported a decrease in their use of alcohol variously explained this change in behavior. Typically, the husband was the referent for the change and implicitly the wives wanted to avoid an anticipated negative self or "anti-model" (Francis 1963). Consider the following accounts:

When we were dating and first married, I could maybe take two or three drinks, to the point where I felt kind of silly, having a good time. And then after my husband really got going, when we would be out, I felt like I couldn't even get to that level, because I would have to watch that he was okay and maybe drive home. And then I got to the point where I might have a drink when people were over, but I was just really—it was getting to be a pain in the neck. I hated it.

As a kind of a response to his drinking, I would try to not drink or drink less. It was kind of like, "I can do it, so you can do it" or "if I'm not drinking, then it will be easier for you not to drink"—that was my reasoning behind it. Because if I'm sitting there and drinking and having a good time, then isn't he going to want to do the same thing?

When I met my husband, I didn't drink much, but I noticed as time went on, I even cut down more—one or zero when we went out. And I've stayed away from it, other than a few times. I didn't want to proceed in the followings of him.

One woman did what others might muse about, taking a bold and short-lived stance toward herself, her husband, and their problematic situation by mixing seductive oblivion with "demon alcohol":

I think I went through a crisis of becoming close to [being] an alcoholic for about twenty-four hours. When my second was born . . .

she was a very difficult child. Both my husband and I would sit down and have a drink each night. I thought if I was calm, the baby would be calm. And then through this last crisis that we went through with him unemployed, I was real depressed, was overweight. . . . I call it "my twenty-four-hour nervous breakdown"—that's all I could attribute it to. He came home one day, [and I said], "Take the kids. . . . Here is some money; go get me a bottle." I locked myself in the bedroom, took a book and ashtray and cigarettes, drank until I was sick to my stomach—threw up. And I was fine the next day. He took the kids and went over to my mothers's house, very upset about what was going on—had a couple drinks before he went—and . . . told my mother . . . "This isn't [her]. What's wrong with her?"

But whatever it was, that's what I said, it was a twenty-four-hour nervous breakdown. . . . I was fine the next day. And I'd never do it again as long as I live; I was so darned sick. I think what it was was just putting on a face for him—and it was everything piled up on top of me. And I just had to have this release, and that's what happened with me. I was always the type who . . . would take . . . an hour to two hours to finish one drink. I kind of scared myself when I went in that room. To me, liquor has been dead ever since. I may have a glass of wine once in a while, but . . .

Other women responded to their problems and their husbands' drinking by drinking more themselves, again using their husbands as referents for their changing actions. These women gave two main reasons for increasing their own use of alcohol. The first reason centered on notions of compatibility, relationship, and sociability, and the second emphasized the problematic nature of their lives and drinking as a coping strategy. By the time their husbands entered treatment for alcoholism (proximal treatment phase of the moral career), however, all of them reported a reduction in their drinking, often to a low or an occasional level. Illustrative of the augmentation-then-diminution dynamic are the following accounts:

We had sort of a system worked [out] at home. He would sit down and talk with me if I would drink with him. Oftentimes if he was not out of town, the stress for me would . . . start to be unbearable by about five o'clock, approaching the time when he should be coming home—stress in terms of whether or not he is going to come, what sort of condition he's going to be in, or he's not going to show up until three in the morning. The stress was just awful and I would . . . drink to alleviate that stress. I think I was very close to going over the line myself.

When I married my husband, I went through a time where I think I was drinking to keep up with him just because he was doing it, but I would get sick. And I also didn't like being nonfunctional on some days, being slowed down. So I stopped doing that and now I've almost entirely stopped drinking.

I was working. I was drinking. And when I was working part-time I was drinking at night . . . just to try to reach some point of oblivion so I could go to sleep. And then I really got into school, into work, and found other ways of feeling pretty good about myself.

In these instances, the women fit their own experiences of drinking to the changing character of their everyday lives. By reflexively viewing themselves, they anticipated and responded to their drinking selves, variously approving, rejecting, and accounting for their performances of self.

In the emotionality and stances the women express, they personalize the significant presence of alcohol in their alcoholic-complicated marriages. The challenge of sorting the definitional ambivalence is met by personalizing it (along with acknowledging and valuating it) and coincides with an increased complexity and presence of definitional ambivalence in this problem amplification phase of the moral career. The maintenance of rather high levels of definitional ambivalence throughout this phase is explored in the next chapter, which addresses implicit questions of why the ambivalence persists.

Notes on Maintaining
the Ambivalence

Why do these marriages and interactions go on (and on) as they do? Why doesn't someone put a stop to this? In other words, what contingencies help maintain definitional ambivalence? Stereotyped ideas of alcoholics as skid-row bums rather than as employed family members may stave off designations of husbands as alcoholics. Similarly, cultural norms, the reification of experiences, or repetitive threats to the husband with little or no follow-through may become part of enduring interactional patterns. In some instances, third-party professional "helpers" initially target a medical or psychiatric problem rather than one of alcoholic drinking. Effective communication may be blocked by a variety of defensive and offensive styles of interaction. Social conventions encourage family and friends to minimize drinking problems and to give the benefit of the doubt in most cases of wrongdoing. These are some of the many interactional and cultural factors that have been presented as part of the amplification of problems and the definitional ambivalence around them. Two pronounced interactional contingencies, however, appear especially to maintain definitional ambivalence; these are *bargaining* by the husbands and *hoping* by the wives.

Bargaining most often involves some form of admission of guilt by the husband, often accompanied by remorseful pleadings or acts, with promises for the future; in short, these are often apologies. Apologies can be thought of as *remedial interchanges* (Goffman 1971) and, like accounts (Scott and Lyman 1968) and other aligning actions (Stokes and Hewitt 1976), as ways of restoring disrupted interaction or relationships. Apologies most often occur after a behavior in question, and they symbolically divide a person into a blameworthy part and a part that sympathizes with the blame giving; by implication, this second part is worthy of "being brought back into the fold" (Goffman 1971, 113). As elaborated, a "full" apology includes "clarification that one knows what conduct had been expected and sympathizes with the application of negative sanction; verbal rejection, repudiation, and disavowal of the wrong way of behaving along with vilification of the self that so behaved; espousal of the right way and an avowal henceforth to pursue that course; performance of penance and the volunteering of restitution" (Goffman 1971, 113). Notice the presence of these various elements in the following examples:

He didn't like his behavior; he felt he had hurt me and his children. He embarrassed himself.

If I said anything while he was drinking, then it was a fight. And then the next day it would be an apology; and then he would be a good boy for awhile, the model husband or whatever. He said, "You were right, I was wrong. I guess I did have too much to drink and I didn't know it."

He's great at asking for forgiveness and [saying] "I love you" and "Let's try again, I really care about you, you care about me; and there is only the two of us."

Oh, he's very remorseful . . . the whole works: roses, dinner, phone calls . . .

In reviewing the components of an apology in its fullest form and sampling wives' reflections of apologies, the seemingly simple apology is revealed to have intricate, ritualistic, social, and self implications. Fundamental to apologies, or remedial interchanges, is that they provide a way of dealing with infractions of ordinary rules and of sustaining the understandings related to such rules. An apology carries with it an implicit message that the offender still upholds these rules and is intending only "a single exception to restrictions and standards he is ready to continue to accept . . . the victim is being asked to accept a single exception, not a permanent reduction of his rights" (Goffman 1971, 165).

An apology given and accepted carries with it a tacit expectation that the transgression will not occur again; "that it will be the end of it is the basis for allowing that particular ending" (Goffman 1971, 165). As happens more often than not in these alcoholic-complicated relationships, however, the husband soon commits a similar offense, after several instances of which the couple really can no longer gracefully deal with the matter through a remedial apology. Repeated infractions and compensations for them go only so far. The husband ceases to appear to be the repentant self implied by his apologies, and the honor paid to the wife by deeming her as deserving of an apology now borders on mockery.

Goffman (1971) suggests that this leads to interactional "disorganization" and that "it is here we find that the patience and good will of the victim are likely to be meager and fitful, for no pattern exists in this particular structural nexus to provide a mold for accommodative response." He further suggests that when assessing any group's capacity for remedial ritual, we must examine what "forbearance in depth is provided for repeat offenses" (p. 166).

Marriage and family relationships are interactional contexts that provide extraordinary forbearance for repeat offenses. Certainly the considerable emotional, financial, and shared-status ties characteristic of these intimate relationships create a good measure of capacity for forbearance. But I wish to emphasize some of the more subtle ways in which a marriage may provide for the absorption of offenses.

Norms of performance (Gross and Stone 1964) operate in any interaction. These norms, which allow for flexibility and tolerance and for giving the other person the benefit of the doubt, can be especially salient for significant others. Indeed, a spirit of flexibility and generosity in interaction is the stuff of which enduring relationships are made. Thus, the symbolism and structure of marital relations encourage the forbearance of offenses in two special ways.

First, marriage and family relationships are viewed as enduring relationships, often as lasting long after any particular problems have dissipated. Family relationships project back into an inherited or shared history and forward into a projected future, spanning lifetimes. Therefore, we may be less insistent on the immediacy of problem solutions or changes in our loved ones; we and they have time to work things out (Weiting 1982). Endurance of a relationship is also associated with the development of a commitment to it: "Intimate relationships often develop a momentum as a result of sheer endurance" (Karp and Yoels 1979, 13). In light of this kind of commitment, people may stay in a relationship even when it becomes a painful one for them (Becker 1960). Thus, the special symbolism and structure of family relationships create a context for added forbearance of offensive acts.

Second, the traditional norm of female role performance requires forbearance. Wives, especially, are expected to soothe marital wounds and nurture the relationship. When these features of marriage/family relationships and female role performance are coupled with an apology that characteristically creates closure on an undesirable encounter and calls attention to the ties of the relationships as well, the subtleties and selves at stake in offense-apology cycles become clearer. Consider these examples:

It was because of this and that . . . he would have all the excuses and all the reasons. And he would come in with the "I'm sorrys" and . . . "I won't do it again" and "I love you" and "I'm sorry I hurt you." And it's damn hard to stay mad at somebody who's coming up to you and apologizing and saying "I love you; you're a good wife . . . you really do a nice job." . . . Well, shit, that's all that was . . . an excuse to go out the next night and get loaded again, you know. And I kept buying it.

I went to the hospital then, and I said . . . "I am not going to live with alcohol anymore. I am going to move out." So he cried and begged, and he said, "Well, I just don't see how . . . we've lived together for so long." So then he conned me again; and he begged, and he cried, and he said that he would be coming home and he wouldn't drink. And he could control it and . . . "What's a drink or two at night?" And he went into all of that stuff. None of it was true; he just went back into the old ways.

Such apologies imply contrasting claims for defining selves—for example, a proper, responsible, sensitive husband versus a difficult, uncaring, exploitative one; a forgiving, open-minded, understanding wife versus a dogmatic, selfish, uncompassionate one. Apologies highlight and add to the definitional ambivalence in these marital interactions; as a type of definition-bargaining strategy, apologies keep contradictory but plausible expectations prominent in interaction and thus maintain definitional ambivalence.

Another effective strategy in the bargaining of definitions of selves and situations is a sort of anticipatory modeling. By this I mean that the husband may periodically exhibit a "nondrinking" (if not "ideal") self, and the occasional revelation of this enhances the wife's (and perhaps the husband's) image of such a self as a believable possibility for the future. Seeing the husband performing in socially appropriate ways—perhaps even while having a few drinks, or ceasing to drink periodically—helps the wife to foresee such behaviors as future possibilities. This phenomenon is undoubtedly related to the wife's frequent view of her husband's drinking as a matter of choice and self-control and reflective of his interpersonal relationships.

Some husbands exhibit their nondrinking selves or "better" selves sporadically; others do so regularly. If a "better" self performance does not accompany periods of abstinence, it nonetheless raises the possibility of nondrinking (perhaps as a "first step" in change). Combining abstinence with better self performance gives all the more fuel for the vision. Illustrations of these kinds of anticipatory modeling follow:

> He turned religious and he gave up drinking for it. I'd say [it was] a period of one or two years, and that's been *it* out of the eleven. And he was a different man. He became a family man, a loving man, a caring man.

> He was proving to himself he didn't have a problem with his drinking. It was something that he could throw back at me. As I look at it *now*, it was ten weeks out of fifty-two and the other forty-two weeks he drank and did his thing. Ten weeks he was home after work, but he did not take part in family things. He has done this for maybe the last three or four years. Also, he would have a bet at the tavern: "If I can be sober from this time until springtime." He was going to show a lot of people he could take this pressure. But he always knew, and he would always say how they would even have a big "welcome back"

sign because they knew the exact date he was going to be back. It was just a very short time.

As long as the wives can imagine their husbands as "other" (better) selves, they are unlikely to have attitudes and definitions, or undertake actions, that eliminate or discount these imaged possibilities. One possibility calls up more possibilities. In this way, definitional ambivalence is maintained; stable designations of problems, and actions for resolving them, are stymied. Sometimes husbands bargain more directly about their drinking. Though more specific in content, such bargaining strategies still allow new visions of who and what they may be in the future:

He would always tell me that he would quit "after this weekend" or he would quit "after this bottle"—he always called them jugs: "after this jug"; this was his last jug. And he would start out tomorrow and he wouldn't have anything to drink . . . or he would quit as soon as the vacation was over. The trouble is, we never made it to vacation most of those times.

He promised me when I was pregnant that he was going to quit by the time that [the baby] was born. He didn't quit, and then it was, "Well, when he gets old enough to know, I'll quit." And then he tried bargaining with me: if I quit smoking, he would quit drinking.

He kept saying that he was afraid to quit, and the reason is he is labeled as a chronic alcoholic. He does have liver disease and high blood pressure and bleeding in the stomach and the esophagus from drinking. He had had alcohol hepatitis before which hasn't really ever gone away. During the course of withdrawal, he's gone through seizures, so . . . he's really afraid of withdrawal.

The plausibility of these bargaining strategies helps to maintain definitional ambivalence just as the women are intensifying attempts to sort through it in this problem amplification phase.

The husbands' bargaining strategies are coupled with a second ambivalence-maintaining contingency, their wives' seemingly unfailing hope (at least temporarily) that the apologies and ideals, are, or at least *could* be, true. Along with the husbands' bargaining, the wives' hoping for the way things could be ("if only . . .") keeps the wheels of definitional ambivalence spinning. Often expressed in terms of endearment, "never losing hope" is illustrated in the excerpts below:

> It was just the same type of things over and over and over: [I would ask myself], "Why me? I was brought up to live better than this . . . this is not my class of a person; why did I get hung up in this?" Until he would sober up, and then I would say, "Well, he's not so bad after all; he's got a problem, but he'll be okay." And then before you would know it, it would be the same old thing again.

> Under all of that horrible, crummy behavior and the alcoholism . . . I really did care for him. He's a *fascinating* personality. When I married him I didn't love him, and he knew that. I like him more than any person I've ever met in my life, and that remained for me even [during] all those drinking years—I respected him. He's interesting, intelligent. . . . I like to be with him. I think I made a wise choice, although it took a lot of crap to get out of the way before I started to feel any payoff. [Author's note: This woman was attending the family program some months after her husband had gone into treatment and had been maintaining sobriety, so, indeed, she did feel a payoff for her troubles.]

The women's persistent ray of hope has an emotional component that is related to compassion or empathy for their husbands' difficulties with drinking. It calls forth sensitivity to the couple's entwined experiences and selves and urges a peculiar sense-making, but on the surface it begs the question, "but why?" Denzin (1984) explains that

> appropriation of the other's feelings is based both on the emotional imagination of the subject and on her willingness to suspend doubt or disbelief regarding the other's feelings and state of mind. Emotionality overrides cognitive doubt. It produces sufficiently plausible reasons for adopting the other's feelings and believing in them. . . . Emotionality depends on the willing suspension of disbelief for its existence, while furnishing the very grounds for that belief. . . . The emotional imagination presumes a willingness to believe in the emo-

tionality of the other. . . . Society is possible, in part, because of the moral foundations of emotionality and sympathy . . . the emotional imagination, coupled with the principle of emotional sociality and moral conscience. (Pp. 242–43)

Thus, we see that the hope so characteristic of many wives of alcoholics is grounded in a context of social expectation, a rich social-emotional context that links human beings to one another—all the more, spouses to one another. So, too, is the forbearance with which these women accept repeated apologies. The bargaining interchanges, and the hope in which they are taken, emerge not from personalities but from cultural rules of conduct and peculiarities of interaction; they arise out of the experience of social life—a socially prescribed moral way of life. Although it may not always be constructive or in one's self-interest repeatedly to accept apologies, or to remain imaginatively hopeful in a deteriorating situation, perhaps we can now better see that the receptive, hopeful path is the morally, interactively, and socially constructed path for these wives to take, at least as historically formed.

Repeated cycles of apologies and acceptances, and the stopping and resuming of drinking, do defy stable definitions of the situation, for time exposes these as only temporary measures. Background expectancies that normally guide interactions and establish appropriate contexts for apology, hope, and emotionality can no longer be relied on. These problematic situations have a shadow of suspenseful anticipation that adds to the definitional ambivalence. Any untoward actions, thoughts, or feelings may precipitate resumption of drinking. Fear may outrun hope; yet hope may outrun disappointment.

This path of moral self-conduct, however, also has other shadows. Another rule of moral conduct is that one has the obligation to maintain a self-respectful, positive "face," not only for oneself but also for others (Goffman 1956). In other words, there are appropriate personal as well as social times and places for apologies and hope, and these are not to be "overstepped." Overdoing apologies or hope could cause a "loss of face" for either or both spouses.

Precisely because there is no social provision for endless accommodation by these wives, they must be leery of "overdoing" hope—yet another task of meeting contradictory expectations. Ultimately, these women must take another emotionally imaginative leap of faith to break the throes of definitional ambivalence, as well as the interactional and cultural contingencies that maintain it. This "leap," realistically, usually begins with one small step that in some way limits the definitional ambivalence.

Part 3

The Proximal Treatment Phase

Limiting the Ambivalence
and Entering Treatment

Some limiting of definitional ambivalence needs to occur in order to facilitate transition from the problem amplification phase into the proximal
treatment phase of the moral career of becoming the wife of an alcoholic.
Interpretations and actions must diminish the viability of competing definitions and of self-doubt in the definitional enterprise. This process may
either begin before professional treatment commences or emerge from it.
The physical obviousness of her husband's drinking, for example, may
affirm the wife's perceptions of it as excessive, abusive, or addictive despite
his continuing counterclaims. Or physical or legal problems resulting from
drinking may limit ambivalence because such complications eventually
require resolution. Drinking may still not be seen as *the* primary problem in
terms of alcoholism, but it is likely to be regarded as problematic in a much
more definitive way. Limitation of ambivalence may first come about
through third-party professionals or through groups like Al-Anon. The
husband himself may give performances too nonsensical to be taken seriously, or he may admit to a problem with alcohol. In other words, a
variety of events and encounters may begin the process of limiting the
definitional ambivalence around these troubled relationships.

One way that limitations on definitional ambivalence play out in everyday experience is related to Stone's (1970) distinction between factors that
are beyond the control of an individual (circumstance) and factors that one

is able to do something about (situation). For example, many of the women in this study began to avoid argumentative conversations with their husbands when they came to view these as no-win encounters. By interpreting such encounters as created by things they can do nothing directly about (like husbands' drinking, attitudes, or actions) and by things they themselves can do something about (their own actions), some wives can change their views and actions. Perceiving interactions as choiceful creations rather than as imposed happenings translates into increased social power, or an ability to effect more positive self-intentionality in interactions—for example, avoiding unpleasant or self-debasing interaction by identifying and avoiding the source of it. When a different and more desired self is clearly envisioned, a foundation is laid for limiting definitional ambivalence.

One might ask why another, even contrasting, expectation of self does not simply add to the definitional ambivalence about self and situation. It is because in this proximal treatment phase of the moral career, the wives are typically moving away from the chaotic mental juggling of contradictory and incompatible yet plausible expectations and performances of self in which they usually come up short. Now there is a qualitative shift in emphasis away from their former downplaying of their own perceptions to increasingly giving credence to them. The wives begin to set limits on the acceptability of their husbands' behaviors; they engage more in self-reinforcing activities and may act more toward self-autonomy. And perhaps apologies and hope have run their course. Thus, while in the problem amplification phase a "new" definition of self born of the imagery of self-doubt and culpability feeds the flames of definitional ambivalence, in the proximal treatment phase a "new" self born of the imagery of survival and self-nurturance douses these flames (whether the impetus be desperation, willful change, or otherwise). In the former phase, the benefit of the doubt is extended to all but oneself, but by the latter phase such forbearance is no longer feasible. The following excerpt illustrates ways in which definitional ambivalence and the limitation of this ambivalence play upon each other in actual experience; it reminds us that we are examining a process that is not necessarily linear:

> When I first spoke of talking to a lawyer, he said, "Well, I'll quit drinking." So I kind of stepped back for awhile, and a very short time

later I knew he was drinking again. So I threatened again, and he said, "Well, I'll join AA." He'd go a little step farther each time that I would make a threat, and it would last for just a short time. I learned through my Al-Anon group that it was my decision to make—that once that decision was made I should stick with it, because I was just giving a lot of idle threats.

I gave him a certain length of time . . . if he hadn't gotten treatment by then, he would have to leave. I just told him, "Gee, I'm really sorry, it's been past the time that I said I was going to have the papers signed, and you didn't abide, and I have to stick by my decision." So I did have the papers drawn, and he moved out for a month. And during that month, my feelings began to change. For the first three weeks I felt real good, and I felt confident, and I felt like I was really coping well. And then all of a sudden . . . I realized that I really wanted him home. And he'd been telling me that Al-Anon was filling my head full of baloney and all this, and I was beginning to think, maybe they did.

I quit going to Al-Anon meetings for about a month. And he did move back home. . . . The first week that he was home, he was out until four in the morning, after bowling. So I realized . . . I was really defeated again. I kind of slipped a little again—I'd argue when he came home. . . . I was back in my old pattern. . . . But, finally . . .

Sometimes a serendipitous awareness creates a clearer definitional path. The very act of designating the problem as alcoholism, of course, diminishes competing plausible definitions and limits ambivalence. In any event, there is a shift regarding definitional ambivalence so that now some events or activities are interpreted in ways that limit the ambivalence and help create a context for recasting problems and definitions. The examples below show this:

It's kind of how you feel about yourself when you're buying into it. I suppose you do believe it when you are being manipulated, but I think it's when—it could be someone telling you, or hearing it on the news, or a poem or something that might click—and you say, "Wait a minute." Then you have to decide, Do I want to keep doing that? Is that good for me? Or am I more important than that? You start asking questions.

I was beginning to get fed up with it. I wasn't willing to accept his behavior and I knew that there was something abnormal about it, whereas before I denied it or I tried to pretend it was going to go away. I think that that's when I began to realize maybe I had to assume some responsibility. I probably was unconscious of thinking that, but it was the beginning of that process, I think.

Two major changes associated with limiting definitional ambivalence revolve around the wives' actions of (1) setting limits on what is acceptable, and (2) refocusing toward self. Generally, the limits newly set by the wives concern behaviors or interactions they are no longer willing to be a part of. The following excerpts represent ways such limit-setting might arise:

He had asked me if I would go on vacation with him, and I had said no. And he asked me why, and I said because of his drinking.

He had been picked up for the fourth time in the last five years on a DWI charge. And I had decided that [if] he got himself into trouble again, he was gonna get himself out. I would not, I guess I say, enable him. They impounded his car when he was arrested, and I would not give him the money to get it out. I would not make any calls for him. I said, "You handle it." And I also told him, "You do what you have to do, and I will do what I feel I need to do for me and the kids."

When he was drunk, drinking at home all day long and not going to work for like days at a time, I bet he would call me twenty times at work and tell me that he was dying and that I better take off work and come home. It was getting to the point where it was affecting my job, and I think that is probably when I really started going to Al-Anon. And that is what really helped me with it: I wasn't responsible, and if I was home, I wouldn't make things any better. I had to put my priorities first, and that was my job. I told him that I didn't want him calling me at work anymore. And it wasn't just like me telling him one time and it worked; it was like telling him over and over, and hanging up on him over and over and over again. It took me many times to get that message through. He has not called me at work once since then.

After I went to the Relate program a year and a half ago, I told him at the time that I would not ever comment on it. It was his problem. I learned these things. . . . It was his problem and I couldn't do anything about it. I knew within myself the only thing I could do . . . was to make my decision. Did I want to live with him no matter what his problem, or did I not want to live with him because of the problem?

By setting limits on certain kinds of interaction, these women stopped taking into account much of the definitional ambivalence they previously had utilized in their imagery and actions—the imagery of self-culpability or "victim," for example. A variety of interactional and cultural factors may stave off confrontation of a problem and its designation and resolution, thus for a time keeping the definitional enterprise quite open to ambivalence. In time, however, certain definitions are less negotiable; the practicality of social cooperation is undermined, and certain definitions emerge with greater plausibility than others. By narrowing the field of definitions, one limits the contradictory, incompatible, and plausible expectations of definitional ambivalence—not only in number but also in kind. In other words, in this phase there is a sort of definitional filtering process. Definitions that rise more dominantly over others are likely to be those that increasingly target the husbands' drinking or behavior as problematic.

As the wives do target their husbands' drinking as a major source of problems, they also change their attitudes and actions toward themselves. They begin to take the role (and attitude) of different "others," more and more discounting the previously salient attitudes of their most intimate significant others (husbands) toward themselves. A new focus on self emerges regarding their own rights, obligations, needs, and the like. That is why this phase is characterized by change and by growth-oriented introspection of self. In ways small and large, the women's lived experiences begin to establish changes in self-imagery and performance. This refocusing on self is represented by the following examples:

I had an accident about a month and a half ago . . . That's the closest I have ever come to think . . . I could have been dead that day, and why am I putting myself through all of this? And why don't I just make a decision, right or wrong, and go on with my life?

My trip this summer was my turning point to my decision that I had to get out of what I was into. I went on a bike trip by myself, and it was beautiful. I really decided I liked myself and my company—being able to stop for coffee instead of a beer, seeing what I wanted to, not the inside of a bar. When I came back . . . I found bottles all over everywhere. [I thought], this isn't what I want every time I turn around. That's when I decided that it was going to change and I was going to do something about it.

I didn't think I wanted to stay in the marriage. I thought I'd better get myself out there and get a job.

My husband came in drunk and embarrassed me so that I could not finish my job. And I left with him and I didn't go back for two or three months, and then I did go back. It was a challenge to me, like I was challenging him with this. I started going to Al-Anon and that was very threatening to him.

I started school. That . . . was a stepping-stone for me, I tell you: just to say, "I'm going."

I wasn't looking for anyone else, but it happened. It had a profound effect on me . . . I started looking at myself . . . *consciously* thinking of what I wanted . . . that I had needs. I wasn't aware I had needs. I just knew something was lacking.

I've learned a lot through these programs and Al-Anon, so I feel I can handle it better now—these last few times when he would drink. We've always done everything together, and so it was really difficult for me to do things on my own. But I find myself doing that now. I decided I had to live for myself.

I only recently really accepted it as a disease . . . and *then*, I got better . . . after I got a little bit of Al-Anon. I was able to not lose my cool when he came home drunk. I was able to enjoy my kids, go ahead with dinner, and spend good quality time with my kids and not be upset or angry and say, "Well, he's not home." Why should I expect anything different? He's sick, he can't—and kind of let go of it, still feeling sick inside but not to the point where it did before.

I have my own problems. I wasn't accepting the fact that I have, but now I realize that I do and I'm taking care of myself rather than him.

Refocusing on self and setting up ranges of acceptability for interaction establish limits on definitional ambivalence. These changing overt stands mark subjective changes in the women's attitudes toward selves as well as significant experiences in this moral career. Changes that limit ambivalence and enhance the self may precede formal help-seeking or treatment, or they may coincide with such activities. In either case, they are closely associated with the proximal treatment phase of the women in this study,[1] a period in which both the wives and their husbands participated in formal rehabilitation programs.

A husband's entry into an alcoholism treatment program signals a pivotal point in the moral career of his wife, for it is now officially and publicly acknowledged that she indeed is married to an alcoholic. From this point on, the work of self-other identity that is central to her moral career is founded on the designation of her husband as alcoholic and of herself as the wife of an alcoholic (sometimes referred to as a coalcoholic or codependent). These new self-images must always be taken into account; the self-negotiations that are such critical aspects of a moral career now have new parameters.

For the husbands of the women in this study, there were several paths leading to treatment: (1) personal decision, (2) family pressure or crisis, (3) medical concerns or intervention, and (4) legal-judicial system. These paths are not mutually exclusive nor do they represent an exhaustive listing. Rather, they are designations based on the events immediately preceding treatment, as reported during the interviews. It is quite possible, even likely, that a person entering treatment for alcoholism as an immediate result of one path may have previously negotiated demands or warnings in one or more other areas.

Some husbands enter treatment by the first path, personal decision, which emphasizes choice over outside influence.[2] I do not mean to imply that those in this category live in a complaint-free or pressure-free environment, only that it is largely left to them if and when they receive treatment.

A second path to treatment is some sort of family pressure or crisis.[3] Family pressure may accumulate over time or spill into a crisis. The crisis could include an apparent breakdown of the whole family unit or of the drinker or significant others. Either looming trouble or a believable ultimatum precedes the husband's entry into treatment. A third path involves medical concerns or intervention.[4] Sometimes the husband's health is deteriorating badly, and he takes action on his own; other times, medical experts exert their influence on the patient. Often, poor health in conjunction with a medical consultation is the moving force.

The final path to treatment for alcoholism is by way of the legal-justice system.[5] Police and court officers may become involved for a variety of reasons, ranging from traffic violations to court hearings to intervention in domestic disputes. The norms, and especially the laws, of a community are at stake here, and even the threat of negative sanctions can be a strong force.

These paths to treatment illustrate the workings of ambivalence. When a husband willingly enters a program for the treatment of alcoholism, he is symbolically declaring an overarching definition of self and situation, in the light of which other definitions pale. Designations by medical and legal authorities likewise carry a weighty definitional influence. The social clout of these definers and their designations is important in understanding the definitional enterprise and this moral career. Legitimated professionals are able to exert great influence on negotiations of the definitions of the situation and on the plausibility of definitions, even despite contrary perspectives the wives might have offered (for example, dropped DWI charges, treating emotional breakdown rather than alcoholism). Interpretations and actions by institutional authorities thus may stave off, as well as target, the designation of problems as alcoholic problems.

It is interesting to note that the wives' influence on their husbands' actual entry into treatment, in three of the four paths characterized here, was usually of a secondary or indirect nature. The single instance in which wives exhibit direct and primary influence—through family pressure or crisis—is born out of a social milieu of impending desperation, not of social status or power. This points to some of the more structural features of interactional and cultural factors affecting this definitional enterprise. This analysis is supported by the study finding that only one of the four reasons the wives entered their own family treatment programs closely reflected their own active stance in limiting ambivalence. This reason—psychological-emotional well-being—indicates their beginning endeavors to limit definitional ambivalence before entering the family program. In contrast, the wives' other explanations for entering family treatment—education, marital relationship concerns, and outside influence or pressure—demonstrate the limitation of ambivalence that occurs *after* entering the program.

The family program the wives attended offers therapeutic rehabilitation for the alcoholic's relatives through lectures, films, small-group discussions, and individual exercises. Such programs are designed to educate the participants about alcoholism, to foster personal growth and change, and to encourage development of interpersonal skills. Of the three centers involved in this study, one held a five- to seven-day residential program for the wives (and other family members), scheduling activities throughout the day and in the evening. The other two centers presented three- to four-hour sessions four evenings a week, running an average of about three-and-one-half weeks per client.

The women in this study spent considerable time, money, and energy participating in the family programs. For those who worked outside the home, it was a particularly demanding schedule—especially when compounded by the singly rigorous job of tending to children and managing a home. So why do wives of alcoholics attend the family programs? To find out, I began the first interview (after brief introductory remarks) with the suggestion, "Let's begin with your reasons for coming to the family program." Their responses highlighted four basic explanations.

One type of reply emphasized a desire to be educated about alcoholism and to gain a better understanding of the husband's past as well as anticipated behaviors.[6] A second reason was that the family program would provide a psychological-emotional respite of sorts.[7] The wives who gave this explanation viewed the program as a chance to focus on oneself—for renewal or growth. Interestingly, though many women noted such aspects of the program later in the interviewing process, it was especially the "program repeaters" (whose husbands had entered treatment several times) who expressed this type of reason in their opening statement.

A third explanation revolved around "marital relationship concerns."[8]

The women citing this reason wanted to resolve marital problems ranging from everyday issues of relationship to dilemmas of marital separation or dissolution. The final reason for attending the family program involved some sort of outside influence or pressure,[9] primarily applied by significant others, peer or reference groups, and people considered to be "expert others." Many of the wives who participated had been telephoned and advised to do so by members of the family program staff, although it was not clear whether the staff at the three treatment centers had contacted all of the wives in the study. Certainly, some of the wives also initiated contact with family program staff.

An interesting phenomenon with regard to family treatment programs generally deserves mention. A small proportion of the wives who attend get more than they bargained for, so to speak. That is, in the process of participating in the program they themselves are identified as being alcoholic or chemically dependent. When this occurs, the wives generally enter a primary treatment program for alcoholism soon after completing their family program. One woman in this study had just this sort of experience when she entered the family program for the first time. Now attending a second family program because her husband was in treatment again, she commented: "I was in three and a half years ago. I spent about a week and a half there as a codependent, and in the year that followed, in aftercare, [I] discovered that in addition to all [the] problems I'm having as a codependent—which, I guess, need to be worked through with him—. . . I was also chemically dependent."

Another woman was attending the family program again after four years of post-treatment sobriety for both her husband and herself. This time she wanted to explore the impact of being married to an alcoholic—an area she felt had been overshadowed during her first family program by the discovery of her own alcoholism. Below, she describes how her drinking problem was identified in the program four years earlier:

> I went as [a] significant person, nonalcoholic, and they picked up on my alcoholism. I had trouble in [the family program] admitting mine, because the counselor said that his [her husband's] was so much worse. I couldn't see mine because I always made sure that I drank with control. I never wanted to get drunk. I just couldn't stand to have

that happen to me, where I couldn't control what I was saying or doing, couldn't walk to bed or take care of the babies. It seemed to me that he was getting dead drunk. I had a hard time seeing mine. You know, he never said anything about my drinking, and he said to me afterwards—after treatment—that if he [had] said something about my drinking then, it would have made him an alcoholic, because he could see that his was worse.

For most of the wives, however, the significance of entering the family program (and of their husbands' treatment for alcoholism) is the limitation of the definitional ambivalence that has so doggedly disrupted their lives. Though the contingencies that give rise to the limitation of ambivalence may differ, the moral (self) implications are profound in the women's lived experiences: self-change and growth, and setting boundaries on interactions. They mark shifts in self-imagery, and they set the stage for changes yet to be established during the process of family treatment itself.

Depersonalizing the Ambivalence

Once the formal treatment process begins, the key challenge to self is one of depersonalizing the ambivalence. The personalization of definitional ambivalence that occurred in the problem amplification phase must now, in a sense, be undone. This requires an introspective resocialization process of unlearning-relearning.

In depersonalizing ambivalence the wives learn partially to remove their personality and individuality from their alcohol-related problems. This deindividuation of the built-up definitional ambivalence is associated with the proximal treatment phase of the moral career because it often coincides with the wives' participation in a family program of rehabilitation. Some women may first begin the process of depersonalizing through activities like Al-Anon or private counseling. The family program (or Al-Anon) introduces the women to ideas that encourage them to generalize rather than personalize their alcohol-related ideas about themselves, their husbands, and their situations.

Depersonalization, the key task in managing ambivalence and the key challenge to self in this phase of the moral career, involves three major changes for the wives: (1) to understand and accept the universality of the disease of alcoholism, (2) to dissociate self from images of selves and situations built up during the problem amplification phase, and (3) to reconstruct a new life based on these principles. Definitions of selves and situations can more easily be depersonalized and generalized when the focus is on similarities (rather than uniqueness), as it is now by virtue of official labeling and the women's placement in the new social category of *wives of alcoholics*. Learning about apparently shared similarities and common experiences (the universality of alcoholism) becomes a significant contingency in the moral career, whether "treatment" begins with Al-Anon, the family program, or other counseling.

Acquiring knowledge about and accepting the universality of the disease of alcoholism usually begins with the wives' awareness that their lived experiences are *not* unique. This is in contrast to their earlier belief that their lived experiences were quite unusual, even abnormal. Even though they are accurate in observing that everyone else does not live with the alcoholic problems that they do, once they are in the family program they learn that other wives who do live with alcohol-related problems share similar experiences. In other words, they discover that they are not alone—that their supposedly private, personal experiences are common to other women married to men being treated for alcoholism. The personalized self-blame and the aura of uniqueness of an earlier phase are now depersonalized and become established as part of a larger, more catholic process of disease. The following excerpts, reminiscent of Matza's (1964) concept of *collective ignorance*, illustrate this discovery of nonuniqueness:

> I'm learning, going to these classes, that I'm not alone, and there are an awful lot of people in the same boat. Some are even worse off.

> When I went to Al-Anon meetings, I thought these people had lived with me . . . that they lived my life, you know!

> When I compare myself to the neighbors and maybe my brothers and their families, I feel that I have a rather abnormal life. It looks okay on the outside, but we really haven't been a "family" family. But when I'm with Al-Anon people and, like, the family center, I'm learning that I am absolutely not alone with the feelings and the situations. So I don't think we are going to be so abnormal anymore.

The wives in these examples have begun to take the role and attitudes of a new group of referent others toward themselves. When they view themselves from these new standpoints, they are uplifted by a sense of self-acceptance and nurturance, as indicated in this statement regarding social support and companionship: "At this time [I relate to] just the Al-Anon people, because they can accept me for whatever I am. It's like a very protective shield."

Along with this initial awareness, there are further attempts to establish the universality of alcoholism. The wives are told that they are okay and so are their husbands, that their husbands have not intentionally hurt them but have done so because they suffer from a disease, and that the wives themselves need help in recovering from the debilitating effects of living with an alcoholic and from their own codependency. Through depersonalization of her alcohol-related problems, the wife is taught to (re)associate her participation in and contributions to problems with her membership in the "new" social category, wife of an alcoholic, commonly referred to as *codependent* in rehabilitation circles. The traditional Al-Anon term *enabler* has only recently been expanded (though not with official Al-Anon approval) into the concept of codependency or coalcoholism, which is viewed for the most part as an objective condition with determinable though not yet completely specified causes and consequences (Asher and Brissett 1988). The wives' contributions to problems are presented as part of the progressive and universal nature of the disease (alcoholism and codependency) rather than as unique to them as individuals. These ideas offer a new way for the women to conceive of themselves; they can now retrospectively reinterpret their lived experiences to align with this new definition of the situation (Goffman 1959). The following observations illustrate the process of depersonalization, by which formerly personalized attitudes and acts are recast and generalized as common to and representative of codependency. Notice how the women begin to use these new reinterpretations of their behaviors as they now speak of themselves:

I know I did support his drinking habit by waiting on him hand and foot. At first I enjoyed it; then I started realizing, Well, he doesn't appreciate this, but I kept on. I felt it was my duty. But now I'm learning that I was just one of his supporters.

I'm finding out now that it's very common for the alcoholic to ask the enabler or [whatever] to become more dependent on them. And

John has always done that. He wants me totally dependent on him, and he doesn't care for my involvement with groups or my nights out. And consequently I had one night out a week, and it was for prayer meeting.

Codependency—it's not obvious right away. It seems like a sharing problem, and it begins to entrap you in a subtle way. I can't say when it was that I began . . . taking over. I never saw it that way. I just saw him busy and stressed and me helping out. Some of my anger was, "Hey, wait a minute . . . I said that I would help you; all of a sudden I've got the whole ball—take your half."

The encouragements and attempts to view themselves as affected by their husbands' alcoholism, via codependency, mark a pivotal moral designation in the definitional enterprise. Where there were once competing plausible expectations and definitions of self, there is now a funneling process through which one particular designation, backed by "experts," is proffered (Goffman 1962). The challenge of depersonalizing is met by changing formerly individuated contradictions into generalized, meaningful inter-pretations under the auspices of the family program and through the teachings of Al-Anon.

Codependency is the vehicle for this conceptual move, in spite of the fact that professional practitioners may believe, on the one hand, that codependency is "manifested by a spectrum of symptoms, signs and problems that range from a lack of symptoms to headaches to suicide" (Whitfield 1984, 16), or, on the other hand, that "the manifestations of codependency are protean, its criteria unclear and its boundaries vague . . . a syndrome for which there are inadequate theoretically established boundaries and mean-ings, and which lacks convincing empirical support" (Gierymski and Wil-liams 1986, 12). Most of the women in this study began using the term during their family program stay and then in everyday conversation, as though assuming that everyone knows what it means. My attempts to pinpoint its meaning, however, reveal considerable confusion. In a separate report of this study, Dennis Brissett and I noted: "Although most of the wives agreed that codependency involves caretaking behaviors and exists by virtue of their association with an alcoholic, they disagreed widely as to its impact on the self, its locus as personal or social, its disease status, its longevity, and whether or not it is distinctive to alcoholic-complicated marriages" (Asher and Brissett 1988, 331).

Painfully aware of such continuing challenges in the definitional enterprise, these women nonetheless struggled to account for their lived experiences through the apparent fact and universality of alcoholism as a disease. Even as some definitional ambivalence was broken down, it rose again reformulated:

> I think it's a weakness for him to drink . . . even though they are telling me that that's not so: "You can't say it's a weakness for somebody to have cancer." It pisses me off. I think it's a weakness for him that he can't control it, because I can say that "I can do it; why can't you?"

> Well, from being here and from what I am hearing . . . there is a program of denial that I just cannot believe. It's just a sickness of denial and I was certainly into it, and he helped me be into it, and he certainly was into it. Of course, I [was] raised [to believe] that you would be ashamed of admitting that there was alcoholism. You . . . just view it as drunk . . . "he's drunk again," you know. I would never think of viewing it as a disease.

> I'm just learning now that it's a disease. I . . . still don't believe it. I believe that you can choose. I feel that I chose not to be an alcoholic. My father is an alcoholic. . . . He had asked me that: "Why aren't you an alcoholic?" And I just felt that I chose not to. But I guess the truth of the matter is that it is not that simple, that he can't help it. And I'm having a hard time understanding it.

Interestingly, after entering treatment, husbands often reveal new information about their alcohol-related expenditures, accidents, activities, and the like that help retrospectively to "fit" the husband to a more generalized image of the alcoholic—constructing or filling out, so to speak, the recent official designation of him. Though perhaps startled by this new information, the wives tend to view it constructively as part of their husbands' "working the program" and as a good sign that they are "getting honest." The following excerpts from the present study illustrate this phenomenon:

Sunday he bawled. He says, "I have to look you in the eyes when I tell you this." And he told me stuff like he dropped thirty-five dollars to a stripper—he wanted to impress her—as a tip, charged it on our VISA. . . . I was just so proud of him for being able to tell me that, because he's been hiding this stuff, and if it's going to help him to get it out, I admire him for being able to do that, because he has never [told me]; he's always lied. I don't know what all he hasn't told me.

When I came and visited him this past Sunday, he admitted to me that the reason why he moved out was because then he could go out and drink and I wouldn't be around to say, "Can't do it," or . . . yell at him when he got home. So there I was believing him . . . we spent a hundred fifty dollars we didn't have for him to stay somewhere to try and get this situated [our problems settled], and little did I know that his underlying reason was so that he could go out and drink more. So that was kind of a shock to me. I wasn't expecting that.

I found out since he's gone through this [treatment]. One of my girlfriends had a slumber party last year and . . . he made a big *stink* about me going. And I found out why: he didn't want me to hear how good other people had it. He admitted to this, and that . . . I mean he had me "right there," you know, and he didn't want me to find out anything that [would wise me up].

I would come home and there was no beer in the house, there was no smell on his breath—he would have his mouthwash and his coffee and everything to hide it. I knew he was loaded, and he would say, "No, I haven't had anything." We had no money to buy liquor so there was no liquor in the house. I knew that. And I couldn't believe he would go out and leave the kids alone . . . and they were in bed—or even take them to the liquor store because they would have told on him. I thought, maybe I'm cracking. You can't find any evidence and you think . . . and I never ever thought that he would . . . hide it on me—good lord! I was totally shocked when he told me that.

Though honesty is supposed to be the best policy, the healing effect of cathartic honesty in these examples seems unduly one-sided. While certain aspects of the proximal treatment phase, such as limitations on ambivalence and now legitimated designations of alcoholism, diminish the difficulties of definitional ambivalence, other aspects of this phase create intense moral experiences for the wives. While some outworn definitional contradictions are laid to rest, new definitions emerge and must be taken into account. They cannot easily be cast aside in the face of pressures from peers and professionals in the family program. These new perspectives have a profound impact on self-imagery in the moral career.

In some ways it may be easier and less painful for the wives to relate, even though unsurely and unstably, to their own relative codependency. Conceptualization of its symptoms allows virtually all of the wives' various attitudes and acts to be subsumed rhetorically within it. Even by partially rejecting the label, they can still use the framework of it to see that there are other ways they could have, or even should have, done things. Self-feelings that emerge from this looking back on self are illustrated in the following reflection, which also shows the continuing moral challenges within these redefinitions of self: "It's so easy in retrospect to see what a stupid, idiotic fool I have been. . . . I was the enabler all these years, obviously—I suppose I was playing martyr, thinking I was doing this great thing by taking [that approach], protecting my family and what have you, and obviously I wasn't. That is the thing that most really [disturbs me]; I am bitter at myself about it now. I have the anger feelings towards myself."

The latter excerpt typifies the irony of wives' resentments toward their husbands, built up during the problem amplification phase, now being turned, in part, toward themselves as they "discover" their codependent characteristics. Feelings of anger, guilt, and so forth reflect not only self-images, but also the women's imagined attitudes of others toward them. As Karp and Yoels (1979) put it, "There is no way that we can experience such reactions as shame or guilt without appraising our behavior from the perspective of others" (p. 38). Those referent others are likely to be the women's husbands, families, and peers and counselors in the family program. It is quite possible that any guilt or shame the wives may feel during the problem amplification phase for "causing" the husbands' drinking or unhappiness will shift in the proximal treatment phase to guilt for previously not responding in the program-defined "right" way. In any event, there are others' perspectives from which these women may appraise and establish implicit "blameworthiness."

Once again moral experiences (like guilt)—those that come up against self and challenge and tug at self—emerge not from within self but out of the interactional and cultural milieu that creates self. As Goffman (1962) poignantly observes:

> Each moral career, and behind this, each self, occurs within the confines of an institutional system, whether a social establishment such as a mental hospital or a complex of personal and professional relationships. The self, then, can be seen as something that resides in the arrangements prevailing in a social system for its members. The self in this sense is not a property of the person to whom it is attributed, but dwells rather in the pattern of social control that is exerted in connection with the person by himself and those around him. This special kind of institutional arrangement does not so much support the self as constitute it. (P. 168)

The emphasis here is on the lived experiences that make this a *moral* career—that is, the experiences that portray and mark significant challenges to the women's images of themselves (and of their husbands and marriages). The following excerpts are representative of the varieties of experiences that challenge women's imagery of themselves and their husbands during the process of depersonalizing their definitional ambivalence:

> I've always looked at him as a very, very secure person. I looked to him for my protection. Even until the day my husband went to treatment, I was still [seeing] the self-worth, the self-confidence, all of the things that I don't have, putting him up on a pedestal. That's been really overwhelming to me—to realize that all these things have gone, and I was so blinded. It's frightening.

> My only hope was that he wouldn't divorce me. I was terrified of the changes. I thought that he would get well and get out of treatment and take one look at me and discover he didn't love me. It was really hard for me to know what to expect. I was terrified.

I sit and listen to these things [in the family program], and I go, "God, I'm embarrassed to say anything." It's piddly compared to a lot of these people; it really is. And it just makes me embarrassed . . . that we can't fix this ourselves. I hope I change it. I feel like somebody else should be in my chair, you know, somebody with a lot worse problems than I have.

In the above reflections, threats, fears, and embarrassments challenge the wives' self-imagery. For these women, this is not simply a period of treatment; it is a time of social, relational, and self upheaval. The next excerpts present a variety of contrasting experiences that can be shared and compared with other wives in the family program (or Al-Anon), experiences that heighten awareness that the women's lives could be different "but for the grace" of contingencies:

I was not able to relax until I saw that he was really here [in the treatment center]. I still heard him coming in in the middle of the night. I still heard the door open and shut. I went through three weeks of this grieving, of still hearing him, and I'm having a real hard time dealing with the fact that soon he will be coming home. I was afraid to express these fears of the sleepless nights to anyone. Finally, I shared it with my children, and they shared with me that they, too, experienced the same things. They heard their dad coming in. They heard the car pull up, and it was all in our imagination. It's just been a real letting go—so out of control and yet a real grieving time for me.

In fact, I feel like I'm breathing free in my own house for the first time. I'm pretty, pretty happy being alone right now. And even my kids said, "Mom, you're sure happier." . . . Even though it hurt them *terribly* that their dad left—they're all close to him—they did realize that I could loosen up.

The following two observations provide another contrast in self-feelings and images:

I've seen him change. I was up there [in the treatment center] yesterday with him, and he reminds me of what he was when I first met him: very outgoing and talkative and—he could laugh and smile and . . . make jokes. It's been so long since he could do that.

When he went into treatment, he started working a *very selfish* program. I had all this anger and frustration, and it never got dealt with while he was in treatment or while I [was in] the family program. And then he was meaner, probably more assertive actually. He just took care of himself and totally ignored the fact that I was there. He shared with everybody but me.

All of these excerpts signify the variety of moral challenges that occur in this phase of the moral career. Each represents a self-challenge as these women introspectively delve into the complexities of their husbands' disease and their own implicated codependency. As the women view themselves from the contrasting standpoints of peers and staff in the family program, they are able to "place" themselves in terms of codependency. The particular contingencies of their own moral experiences influence issues and emotions that now confront them in "recovery."

At this point in treatment, the wives face the challenge of ideologically and behaviorally separating themselves from the images and expectations built up during the problem amplification phase. They are encouraged to reflect on themselves as persons—separate from their husbands—still depersonalizing alcohol-related problems, but also distinguishing themselves as viable, worthy persons in their own right. Who and what they are (or could or should be) becomes important in and of itself, dissociated from their husbands:

Finding out that . . . I am important and I have got a right to say no . . . to have some things that I'm not having and I'm going to go get them . . . knowing that I wasn't here just for everybody else, that I am a person, that I'm not crazy, that I am intelligent—I really got some neat awarenesses about who I am. . . . And I actually got to the point where I like myself—it was what I had gotten out of family treatment. It was neat to be able to stand up to him and say, "Hey, I don't have to take your shit"—because I was safe in that atmosphere to be able to say that. I could say all sorts of things there [in the family program] that I could never say before.

He has been in treatment four other times. He continues to go to AA, and he continues to use and continues to lie about using. And I can't handle it anymore. I've gotten so into his life, I've lost my own. So I need to start living my own again. Exclude him. Detach. Learn to detach. I needed to separate myself from the situation so I could focus in on me, because it's so easy to focus in on him.

In contrast to the uplift that such self-appreciation and nurturance can bring, there are also difficulties and continuing challenges in dissociating from past experiences and images, as illustrated in these comments:

Frustration—my inability to disconnect. I know the program is teaching us to take care of ourselves first. I know that I have to do that for my own health now; it's gotten to that point. But it frustrates me that the solution appears to be obvious, but when it's applied it's almost impossible. He has complete denial. To a man that is aware, [has] education, and deals [professionally] in the problem [as a counselor] is very frustrating to me, and I am very ineffective against him . . . that's frustrating.

I would like to be a person in my own right, and I would like to stop the caretaking role, be free of all game playing. One of the games that we play is, I am always up and he is always down. And I'm supposed to pull him up. And if I don't pull him up, then I am some yuck or something. I mean there is some kind of a game there, so ultimately I always end in the down position, because he's manipulating me. . . . I would like to develop more sensitivities about people, that I am not taken in by them, and more separation, that I have an identity of my own. Also I would like to feel that I am not stuck. I'm working towards getting to the point that I stay in the marriage by choice or leave it by choice.

There is kind of a separation, a death awareness, that I have right now, and it's very sad for me, [what] I'm going through. I try really hard not to take it personally, but I *have* all these years, thinking, what am I doing wrong?

Through the teachings of a self-reflective program the women come to understand that they are not the "cause" of their husbands' behaviors, and they begin rejecting self-images that would have them be so. A sense of relief usually emerges from this experience:

My problem was that I was always trying to please so many people. I didn't want to do anything wrong. I wanted to be perfect, so that they would like me. I finally realized that I am a good person. I do have feelings. I don't have to take all the responsibilities. I don't have to feel so guilty all of the time—just since I have been here [in the family program]. I was totally ignorant about . . . alcoholism. Everything I've learned—I had no idea what it was all about before. It's amazing.

This letting go is a new thing . . . that I had not been aware of until I was reading the literature, so I realized that that was the best thing that you can do, and I didn't do that before. I've been thinking that I could help, and we learn here that you have to let go; it's their problem and not your problem. And it certainly is a feeling of relief to be told that, that you're not responsible for the whole situation.

A woman who had been through the program several times with a husband who repeatedly resumed his drinking after treatment used a slightly different tone: "I've gone past that point of thinking I'm going to help him recover. I realize that he has to do that, that he has to do that for himself. And if he goes back to drinking, or if he stays sober, that has to be his decision, and he has to do it. Whichever way it goes, it's him; it's not me."

The other side of this causal coin is that just as the wife's behavior is purportedly not causing her husband's actions, neither is the husband's behavior causing the wife's. Through the teachings of the family program, the wives begin changing their views of their husbands, and they begin to see that all of their own problems have not been caused by their husbands. Accompanying this perspective is an often-revelatory emphasis on self-responsibility. The wives hear and begin to understand that they alone are responsible for their attitudes, acts, feelings, and interactions. During both program activities and their free time the women share introspectively, suggesting behavioral changes for self and one another; a momentum of personal growth and change spreads throughout the formal and informal activities of the family program. The following excerpts illustrate ways in which this new awareness of self-responsibility translates into lived experience. Notice, too, that typical (codependent) rehabilitation concepts such as *caretaking*, *controlling*, *enabling*, and *resentments* made their way into the vocabularies of the women in this study after just one or two days in the family program, when these interviews took place (emphasis added):

> He knows how to manipulate me, and I allow that to happen. . . . I'm still into *taking care of* him.

> I really realize that I have played the *caretaker role* so much that it is such a relief to get out of it, to not have to *control* and not have to *caretake* anymore. All I have to do is take care of myself . . . and be responsible to my daughter. I always felt I had to, for whatever reasons—my *enabling*. I don't have to do that anymore if I choose not to.

> We discussed that today, I have to be assertive.

> If my husband can quit drinking . . . I hope that I can wipe away all my *resentments*, my feelings that are built up in me. I feel that is just as every bit as important as his problem; I've got to change my behavior. I also don't have as much compassion as I should have for the person who has a problem with alcohol. I mean, heaven knows I have probably had in me for a number of years that it's a medical problem and what have you, yet I find sometimes it very hard to accept that. I need to get some of these feelings wiped out of me.

These examples of learning to accept responsibility for self and the need for self-change, in part, demonstrate the challenge of dissociation from the alcoholic husband, his problems, and the imagery of the pretreatment period. Paradoxically, dissociating one's "self" from the husband and his alcoholism—an attitude and an activity that would appear to release a wife from accountability and liability regarding her husband's disease—is nonetheless a significant factor in linking her to his alcoholism via codependence. Her keen and reproaching awareness and her acknowledgment of her own untoward behavior in the past hold critical sway in this process of accounting for self-responsibility. Common sense also tells her that if she cannot be rightly blamed for his behavior, then he cannot be rightly blamed for hers. Add to this the tremendous relief many of the wives experience as they learn that their imagined "awfulness" did not cause the drinking problem after all, and a very special social climate emerges. It is a climate in which the wives willingly explore other flaws in their own behavior, which by comparison appear to be far less serious than being the cause of their husbands' alcoholism. The following interview excerpt articulates this phenomenon:

I think that working through Al-Anon, trying to work a program—I think that I found out that I'm a human being . . . a decent human being. I used to think that I was a bad person. I went through all of that, and then after finding his drinking had nothing to do with me—I was not to blame for any part of it—helped me a lot right there. And then proceeding on from there, that I could look at myself. I think that if they had said that "yeah, it's your fault," I probably wouldn't have gone back to Al-Anon [or tried] to get any type of help. But just finding out that . . . I didn't have anything to do with it helped a lot. And knowing that—that is sort of the way that they believe—I could look at myself and I could change as they teach it: I could [do it], "Look at yourself and change your own behavior."" I could do that, and I was very happy to say that there is something wrong with me, . . . let's look at it. And I'm very willing to work at it.

The "hook" here is that the wives' admission of untoward acts and attitudes is taken as prima facie evidence of their own codependency. I am not implying that the women do not benefit from the treatment process; they usually do. Rather, I am calling attention to the self-imaging challenges of these experiences and to the implications of a process that seems first to deviantize the women's previous actions and then to medicalize this new-found deviance as the "illness" codependency (Asher and Brissett 1988).

In considering situations involving moral choice, both Chodorow (1978) and Gilligan (1982) found that whereas males are likely to construct moral arguments around the maintenance of social distance, females experience moral conflict and use moral justification for failure to meet others' needs and for failure to nurture and maintain relationships. In the rehabilitative family program, the wives are presented with an interesting twist on these moral stances: an attitude of *tough love*, prescribing a detached, nonreactive stance toward their alcoholic husbands, is deemed to be the appropriate behavior. Thus, a wife learns to maintain a stance that is morally appropriate to her—one of being a loving person doing what is best to mend a wounded relationship and, at the same time, to invoke the traditional male standard of maintaining distance in the relationship. And so, as Haaken (1990) observes, "In the enabling situation, it is noteworthy that the woman's failure to respond to the problems of her alcoholic husband requires justification in terms of *his* need for a different response. It is understandable that many women embrace the enabling construct and experience some relief in being told that to not respond to the demands of the alcoholic spouse is actually more loving than to do so. The underlying feminine ideal of maternal sensitivity to others is preserved by a reframing of the moral issues" (p. 400).

In another activity of the family program, participants begin looking at life goals. Formulating plans for self involves new images of self that emerge during the program. Making such plans is part of depersonalizing ambivalence and refocusing on self as wives separate from their husbands' alcoholism. Setting autonomous goals for personal plans was a new undertaking for many of the women in this study. Virtually all of them had begun their married lives along traditional lines (though some developed individual goals during the course of their marriages). The comments of one woman symbolize many wives' looking-glass views, which they imagine mirror the standpoints of their husbands and society:

> I guess my goals when I got married were that . . . I'm there to serve, take care of my husband. And I'm a good cook, and I take care of my kids. . . . I guess I really didn't have any goals for myself; I didn't need goals. I mean . . . all I needed to do was to say "I do," and that's all that is expected of me. . . . If my husband gets sick and cannot work, then I go find a job and I do what I can . . . within my role. My role is this; his role is that . . . there were really no goals.

The self-imagery suggested in these statements is in stark contrast to that now emerging during the family program: self-responsibility and reliance, taking care of self, and setting personal goals. Though these are positive changes, they nonetheless present dramatic challenges of change to self and can mean profound experiences of inner upheaval.

Program terms like *letting go* relate to the wives' reports of grieving processes and signify the intense and moral nature of participating in a reconstruction of self and life-style, as suggested in this proximal treatment phase. By way of the family program (or Al-Anon), the women learn to change their interpretations of themselves and their lives and to clarify personal goals. Not surprisingly, many of these goals are program-oriented, as represented in the following comments:

> Well, I want to continue going to Al-Anon and I want to continue working this program and trying to recover. I want to attempt to seek out friends and I want to be more open with people, take better care of myself, be a person who is able to cope with problems without falling to pieces and somebody who is—has serenity and peace.

> I'm going to learn as much as I can about this disease and go to Al-Anon—whatever I can do to see what can be done for my husband.

The following excerpt illustrates the Al-Anon idea that "working the program" is a lifelong endeavor: "[I have to work on] character defects, and personality changes, I have to make . . . it took me four years to get where I'm now. I don't think I'll ever be what I want to be in this life; I think that there will always be something that I'll want to change. I think that that's kind of normal. Once you work on one defect, another one crops up . . . you go back to the first one. I don't think that you ever completely [get rid of the defects]. So I think that it's going to be a lifetime for me working at it." Many of the changes cited by the women in this study, although related to the program teachings, are associated less with "working the program" and more with individual goals:

> I want to be a more honest person than I have been, be able to express myself more than I have been—assertiveness. I want to be sensitive to people. And then I want to continue . . . the growing responsibility aspect of it. What I would like to change in the next one or two years is to see who and what I am, and to feel who and what I am, because I haven't felt me. I don't think I've ever really felt who I was and expressed what I want to when [I want to]. I allow myself anger, but I don't allow myself to feel and to know my body in that

sense. . . . And even spiritually, I would like to change those parts . . . so I know what I am, who I am.

What I am really interested in is to understand what has happened to me, because all of the emotions are still entangled. And if I do end up leaving the situation, I want to understand where I was and be able to sort out how it did influence me, and it has . . .

Right now, I'm hurting. I would like to feel that I am loved, that I can give love freely, feel the closeness with someone, no strings. Just to be me, I guess. Just to hold onto me, [to be] strong, responsible . . . also to be weak, to feel the freedom to choose my own [way], you know, that's based on just me. I'll have to learn to go to people and . . . seek help, and not to just keep it inside of me—learn to express myself, accept the fact that I can't handle a lot of things, just with me. I need the help of others.

Anticipation about the future may loom heavily at this time of shake-up in self and life situation. The following examples typify the apprehension that accompanies or overrides the new feelings and thoughts:

[You] asked about the future. I guess that that is where I am at now. Okay, we're both trying to get help. Nobody knows what tomorrow is going to be, and so I wonder . . . what is it going to be? Is it going to be worth it? Five years from now, am I going to wish that I would have gotten out now? . . . I don't want to regret . . .

I'm kind of nervous about being home with him because . . . he keeps wanting me to tell him that I love him. . . . I guess I love him . . . but deep down I'm not sure it's the type of love that I'm supposed to be feeling or I had at one time. I don't want to live a lie, and yet I've always been afraid to hurt him. When he is behaving well, you know, all he has to do is shed a couple of tears and I'll melt. He's always known that, and he banks on that happening, and I can't keep living like that. And he's upset, too, because I didn't cancel the lawyer. . . . He said, "[Why] are you being so skeptical? Are you going to hold this over my head?" And I said . . . "I [am] not really holding it over your head. It's more or less because I'm not quite sure myself."

Of the participants in this study, perhaps the most apprehensive were the wives who had already seen their husbands through alcoholism treatment before and had themselves been through family programs associated with the husbands' previous treatments. (The number of repeat treatments for these couples ranged from two to six.) A woman whose husband had been through treatment six times exemplifies the lived experiences of those in repeater situations:

I see how elated these gals are, [the women] who are here this week. . . . This is their first time through this, and I can look back and the first couple of times, I was exactly the way that they are. To them it's a ray of hope, and they don't understand why I'm not feeling that. And it's because I have been let down, I, not—yes, him—and I've let myself down too many times. And they tell me . . . "You know what I'm doing. My husband has been in here for a whole week now, and . . . I've learned this. You ought to try this; it's working for me." And I think, whoopy ding . . . let me talk to you six months from now—even if he's sober—and let me see if you're still feeling this high. Because I think a lot of these people have a concept that once their husbands or their mates get out of treatment, and they get home, that everything is going to be peachy-keen, and life is a big bed of roses.

They've got a rude awakening because I've seen it happen, and it's happened to me. Even if they do stay sober, you still have the same problems unless you work at them. . . . You might handle them a little differently and cope with them, or you might not. [You] might not be able to handle it any differently, you might still fight, you might still argue, he might still go out and see the gal. He won't come home drunk or whatever—just understand this, that it doesn't fix everything.

In this examination of objectives and anticipations for the future, we see a variety of feelings, self-images, and outlooks on life. In these prospective comments, the women anticipate what they and their lives will be like at some point in the future. They view themselves as social objects, as persons they want to be, anticipating themselves from others' standpoints and imagining the responses of others and themselves to these "new" selves.

In the proximal treatment phase, there is a special link between past and future, between former, ongoing, and projected selves. The past is always close at hand when persons consider future changes, for past images are the referents for the changes to come. Constructing what one wants to be like (or should be like) refers also to what one has been like. Ironically, the program dictum to live in the present and "one day at a time" is impinged upon by the past and future of these women's lived experiences. Now, as they move from this phase into post-treatment, the women face ever-different challenges of ambivalence management in the moral career of becoming the wife of an alcoholic.

Part 4

The Post-Treatment Phase

Transforming
the Ambivalence

Persons create selves as they take attitudes and actions toward themselves and others. In the same manner, the women in this study continue to create their selves—now, in the post-treatment, postnaming phase, as wives of alcoholics. In this final phase of the moral career, the focus is on how women who have become wives of alcoholics—through reinterpretation of their biographies, through resocialization, and through social designation—meet the challenges of ambivalence management by transforming the remaining ambivalence and self-consciously establishing themselves as wives of alcoholics. This entails putting less emphasis on contradictory expectations, thereby transforming ambivalences into choices or alternatives. Descriptively, the formerly exasperating dilemma of "he's this . . . *but* he's also that"—the implication being, "so which is he, really?"—is transformed to a more harmonious statement of "he's this . . . *and* he's that"— the implication being, "and that's okay." The disruptive ambivalence of earlier phases is reinterpreted in ways that allow for more stable, even if initially difficult, definitions of selves to emerge. This relative "routinization" of definitional ambivalence involves transforming it; reconciling it and philosophizing it comprise this transformational process. Transforming the ambivalence is more than simply changing it; it means refashioning it into something new and meaningful.

Why is it necessary to transform ambivalence? It is because many contradictory and incompatible expectations and courses of actions are left unresolved in the aftermath of the problem amplification and proximal treatment phases of the moral career. The interpretive challenges of depersonalizing ambivalence during treatment, for instance, leave other ambivalences unaddressed. The women are told about "how things are" (for example, the universality of the disease alcoholism and their own codependency) and about "how things could or should be" (for example, dissociating from husband/his alcoholism, creating a more autonomous self), but little attention is given to the actual images, attitudes, and emotions the wives may have that are incompatible with these new expectations. They are told they should be more responsible for how they negotiate and experience situations and they should be honest about their feelings, but they seldom hear about the interactional and cultural factors that influence (help or hinder) these kinds of self-performances.

In the face of learning that alcoholism is a disease and that their husbands could not help what they did, the wives are left to find their own outlets for hurt and anger—for lashing out at a "sick" person is a socially inappropriate choice. Participation in Al-Anon may be, for some, a way of dealing with such unresolved, relationship-related emotions and issues—a sort of steam escape valve. The task in the post-treatment phase is to create an interpretive framework for managing any remaining definitional ambivalence, for retrospectively comprehending their lived experiences as wives of alcoholics. Their career-long struggle to manage definitional ambivalence requires a major transition as they transform the contradictory expectations into an operative explanatory framework for living. This is accomplished primarily under the tutelage of a family treatment program and Al-Anon, directly or indirectly, through interpretations that transform the disruptive features of ambivalence into something with which the women can live. Two methods the women use to create such a milieu for themselves are reconciling the ambivalence and philosophizing it.

An illustration of a specific instance of ambivalence vis-à-vis ideology demonstrates the dramatic moral predicaments the wives encounter. The concept of *detachment*, taught in family programs and Al-Anon, symbolizes a variety of definitionally ambivalent expectations with which the wives may be left to deal however best they can. The following excerpt typifies

personal, interactional, and ideological struggles with definitional ambivalence:

> I don't know how Al-Anon people detach. That's why I quit going.
> I said, "Tell me what it is that you do [to detach] . . . this Al-Anon . . .
> what. Why is it that it does this [tells you to detach] to you?" Well, no
> one had any answers for me. And I don't know if it's that they just kind
> of block it out and just, well . . . like they say, you just continue your life
> without them [a drinking alcoholic husband]. I said, "Well, you've got
> this 'crazy' in and out of your house. . . . How do you get away from
> it?" [And they told me], "You just detach yourself." I said, "God, if you
> say that to me one more time, I'll die." "You know," I said, "I just don't
> understand it." So, I don't know.

This excerpt is from the woman's third interview, a considerable time after
her participation in the family program. Her questions remain unanswered,
her struggle still rife with incompatible expectations. This is one way in
which definitional ambivalence is left unresolved. The family program and
Al-Anon define a way to manage the ambivalence—not by addressing it
directly, but by attempting to transform it. The transformation of ambivalence involves a strategic reinterpretation, a new way for the women to view
their worlds—-a way that offers apparent social comfort and comprehensibility that other ways cannot.

In discussing detachment, a book of daily readings much recommended
by the family program and Al-Anon advises wives not to waste energy or
time attempting to figure out what makes their husbands drink or behave
poorly. That these men suffer from a compulsive disease and should have
their wives' compassion is enough for them to know. The women are
reminded that they do not have the right to control their husbands and that
to treat them as if they are naughty children only makes matters worse. The
reading includes a promise to self and to God to let go of the problem, and a
prayer for detachment from the situation rather than from the drinker. It
also suggests that compassion and changes in attitude by the wives may
help their husbands to gain sobriety (*One Day at a Time in Al-Anon* 1979, 3).
In this daily reading selection, we see continuations of the earlier resocialization themes along with suggestions for accepting and harmonizing atti-

tudes and actions. These are the kinds of changes that emerge in transform-ing definitional ambivalence by reconciling it or by philosophizing it.

Reconciling something implies the act of harmonizing, bringing it into agreement or acceptance. It is a significant task in the moral career because it dissipates lingering definitional ambivalence. Reconciling attitudes to-ward the ambivalence transforms the contradictions and incompatibilities of selves and situations into a conciliatory, interpretive framework. The reconciliation of ambivalence focuses on acceptance and change, often through expressions of acceptance of self and husband as individuals and through declarations of personal change. This may include actualizing previously imaged or desired characteristics about selves or the marriage relationship, or, in the absence of actual changes, it may involve concilia-tory acceptance.

Certainly one important factor in reconciling definitional ambivalence is having a husband who now abstains from drinking, particularly when abstinence is backed up by introspective change on the part of the husband. The emergence of this kind of situation in the post-treatment phase is perhaps the most logical and rewarding for comprehending and reconciling definitional ambivalence. It is a "happy" solution to the puzzles of lived experiences, as one of the women pointed out: "What's distinctive about a couple who are recovering together is that they learn to be flexible. There is a real strengthening of the relationship. . . . There is sort of a resiliency and you don't . . . have a breaking point any more. Everything just seems much more manageable. There aren't crises anymore; no matter what happens you can take life as it comes."

Husbands can enhance their spouses' task of reconciling ambivalence by taking actions besides abstinence. One way is by exhibiting attitudes and actions that help their wives to overcome residual feelings of distrust or hostility toward their husbands, as these interview excerpts suggest:

I've seen not only a willingness to change, I've seen a change. My husband is a new person. [Before] I said he was a bastard.

It was just a big heavy thing. And, of course, with that all taken away . . . you can't help but be a happier, more confident person. A person that is an alcoholic in his worst moments is not going to be real complimentary and probably likes to put people down because it makes him feel better. And now . . . there just isn't any of that, being put down. . . . He is sweeter and . . . he just can't be thoughtful enough, and he's thinking all the time about what he can do for people and for the family. The part about putting people down, he used to be real bad about that and [about] being sharp and sarcastic. And thinking back on it, why, that was one of his methods of upping his own ego.

Notice in the last example how the previous pain and turmoil of competing definitions of selves and situations are made acceptable in light of the present. The past is made consistent with the present as the newly legitimated definitions of selves and situations are eased into explanations of past selves and situations (Goffman 1962; Berger and Luckmann 1967; Schur 1971). This reinterpretive aspect of the definitional enterprise provides a way to view the past as consistent with the present; it harmonizes contradictory definitions between the past and the present. In short, reinterpretations reconcile the definitional ambivalence.

The husbands' affirmation of incompatible expectations that existed in the past appears to be another significant factor in the wives' ability to deal with or discard accumulated resentments, thus facilitating the reconciliation of definitional ambivalence. The following comments reflect one husband's conciliatory affirmation of troubling past experiences: "Every now and then he'll still say to me, 'Gee, we never could have done this if I was still drinking.' Or he'll say, 'I was such a fool' or 'I feel really bad about some of those things.' He still says it to the children."

Wives more easily accept and harmonize contradictory and incompatible expectations from the past when their husbands, formerly denying these, now acknowledge them. In a sense it is self-vindication for the wives, acknowledgment not only of the definitional ambivalence but also of the struggle they encountered. After all, their vexations with definitional ambivalence resulted partly from dealing with the contradictions and incompatibilities of ambivalence itself and partly from the struggle in illuminating these ambivalences to others, especially their husbands.

Changes in the attitudes and actions of the husbands are just one element in reconciling definitional ambivalence; changes in the wives are another. Changes in the wives' attitudes and actions also reconcile definitional ambivalence because these revised interpretations of selves and situations can harmonize ambivalent definitions. Such changes are moral experiences because they challenge the self in a context of change, representing changes in self-definition, self-feelings, and ideological views. The following interview excerpts illustrate such changes:

> Without Al-Anon I know that I wouldn't be feeling good about myself. I mean, I am feeling comfortable about myself and I feel good about where I am today and who I am. I really feel that I am a good person. . . . I'm a much more caring person, I'm a much more empathetic, outgoing person because of sharing in Al-Anon and having people share their lives with me. I'm able to get close to people now, where I was never able to do that before. I mean I can actually hug somebody . . . and it really feels good. I could never do that before.

> Again, [my increased] self-confidence: he is home now, he's not drinking, and he's not spending all kinds of money that we don't have on drinking. And I find it easier for me . . . I won't let things bottle up inside of me anymore. If I have something to say, I'm going to say it, whether he listens or not. . . . I'm going to get it off my chest. Whereas before I . . . was afraid to do it . . . well, [I thought] that it wouldn't do any good. . . . I didn't want to if he was [sober]; . . . when they're drinking you're angry, but when they're sober you [think], Why bring it up now? He's not drinking now. . . . And you just put it off and let it build up. And now if it happens once, I say something. . . . I don't carry that around with me anymore.

These examples suggest that when the wives view themselves as changing for the better, they can assume more harmonious or conciliatory views of the disruptive ambivalences of the past. Such changes are often along lines indicated by the teachings of the family program and Al-Anon, including learning to take good care of themselves or to perform in desired ways. It certainly helps, too, when these ambivalences can be seen as belonging to the past and as unlikely to arise in ongoing interactions. Declarations of changes in selves and situations symbolize differences between the way things were and the way things are, paving the way for conciliatory attitudes and actions.

Other conciliatory changes emphasize acceptance of conditions as an adjustive kind of action, so that life can go on, somewhat in spite of definitional ambivalence. This kind of reconciliation, by learning to live with the ambivalence, is demonstrated in the examples below:

I know that he was sick. I understand that, but don't keep doing it to me, because I won't stay a whole lot longer. I can learn how to forgive and forget: you know, if you don't do it to me, then I don't bring it up or . . . it will just eventually go away. It's a growing experience. You grow from it because you've been slapped in the face so many times and kicked and stomped on, and you finally learn how to deal with it. Those kind of things I can deal with and understand.

The sex [abuse] was difficult for me. [The family program counselor] got that out of me. That was awful for me to say . . . the things that have happened. I never told everything that's happened. It's over now, and I got it out once, you know. But different things will remind me of it—rape scenes on TV or . . .

As he progressed with his drinking it was kind of hard to accept, and I guess I felt sorry for myself: why did it have to happen to me? I used to do a lot of hollering at him. I try to keep that down now. [It] just gets real depressing at times when I look at him and wonder why. . . . After each treatment period I think I've been more accepting of it. I realize that it doesn't do any good. He realizes himself what he's doing to himself. I don't think he sees himself as being obnoxious as he sometimes gets. But . . . we do talk about it; we can sit and talk a lot better.

A certain pragmatism is implied in these accounts. In the process of the moral career, reconciling ambivalence eventually becomes the practical thing to do. The full-blown disruptive definitional ambivalence of the problem amplification phase simply cannot be sustained indefinitely. During the post-treatment phase, all of the wives in this study engaged in reconciling activities, whether or not they remained married to their husbands, whether or not their husbands abstained from drinking, and whether or not the reconciliations corresponded with the ideology of the family program and Al-Anon. Just as the importance of an event to a person can be

measured by her reaction to it, the moral significance of definitional ambivalence can be symbolized by the reconciling stances taken toward it.

A second and closely related way of transforming definitional ambivalence is to philosophize it. Philosophizing refers to applying "guiding
principles" to situations of living. The change-challenge of philosophizing
the ambivalence goes hand in hand with reconciling it; they are comple-
ments in transforming ambivalence into a satisfactory interpretive framework for explaining the lived experiences of this moral career. Philosophizing renders the lived experiences in the moral career comprehensible, not
only in the sense that they can be understood per se but also in the sense
that they can be understood as fitting into the larger scheme of things and as
explaining, in part, the nature of life itself.

The challenge to interpret the moral experiences of definitional ambivalence philosophically is met by interpreting the past as a significant learning
experience. Because it is learning, the emphasis is on its benefits, such as
increased empathy or increased appreciation of life. The overwhelming
praise of personal growth expressed by the women in this study is testi-
mony both to the intense moral nature of definitional ambivalence and to
the significant challenge encountered in defusing it. There are three major
philosophizing themes: qualities gained, good coming from bad, and fortuitous destiny.

The theme of *qualities gained* refers to attributes the wives feel they
obtain through their experiences with an alcoholic husband. The implication is that such qualities better equip them to deal with life:

> Well, it is certainly a traumatic experience while you're going
> through it. I think it makes you stronger when you realize you lived
> through that. And it makes you think ahead. . . . I guess it makes you
> examine, deep down—really examine your life a little closer and think
> about if certain things happened, how you would cope. There are a lot
> of support systems out there for you to go to, should you need [them].
> With the different things that happened, that gave me strength. I
> mean, I am much better equipped to cope than he is, because I've
> accepted the responsibilities. I've accepted the challenges of my life,
> the bad times, and I've survived them. I haven't let them get me. I
> never ended up in a mental ward, you know, and I could have. I came

close, but I didn't. I kept hanging on, I kept treading water, and I kept overcoming. . . . That gave me strength and character.

And if [you've] gotten through that, then golly, you can just kind of take a look down that road and say, hey, that's got to be good. . . . I've got more reason to be hopeful now than I ever had. I mean shit, I was hopeful when there wasn't any reason to be hopeful. I don't have to hope anymore; I just know it's going to happen. And if it doesn't, I'm going to make damn sure that it does.

I think I can maybe feel some real true compassion for people who do have illness. I think all the pain and whatever I have had in my life has made me a better person. I think now that something very, very tiny and very, very simple that most people would turn [up] their nose at, I can say I find beauty in, and I don't think I would have been able to say that twenty-six years ago, because at that time . . . I took a lot of things for granted. But in having to sacrifice and to do without, I would say just a pretty tree or a flower, just something that is really beautiful [I really appreciate now].

Among these expressions lies a large array of qualities gained, but the unifying theme is that the difficulties of this moral career have made these women better persons.

Another means of philosophizing the ambivalence is found in the related theme of *good coming from bad*. This emerges from ideas about good fortune arising out of adversity and is a cousin to the popular motto, "no pain, no gain." Illustrating this theme are the following excerpts:

I just can't believe at thirty-five I finally feel like I should have when I was twenty: up and raring to go. . . . So, I guess, if I can get something good out of a bad experience, that's all I'm asking for. . . . Hopefully, my ex-husband is going to be happy, too. I mean, I don't hate him, but I can't stand him . . . for just the things that happened. And you can't completely blame it on him. I was codependent for sure. I know that now.

Looking back on all those years, I can't see any bad. I see only good. And the reason I see the good is because it's been a learning experience, and everything that's happened to me has been a little piece of where I am right now. . . . I never thought that I could ever say that. . . . I mean, five years ago or three years ago, I never would have been able to say that.

There was no being educated as far as some of my problems [were concerned], and maybe it took going through a really bad experience like that . . . to become educated. You know, I'm kind of glad that we had to go through all this. I'm selfish, I guess, because I got a hell of a lot out of it: I got my life, you might as well say, because I was doomed, really. I was really, really screwed up.

To account for problems, once crises are past, as having improved oneself and one's life in the long run lends comprehensibility to having had the problems. They stand now, in hindsight, as experiences with special meaning and purpose. Paradoxically, the problems of definitional ambivalence and moral experience that once represented a kind of personal-social disorganization now come to represent a kind of organizing principle to the scheme of things. What the wives of alcoholics were once working against, they are now working with, and it is working for them.

The third philosophizing theme, *fortuitous destiny*, alludes to the fate of life, a kind of fatalistic working out of life and problems:

I think we had everything in the world going for us. The only [problem] . . . was his drinking, and when that drinking got out of the way, why, we just—we're very fortunate people. There's no doubt about it. I mean, that's our feeling; we think we're very fortunate. Sure we had that, but I guess everybody has something. We're sorry it took some years of our life and toll from us, but we still have got—as I say, we care for each other, we have a loving family, we are financially sound, we have our future. And I just retired and he's about to.

I consider myself to have gone through three phases: . . . ignorance, discovery, and recovery. . . . And [of those phases], probably from one to ten years . . . was ignorance.

I guess I'm real sad that it happened, but I think that by going through all this—if [he] stays sober—that it's probably going to bring us together a lot more than before. It was a stroke of luck. I don't know how we would have gone about this if the police hadn't brought him in. . . . I guess I can just be happy that maybe there was someone up there rooting for us . . . that knew that we . . . really wanted to stay together. And it just fell into place, because we're one of the lucky ones. . . . I've seen a few people now that have gone through twenty to thirty years and [just] now have been doing something, so I consider myself lucky.

It's hell. Change hurts. It's very painful. It's scary and it's tough to this day . . . but I have no regrets: no regrets for marrying him, no regrets for being involved with him, no regrets for anything I've done, no regrets for where I am right now, today. I don't know that I'd say I'd go and do it all over again, but I don't regret. . . . He was just something that happened, and . . . I was glad when I married him. We had a lot of happy times together, and I'm glad now that I'm out of it. Glad I don't have any kids.

In these examples of philosophizing the ambivalence, the contradictory and incompatible definitions of selves and situations that once loomed very large are now reinterpreted as happenings that a rather fateful good fortune has overcome. It is as though alcohol-related problems are now interpreted as interruptions in an otherwise good life, as a chance negative part of a positive whole, or as a harbinger of a fatefully good change. Each of these reinterpretations of the definitional ambivalence implies getting back on track with one's fortuitous destiny—truly a transformation from previously imagined views.

One more aspect of transforming definitional ambivalence deserves mention. It involves the women's post-treatment interpretations of themselves and their own experiences in this moral career vis-à-vis other women who are presently undergoing what they have already been through. In the following examples from this study, the wives' attitudes and actions reflect a sort of "mystique of knowledge," a disdain for the lack of self-defensive actions, and adoption of an empathic-teacher role:

I have a girlfriend [who's] calling me regularly . . . she's got this drunk: da-da-da-da, same story, everybody's story, you know. And I keep trying. I say, "Debbie, if I could only explain this to you; if you'd only listen and try to understand this." . . . She's in the state where she just . . . I mean, it's like he's done just these horrifying things to her and she just hasn't figured it out. And I say, "Just wait until you figure it out." I said, "I can't help you. . . . You're going to have to figure it out for yourself. . . . When you're ready, you'll leave. Or you'll get rid of him."

There was one [Al-Anon] group, specifically. . . . I just thought, what are you people doing? . . . Then there were other groups that were real supportive no matter what you did—[that's] what I liked— and a lot of people there had smartened up. . . . They may have stayed with the person, but [they] at least had different lives. . . . But mostly the impression of Al-Anon for me was real depressing. Just listening to what people said, and they'd come back and say the same thing, like they just wouldn't make the change. That would depress me—that they were under that control, that they just couldn't get away from it. . . . [There] comes a time when, if you've got a good counselor, the counselor will tell you, "Hey . . . it's graduation time now; get your ass out there and start living it." . . . And that's kind of where I am with Al-Anon, I'm very involved; I'm chair of the group. I have been for six months, and I'm just taking on the position again for another six months. I'm involved in Alateen. I find that Al-Anon for me now has been more of a sharing what I've gotten and I'm giving back now, not taking as much. I'm giving back in gratitude, hoping that I can help somebody else with my experiences.

Though these examples portray varying ways of transforming definitional ambivalence, each portrays a stance that symbolically distances the women now transitioning out of the moral career from women currently in the throes of it. The overt stances they take toward these other women mark the changes in their own moral careers and self-imagery that differentiate what they were in the past from what they are today. For the wives whose moral careers are drawing to a relative close, the women who are currently living out the earlier phases of the moral career of becoming the wife of an alcoholic may represent all too painful reminders of their own not too distant "anti-models" (Francis 1963) of selves.

All of the illustrations of reconciling and philosophizing ambivalence symbolize a transformation of what is problematic into an explanatory framework for interpreting lived experiences. These interpretations become ways to make a kind of pragmatic peace with their intense moral experiences. The challenge to the wives in the post-treatment phase of this moral career is to rein in the ambivalence that has run rampant and been so disruptive in the phases leading up to (and partially including) proximal treatment.

Whether couples separate or stay together, whether they continue—alone or together—to attend Al-Anon (and Alcoholics Anonymous) meetings or decline to participate, and whether or not the husbands maintain alcohol abstinence, the women have left the family program with new, objective knowledge and subjective awarenesses about alcoholic-complicated relationships. Changing attitudes and action patterns begins with the rudimentary skills developed during the relatively brief treatment period. Some continue to use and expand these skills of their own volition, with the support of their husbands, friends, Al-Anon, or other support groups, and a few appear to set them somewhat aside. Some of the women's actions and interpretations revert to those of earlier phases of the moral career—often coincident with their husbands' resumption of drinking—repeating participation in what were earlier referred to as stultifying interactional contexts. Such events perpetuate the moral and careerlike features of their lived experiences.

The big difference now, though, is that their selves have recently been affirmed as worthy and the women as having certain "natural" rights, if even responsibilities, as human beings. They may not fulfill these expectations, but the presence or desire for them has been validated by others as well as themselves. And for this morsel of self-nurturance, alone, the women are grateful. Regardless of their present circumstances, nearly all of the women in this study indicated that they liked themselves more, felt increased self-confidence and autonomy, and believed that their lives had improved by their third (and final) interview. Even those who were interacting with a drinking husband viewed themselves as having more choices, self-awareness, and rights now. Transforming definitional ambivalence, through reconciling and philosophizing it, contributes to these kinds of imaged-improved selves and situations.

On leaving the family treatment program, the wife of an alcoholic faces the practical challenge of fashioning a new life for herself as best she can. Thus, transforming her definitional ambivalence into a framework for interpreting problematic experiences, while going on with life, simply becomes the pragmatic thing to do. It is practical not only because it appears to work, but also because in the course of life there is usually little else to do. During treatment and in the ideology of Al-Anon, this is what one must do. If success does not come right away, one can, indeed must, keep trying. As Shakespeare cautions, however, "therein lies the rub."

Conclusion

Sociological Insights, Implications, and Speculation

What distinguishes codependency, objectively or subjectively, from passivity, powerlessness, altruism, or even social courtesy? An instance of the latter emerged recently when one of my friends was giving a coffee party—busily refilling cups, passing trays of snacks, and otherwise serving her guests. At the end of the party a guest commented, "Susan, you were so codependent today!" In recounting the incident to me later, Susan Smith observed with dismay, "Since when is civility defined as codependency!" The guest had evidently equated Susan's civility with servility and then made a conceptual leap to codependency.

This simple story of a casual conversation alludes to the important issues raised by this study of women married to alcoholics: definitional ambivalence, moral career, and, ultimately, the social use and meaning of the term *codependency*. Several questions about codependency remain. Why, for example, is codependency such a buzzword at this time? Why is something supposedly integral to a particular kind of relationship and interaction refocused on the identity of one of the individuals in that relationship? Why is the concept spilling over to areas of interaction and relationship not necessarily associated with chemical dependency? These are points to keep in mind as I take a final look at the findings of this study in light of (1) other research on the wives of alcoholics, (2) a sociology of ambivalence, (3) the politics of codependence, and (4) the concept of a moral career.

Wives of Alcoholics

The present study suggests that the term *moral career* aptly represents the lived experiences of women married to alcoholics in several significant ways. For the purposes of this study, the moral career begins with the wives' first perceptions of problems caused by their husbands' drinking and ends with official recognition of and treatment for themselves as wives of alcoholics. Major attributes of the moral career include the following: (1) the experiences of a woman married to an alcoholic are distinguished as part of a class of "special" troubles, outside of the usual problems of living, that seriously challenge and change her self-definition over time; (2) being married to an alcoholic entails an often long and trying process of social interactions and contingencies that serve variously to enhance or to bypass the designation of alcoholism as the source of the special troubles; (3) this process is dominated by definitional ambivalence: contradictory or incompatible attitudes, beliefs, expectations, and performances involving roles, which result in multiple plausible definitions of situations and selves; (4) due to the prevalence of definitional ambivalence throughout the moral career, the major challenge to women married to alcoholics is the task of managing that ambivalence; and (5) women whose husbands are formally designated as alcoholics and who seek support groups or rehabilitative family programs related to their spouse's alcoholism are introduced to and encouraged to engage in retrospective designation of themselves as codependents in need of ongoing activities toward their own recovery.

In his "argument against specialism," Orford (1975) claims that alcoholic-complicated marriages are simply one component of a broader grouping of troubled and stressed marriages. The present study also suggests that interactions in such marriages are not unlike reports of other troubled relationships (for example, Straus, Gelles, and Steinmetz 1981; Orford 1975; Hill 1949). Related to Orford's argument against specialism is the issue of categorical typing. The women in this study were married to diagnosed alcoholics and they shared a range of social experiences, but neither these attributes nor my use of the terms *women married to alcoholics* or *wives of alcoholics* should be taken as defining features of them as types of individuals or as a group.

Because cultural and interactional factors play an important part in defining selves and problems in alcoholic-complicated marriages, an interaction-based social model is a more inclusive and effective tool of analysis than the personality-based models that have been popular in the past. For example, as cumulative and more serious problems arise from their drinking, alcoholic husbands tend to shift their explanations for their behavior from reasons outside the family to reasons within the marriage. This shift to motive offerings based on the marital relationship or on attributes of the wife or household is especially associated with the wives' feelings of self-blame, which bear an uncanny resemblance to later feelings and expressions of self-culpability in their acceptance of codependency. The need for an interaction-based social model is further indicated by my finding that the social processes of law enforcement, medical practice, work relations, and the alcoholism treatment industry have exerted influence in the defining or bypassing of designations of alcoholic problems.

A persistent question about the wives of alcoholics is whether they go through distinctive, sequential stages of adjustment to their husbands' developing problems with alcohol, such as Jackson (1954) described. Although her findings are still widely used in rehabilitation circles, they were unconfirmed or were modified by Lemert (1960) and Sundgren (1978). The present study suggests a series of broad interactive phases, not necessarily sequential, within which individual paths emerge and vary according to social contingencies. As in Wiseman's (1980) report of "home treatments," the emphasis here is on general interactive features rather than sequential or developmental orderings, on emergent actions rather than reactive responses, and on definitional enterprise rather than predetermined behaviors. Though somewhat descriptively similar, the evidence presented in this study does not support Jackson's claim of stages of adjustment.

Some researchers have posed the question, What kind of women marry alcoholics?—the implication being that women with certain characteristics (even pathologies) find (even seek) men who have or will develop alcoholism. This approach was dominant in early studies of wives of alcoholics. The data presented here lend support to the conclusion that "adjustment to a mate's alcoholism is almost totally a post-nuptial phenomenon" (Sundgren 1978, 215). A more incisive and less biased question is whether there are kinds of interactions or circumstances that preclude or facilitate a relationship with an alcoholic (or perhaps any problematically self-indulgent) significant other. As my data indicate, the answer to that question lies in future studies of interactional contexts, self-formulation and negotiation, traditional gender socialization, the social structure of gender arrangements, and family patterns.

The early thrust of research on the wife's possible personality disturbance (and on her role in the development of her husband's alcoholism) has so biased the field that researchers seem obliged to address this issue even though there is mounting evidence that personality disturbance is not a distinguishing characteristic of a woman married to an alcoholic. Perhaps the role of the wife in her husband's alcoholism has been overstated. After all, men who are single nonetheless manage to maintain and intensify their alcoholism. As this study demonstrates, it would be more useful to investigate survival resources and strategies activated by women married to alcoholics.

Sociology of Ambivalence

The concept of definitional ambivalence provides a better grasp of the character of moral experience. In understanding the seriousness and disruptiveness of the challenges to self arising from definitional ambivalence, it is possible to appreciate how such challenges feed into a moral career. It should be evident that situations of definitional ambivalence—those involving incompatible or contradictory expectations or a multitude of competing plausible definitions—present special challenges, especially when interpretations, decisions, and actions are crucial to selves and to significant others. Often over prolonged periods, the women in my sample found it difficult to reduce the burden of conflicting expectations. In order to manage, they needed continually to reformulate views of self, husband, marriage, and "the problem," the very process of reformulation adding to the strain of the situation. Indeed, the definitional ambivalence encountered by the women so challenged the self and interpretation of the situation that the management of ambivalence became the central task of their moral career.

The experiences of these women suggest that ambivalence is an important element of human social life generally. The concept of definitional ambivalence identifies the special situations and the emotional and interpretive difficulties with which we sometimes must contend in facing contradictory or incompatible attitudes, beliefs, expectations, and performances concerning social roles. Such ambivalences can range from the choices and equivocations of everyday experiences to the crises of self-definition exhibited, for example, by women married to alcoholics.

Interestingly, sociologists have a tendency to ignore ambivalence, despite the foundation that Merton (1976) established some time ago for a sociological approach to it. By adapting his functionalist conceptualization of sociological ambivalence to the insights of symbolic interaction, the concept *definitional ambivalence* can account for both structure and process as important ongoing aspects of experience and can help in understanding how they both affect people's lives. As a rule, sociologists have focused on one over the other and have lacked a way to address the interface between them; the concept of definitional ambivalence allows researchers to apprehend and utilize both social structure and interactive process in their observations and analyses. As illustrated by the typology of ambivalence management presented in this book, a sociology of ambivalence can provide a new lens with which to view experience.

Aside from its value in understanding ambivalence as a generic feature of human life, the concept ought to be useful in research on a variety of serious problem behaviors. Since the very definition of moral career means that there are serious disruptions and changes in self-definition, it seems impossible to think of a moral career without definitional ambivalence, although not all situations of definitional ambivalence necessarily point to a moral career. Perhaps the present typology of ambivalence management is most appropriate for the growing numbers of behaviors and relationships that are defined as addictive. It seems reasonable to suppose that definitional ambivalence and the related concepts and dynamics outlined in this study may be applied to behaviors and relationships involving social stigma and tension in the attempts to expose and mask such problems. I have in mind behaviors that are designated as addictive or compulsive, like gambling, eating disorders, promiscuity, and such. The interactive dynamics between the involved significant others and, in turn, between those couples and treatment agencies, would be similar, I suggest, to those illustrated here in alcoholic-complicated marriages and to those previously depicted in cases involving the designation of mental disorders (for example, Goffman 1962 and Yarrow et al. 1955). In social processes of this kind, studies of the construction of objective-subjective "realities" and self-other relations can be guided by the analytic concepts of definitional ambivalence and moral career, and by the sensitizing concepts of stultifying interaction and deficient negotiated-self.

The Politics of Codependence: Labeling and Medicalization

As part of their rehabilitation in the family treatment program, women married to alcoholics are taught that there are seemingly universal aspects of alcoholism, and they are encouraged to detach themselves emotionally from their husbands, accept responsibility for self and for change, and construct a new life for themselves based on these teachings. In this process a women's behavior is characterized as *codependent* by virtue of her being married to an alcoholic. Thus, studying the moral career of women married to alcoholics also becomes a study of the meaning of codependency. But to grasp its meaning we must view the concept within the larger social context of the labeling and medicalization of *deviance*, since the codependent label carries both the stigma of deviance and the medical trappings of sickness and recovery.

Though much of what has been said about labeling and medicalization goes beyond the immediate concerns of this study, it does offer an important framework for understanding the experiences of women married to alcoholics. In turn, the lives of these women can provide new insights into the dynamics of labeling. Sociologists have long been interested in the sociopolitical processes of designating and labeling deviance and especially in the interactions between the labelers and the labeled (for example, Becker 1963; Erickson 1962; Kitsuse 1962; Lofland 1969). To the extent that a type of behavior is viewed as a departure from normative expectations and efforts are made to treat it, that behavior is considered deviant (Schur 1971).

Attempts, then, to treat and rehabilitate wives of alcoholics carry implicit assumptions about their deviance. Significantly, it is usually in family treatment programs (and in Al-Anon) that these women first learn of their own need for rehabilitation and of their deviance implied by this need. Their "problem" is identified as codependency, which in treatment circles and the popular culture is characterized as a sicknesslike condition. Dynamics such as these are what I refer to when addressing the concept of codependency in terms of the designation, labeling, and medicalization of deviance.

It used to be thought that wives of alcoholics manifested the psychological pathology of controlling behavior, as evidenced by their taking over the supposedly masculine role of breadwinner or by doing so-called manly household chores. The present concept of codependency retains the "symptoms" of controlling behavior, but it is no longer couched in terms of the women's "masculinized activity." Today's more androgynous gender roles depict such behavior as normal, not pathological, revealing the arbitrary social and political dimensions of the wives' previously supposed pathology, and confirming observations that designations of deviance are culturally relative and change over time (Conrad and Schneider 1980). Conrad and Schneider (1980) note that designations of deviance have become dominated by a medical paradigm, with social control provided either through medical intervention or modification of deviant behavior. They add that conceptualization of a behavior or condition as an illness becomes a form of medical social control that can serve either individual or societal interests. If medicalization refers to the broad cultural trend in the United States of increasingly defining nonnormative or deviant behavior as a medical disorder, codependency is a specific instance of that trend.

Whether or not one agrees with the medical model or the idea of codependency as a disease, the consequences of the model in the lives of women married to alcoholics are genuine. Surely, the medicalized concept of codependency becomes a major point of definitional ambivalence in their moral careers. On the one hand, it offers a way for these women to manage the ambivalences that they face; but, on the other, it creates disturbing new self-definitional ambivalences and challenges with which they have to contend. Ironically, "wellness" is achieved at the price of proclaiming "illness"! My findings suggest that contact with rehabilitation agents plays a primary role in designation of the women's behaviors as deviant and as symptomatic of codependency. The apparent fact of codependency among these women is the outcome of a social process of constructing a medical reality, rather than of discovery or identification of an objective, preexistent, distinguishable illness. Through rehabilitative programs, the culture of codependency is introduced, negotiated, and relatively stabilized in the women's lived and ongoing experiences. Family programs of rehabilitation, Al-Anon, therapists, and the popular literature on codependency support the apparent (though constructed) reality of this "condition." And Schur (1984), in his study of gender stigma and social control, reminds us that "until women collectively have acquired an equal share in the power to develop and impose labels, the controlling of women through an imputation of spoiled identity will persist" (p. 235).

The women's initial self-blame, emanating from the negative self-imagery and marital estrangement so evident in the problem amplification phase, may make them more receptive to reformulated ideas of their deviance in terms of codependency and may, in part, explain why the codependent label tends to stick once it is applied. Minimization of blame is said to be one of the brighter social consequences of medicalizing deviance (Conrad and Schneider 1980). It seems that many women, however, merely shift from blaming themselves as the cause of their husbands' drinking to faulting themselves for behaviors that are judged to be inappropriate once these behaviors are conceptualized as codependent. Overall, my findings suggest that the interactions leading up to labeling are as worthy of inquiry as the processes, more often studied, that occur during and after designation of the label.

One of the first warnings about the conceptualization and labeling of codependency was issued by Schreiber (1983); he cautioned women to stay away from chemical dependency treatment centers, likening them to old boys' clubs. Similarly, a recent book by Katz and Liu (1991) speaks of the conspiracy of codependency. In an earlier report based on data from this study, Dennis Brissett and I concluded that the reconstruction of lived experiences during rehabilitation establishes the plausibility of codependency and coincides with an emerging identification of the self as codependent. The influence of the (alcoholism treatment) family program industry in this reformulation of experiences and identity and its assertion that spouses of alcoholics are inevitably codependent are the significant elements in the widespread acceptance of codependency. Not only does the broad range of supposedly codependent behaviors allow for individuals to choose or identify their own brand of codependency, but also its sweeping generality and vagueness make individual resistance to or rejection of the label difficult. Burdened by the circumstances of their lives and anticipating positive changes through participation in a family program (or perhaps Al-Anon), women married to alcoholics are especially receptive to ideas for resolving their difficulties and vulnerable to assumptions of their own codependency. By virtue of recommendations for treatment and ongoing recovery, and as a result of the evaluation practices of the rehabilitation industry, these women's behaviors are deemed "deviant." That deviance is then "medicalized" by the implication of sickness or disorder in the label *codependent*. The efforts by some to rename codependency as coalcoholism can be viewed as a further step in the trend toward medicalization (Asher and Brissett 1988).

We need to recognize codependency as a construct, as a way of talking about modes of thinking, feeling, and acting. We have barely begun to examine how naming these ways of being in the world is itself affected by the ideological context of our lives. The distinction between disease as a metaphor and disease as a reality is confounded and requires far greater scrutiny. As it stands, codependency is a broadly defined catchword symbolizing, I suspect, much more about social process and structure than about disease or individuals.

Conrad and Schneider (1980) caution against assuming that the institution of medicine is morally and politically neutral, and they also caution against refocusing complex social problems on individuals; these are among what they call the "darker social consequences" of the medicalization trend. In a similar vein, Schur (1976) warns against the "awareness trap"— the recent popularization of concerns with consciousness-raising, self-development activities—a movement that includes, for instance, the recovery from codependency. He argues that in the midst of such personal growth activities and movements, people risk losing sight of the institutionalized, societal-level sources of individually expressed inequality or constraint:

Oppression is not . . . simply a matter of certain individuals behaving in unloving or unliberated ways. It is systematic, socially structured, and culturally reinforced. To understand and change it, we usually will need to focus on a great many sociocultural factors—ranging from economic structure to the mass media, from status hierarchies to the legal system, from unemployment opportunities to child-rearing attitudes. When problems transcend the personal or interpersonal levels, so too must the solutions. . . . In such situations, no amount of self awareness will suffice. (Pp. 4–5)

In light of such claims, it would be prudent to consider the social and political dimensions of the construct *codependency* and their moral implications for women married to alcoholics.

The concept of codependency undoubtedly is pragmatic and has value for many women who are married to alcoholics. Certainly, the process of recovering from codependency provides new meaning, intensity, and focus to their lives. Also, the designation of a (deviant) "condition" and the offer of treatment have the aura of medical legitimacy. Medicalizing problems allows people to feel that their "sickness" can be explained and justified; it enables them to be more optimistic about the potential for change (Conrad and Schneider 1980). Besides being a way to name existing troubles, codependency offers a framework for understanding them and for resolving ongoing problematic situations. When "codependents" come together in a family program, Al-Anon, or some other rehabilitation-support setting they can share common experiences, develop social ties, and walk the path of self-recovery and personal growth in like company. Being "in recovery" is presently fashionable in our culture, and so this process of self-remaking often evokes social approval. All of these attributes can help to stabilize and enhance the lives of persons in alcoholic-complicated relationships.

Despite the positive aspects of the process of recovery from codependency, I have several misgivings. To begin with, I question whether application of the label is really necessary. With its medicalized connotations of affliction-malady, the label requires specified "recovery" and precludes alternative avenues of help. Without the label, people could simply obtain help with reorganizing their lives, by engaging in any variety of self-rehabilitating programs, as they saw fit. As demonstrated in this study, when the label is applied, lives do get reorganized, but along the lines of (1) a designation of deviance, (2) treatment of an ambiguous psychological/ behavioral medical disorder, and (3) use of an ideology recommending a lifelong process of recovery.

An important aspect of current guidelines for recovery is attendance in Al-Anon (or the newer Codependents Anonymous) groups, the most widely known rehabilitative program for spouses of alcoholics. Before leaving the family program, the women are routinely encouraged to finalize arrangements for attending a weekly Al-Anon meeting as part of their aftercare goals. In separate research on Al-Anon groups, which I view in both the best and the worst sense as "communities of commiseration," my other misgivings emerged. These misgivings stem from features that I refer to as the no-exit model, rhetorical participation, the struggling self (Asher 1985), and marginalization.

By the *no-exit model*, I mean that there is no legitimate way out of Al-Anon. If a woman stops attending meetings, that is viewed as an implicit sign that she is "sicker" and needs the group more than she realizes. There is a "knowing" assumption that "she'll be back" (because eventually she will need to be). Most other therapeutic or rehabilitative programs seek to build clients up to a level of relative self-sufficiency, eventuating in a termination of the therapy, but this is not so in Al-Anon. The assumption of lifetime membership in Al-Anon easily translates into the idea that codependency and recovery are also expected to be lifelong. Thus, long after the initial application and acceptance of the codependent label, the women continue to face the moral implications and challenges of their presumed condition. In practice, then, both Al-Anon and codependency present a no-exit feature.

Another phenomenon, *rhetorical participation*, may well be related in part to adaptation to the no-exit model of Al-Anon and, by extension, to the "no-exit" from codependency. It seems to me that there are two extreme categories of long-term Al-Anon members: what might be called *transcenders* and *treadmillers*. The transcenders seem virtually to blossom with the new teachings, which often appear to serve as a springboard for them in developing later interests that involve a "new consciousness" (especially of self development and spirituality, like New Age). One newsletter, aptly titled *Stepping Up*, has precisely this focus of going beyond the "Twelve Steps"—the twelve philosophical-behavioral guidelines for changing oneself and one's life that are the foundation of Alcoholics Anonymous, Al-Anon, and now many other groups of types termed "anonymous."

Other members of Al-Anon, the treadmillers, voice the rhetoric of Al-Anon teachings and slogans without apparent conviction and without embracing the new self they imply. They keep echoing the jargon of the program in meetings but do not appear to gain much insight, growth, enthusiasm, or cheer from it. I am thinking especially of members who have been in Al-Anon for many years, say, from twelve to twenty years or more. Their nearly lifeless comments at meetings left me with a sense that they were probably there only because it was expected of them. Perhaps it was a pattern established long ago when they and their alcoholic husbands first started driving to their respective meetings together. Although, for some, rhetorical participation might be a rather detached expression of belonging to the group, for others it may represent a sense of obligation about which they are ambivalent. If the latter is the case, rhetorical participation may be an adaptation to the no-exit model and may not be in the best interests of members.

Another misgiving I have about recovery from codependency via Al-Anon (and, by extension, via the twelve-step movement in general) is the emergence of a *struggling self*. I believe this arises particularly through the practice of what I call *dichotomous introspection*, a separating of self into desirable and undesirable attributes. Efforts to strike a balance between these competing aspects of self-feeling and expression, or to overcome personal liabilities with assets, can engage the self in a continuous struggle. This is what the work of recovery is about; the struggling self becomes the hallmark of "working the program" and being a good member of the group. "To the degree that voluntary self-help groups foster these dynamics they may also foster the struggling self as a new ideal in contemporary life" (Asher 1985, 29). The currently fashionable status of being in recovery honors a struggling self.

Christopher Lasch (1984) tells us that the essence of selfhood is expressed in "the painful awareness of the gulf between human aspirations and human limitations," and that there is value in defining the self as "tension, division, conflict" (p. 258). By this reasoning a "self in struggle" would appear to be a state of being involving the fullest expression of selfhood, and, indeed, philosophical pragmatism may bear this out. But between theory and practice, the dynamics of recovery transform selfhood into a Sisyphus-like challenge: Sisyphus, struggling to bear the weight of the huge boulder, pushing it up the steep hill to the summit, only to have it continually roll back against him (Camus 1965), becomes the model for self, struggling to bear the burdensome mix of defects and assets of one's character and to accomplish the seemingly never-ending task of maintaining balance or, better still, of replacing the defects with positive attributes. The feature of self as a burden one must struggle with may lead, I suspect, to a subtly emergent disconnectedness or distancing of lived experience. In the case of the Al-Anon members I observed, it was as though they did not perceive their flawed emotions and behaviors as their selves in direct action, but more as the consequences of their codependency intervening and intruding on their (otherwise better) selves. Some vital connection to the vicissitudes of existence, some intimate grasp of the vagaries of living, is lost, I think, when undesirable or unplanned feelings or actions are said to result from one's behaviorally intrusive condition—in this case, codependency. To say, "That's my codependency kicking in," separates action from self and self from emotional life. It reinforces a sense of disconnection from the exigencies of experience; it reinforces, in a subtly reformulated form, a sense of being a victim.

Perhaps a more generic concern than the no-exit model, rhetorical participation, or creation of a struggling self is the *marginalization* of selves from society that is incurred by participation in Al-Anon (and other twelve-step groups). It is in the nature of the philosophy of Al-Anon that members view themselves as somewhat different, as somewhat marginal to the mainstream, due to the "condition" they have. In recent years there has been a proliferation of new twelve-step groups for an ever-increasing number of behavioral "conditions." We do not know what effects there might be in the general social fabric if increasing segments of the population gain personal identity and small-group solidarity through diminished identification with the mainstream of society. Social solidarity is a central concern not only for sociologists but also for any society of interacting persons. Are we creating pockets of personal solidarity at the risk of a greater social marginality? And if so, to what effect?

My intent is not to malign Al-Anon, Alcoholics Anonymous, or other twelve-step organizations; they have helped thousands of persons to create better lives for themselves. These organizations, however, have been in existence long enough so that their latent functions—unintended or unforeseen consequences—are more apparent than in their early years. My misgivings center on aspects of these groups that may operate, in an unintended way, against the best interests of members. My purpose in raising these misgivings is in the hope that prospective and long-standing members may attend groups with a heightened awareness about participation.

In any event, the twelve-step model has both redemptive and restitutive qualities that may have great initial, if not lifetime, appeal for women whose lived experiences with their alcoholic husbands have become moral careers, experiences that ask of them not only who they are but also what they are and how they could have been drawn into this "crisis of self." Their answers usually refer back to their apparent codependency and thus may seem to provide a logic, however circular, to their lives. Yet their answers to such questions also point to the larger social implications of the concept of codependency.

These implications are suggested by the hypothesis proposed by Conrad and Schneider (1980): as a particular kind of deviance becomes a middle-class rather than solely a lower-class problem, the probability of medicalization increases, and that medicalization increases directly with its economic profitability. It is interesting to note, for example, that members of the rehabilitation staff not only recommended that the women in my sample participate in the family program but also often actively recruited them. This is not to say that the women did not benefit from the program; most of them felt that they did, and many even praised it. The fact remains, however, that an entire industry has grown up around and is maintained by the treatment of the wives and families of alcoholics, and the rehabilitation industry needs codependents as much as codependents may need the rehabilitation industry.

I think we need to be keenly aware of the relationship between conceptualizations of codependency and historical attitudes and actions toward
women. There has been and still is a staggering flow of cultural messages
about women's second-class citizenship, such as women's vulnerability,
subservience, caretaking, passivity, self-sacrifice, sexual degradation, and
affective and economic dependence. There are burdensome social expectations for women to keep families together, and to bridge and smooth
discrepancies between private and public family life. Until recently, there
has been a virtual absence of cultural mandates or socially structured opportunities for females to develop resources and skills of emotional and economic autonomy, assertiveness, and psychological or social empowerment.
All of this fits disconcertingly well with the characterization and implications of codependency. Given this cultural context, I believe it is primarily
women who are labeled codependent, and it is primarily female spouses of
alcoholics who experience life with their mate as a moral career. Much of
what can be said about female socialization and experience also pertains to
codependency, and those fundamental experiential aspects of a woman's life
predate any later encounter with a moral career of being married to an
alcoholic.

Moral Career and the Experience of Gender

To me, one of the most valuable results of this study is that it is a record of
women's experience in their own terms. Gilligan (1982) calls for just such a
"voice" to fill out our thinking on adult experience and maturation, which
is now predominantly based on the experience of men. Her work informs
us that women view their identity as including "the experience of intercon-
nection," and that moral appropriateness for women means "the inclusion
of responsibility and care in relationships" (p. 173). Given this, it is not
surprising that wives of alcoholics experience definitional crises of self in
relation to husband and marriage, thus "engendering" a moral career!
    In light of these findings, a different understanding can be drawn from
the tendency of the women in my sample to downplay the idea of alcoholism in their mates, and to focus on marital issues as the source of

problems and their domain of responsibility. Bepko and Krestan (1990), for instance, note that the confusing thing about the label codependent "is that women have always adapted, accommodated and focused on others." They go on to ask, "If making relationships work is so much a part of a woman's definition of herself, so strong an element of the code, what makes the kind of overfocus that is a response to addiction so damaging and dysfunctional?" We might better view such behaviors as "good behaviors that go to an unbalanced extreme in certain situations" (p. 68). Such actions might be viewed simply as the way these women felt they were supposed to behave.

The designation of actions of this kind as codependent means that women's experience is being judged in terms of "appropriate" male experience (see Haaken 1990), which is based on standards of independence and separation, as Chodorow (1978), Gilligan (1982), and Rubin (1983) have established. This explains, in part, why the women in this study had to be taught (in the family program) that some of their actions had been codependent in nature instead of protective, caring, or a form of marital obligation, which were what they had often initially perceived them to be. The voice of these women was not heard as the valid account of their experience. Not counting their experience as what they say it is for them is one instance, among many, of ways in which women's experiences are rendered "socially invisible." Besides Gilligan's (1982) work, Marilyn Waring (1988) has written a book aptly titled *If Women Counted*. If the voice of the women in my sample "counted," the later redefinition of their behaviors as codependent might be not only unnecessary but also irrelevant. In this way we would not be stigmatizing women for responding to events as they have been taught to do, and we would not be judging their actions and experiences on the basis of male standards for relationships. Familiar mandates used in the family program and Al-Anon, like detachment and tough love, might well be reconceptualized and renamed if they referred to extremes of good behavior and valued moral efforts to maintain relationships in the face of serious adversity. The focus could, for example, be on questions of balance as Bepko and Krestan (1990) suggest—on imbalanced caring and on balanced love, for instance.

The most significant and far-reaching conclusion I draw is that a woman may undergo a moral career as the spouse of an alcoholic precisely because she is a woman. What now manifests as a profound moral career for women could be far less disruptive to self-definition and lie more in the realm of solving problems, albeit serious ones, if life experiences did not vary so markedly by sex. Remember the near "negative case" presented in chapter 2? That wife, a long-term careerwoman with an advanced college degree, acted with confidence and assertiveness—though at times also with uncertainty, emotional confusion, and hurt—in taking relatively quick action (eight months) to solve the problems created in her marriage to an alcoholic husband. In contrast, the rest of the women in the study experienced a prolonged and arduous moral career that shook the very foundations of their self-definition and social worth.

If, on the other hand, such women felt and exercised a high sense of social value, social power, and autonomy, I doubt that they would participate in the lengthy interactions that shaped the intensely moral careers presented here. This speaks not to personal inadequacy or an inherent gender pathology, but rather to a great need for the institutionalized social empowerment of women. It is widely assumed that it is women who best can (and should) delve into the underlying elements of personalities and relationships, and that they are predisposed to taking a holistic, processual approach to fixing problems. In contrast, men are generally expected to take timely, efficient action in dealing with problems, to get "back on track" and not to let matters become too disrupted. The expectations related to women have to do with self-involvement and mending the whole; those concerning men have to do with problem solving and mending parts. Regardless of the natural or social origins of these differences, it is not surprising, in light of them, that the lived experiences of women married to alcoholics become a self-definitional moral career. My conclusion is supported by Sundgren (1978), who found that husbands of alcoholics begin the process of adjustment later but proceed more rapidly and come to a resolution sooner than do wives of alcoholics.

Two questions for scholarly feminist investigation arise from these thoughts: (1) to what extent is an introspective, all-encompassing approach to problems women's endogenous or natural way—thus to be honored and preserved as their unique contribution? and (2) to what extent might this be a socially created, institutionalized gender pattern that confines women's energy and choices—thus to be examined, exposed, and perhaps modified? Theories of androgyny suggest that all persons have both feminine and masculine elements, which are also variously referred to, respectively, as aspects or energies called intuitive and rational, receptive and active, expressive and instrumental, and being and doing. If this is so, both sexes ought to be able to choose either the stereotyped "feminine" approach of deep self-involvement or the stereotyped "masculine" approach of relatively detached efficiency toward issues in their lives. To the extent that expectations largely confine women or men to only one mode, not only are their social experiences and skills in meeting the demands of all kinds of situations restricted, but so also is their very self-expression restricted.

As the situation stands, it is unlikely that a study of the experiences of men married to alcoholics would yield results that could as easily be cast as a moral career. According to Goffman's (1962) outline of the moral career process, dramatic challenges to and changes in self-definition occur in such a way as to disrupt social interactions and relationships, ending in the individual being placed in a new social category—in this case, codependency. Yes, men would face looming problems and emotions (much as the careerwoman in the near "negative case" did), but traumatic problem solving is not the same as having to confront basic questions about the very viability and definition of self. Ordinarily, men married to alcoholics do not find that their sense of self is at stake; their relative social value, identity, anchoring, and power do not make it so. Thus, I suggest, in the case of spouses of alcoholics, the emergence of a moral career is marked by gender: the moral career is one of becoming (and being) the wife of an alcoholic. This moral career is gendered when self-involvement becomes a moral career primarily because it is the experience of women, and when its culmination in codependency is rooted in standards for male experience and morality.

Generically, of course, the concept of a moral career applies without reference to gender to any situation that seriously disrupts, challenges, and changes self-definition and social categorization. Becoming old, for example, or living with AIDS, or being brainwashed or deprogrammed could all be moral careers. Efforts to counter the effects of childhood abuse by initiating changes in self-definition, with both help and resistance from others, could also present many of the same issues that I have explored in this book. Because the concept of moral career is focused on both personal and public dimensions of experience, it can greatly enrich our analyses and understanding of social process and living experience. The moral career studied in the present work provides an empirical account of the processes by which women married to alcoholics may come to accept themselves and to be accepted by others as codependents. It would be interesting to see if other areas of experience form moral careers that are distinguished by gender, not to mention ways in which a moral career would play out differently by gender.

Part of the value of any research is the insight it provides in substantive areas of study such as, in this case, the sociology of ambivalence, the concept of a moral career, and alcoholic-complicated relationships. Another value of research is in the broader understandings gained through investigation and elaboration. In that sense this study perhaps helps us better to appreciate ambivalence as a feature of everyday life, and social and sometimes moral experience as gendered experience. The idea of self-development inherent in recovery from codependency can be seen to reflect a larger value of self-development built into the general culture, and the emergence of the "good-bad struggling self" as indicative of the duality so popular in Western thinking—particularly in what Schaaf (1981) calls the White Male System of thinking. And, above all, we can appreciate that the social experience and status of women married to alcoholics say something important about the collective experience and status of women in our society.

It is good, I think, to view this study in light of C. Wright Mills's (1959) call for exercising a "sociological imagination." He reminds us to see individuals' apparently personal troubles in a context of larger social issues, "to understand the larger historical scene in terms of its meaning for the inner life and the external career of a variety of individuals" (p. 58). To activate the sociological imagination, he recommends that we consider fundamental questions—our answers to which reveal, I believe, the heights and depths of social experience and collective conscience. "What varieties of men and women now prevail in this society and in this period? . . . In what ways are they selected and formed, liberated and repressed, made sensitive and blunted? . . . What values are cherished get threatened and what values are cherished and supported, by the characterizing trends of our period?" (pp. 7, 11). I hope that my study of the moral career of becoming the wife of an alcoholic will prompt others to ask how we can answer these questions anew.

Appendix

Research Design and Methods

There is an intricate and appropriate link between research theory and methodology. The questions the researcher ponders shape the design of the research project. In this study the implicit overarching question, "What does it *mean* to be a woman married to an alcoholic husband?," has an affinity for an inductive approach and qualitative data collection and analysis. The purpose of this inquiry is to understand how meanings of certain kinds develop and how they relate to biographies, to further meanings, and to actions—taken collectively, how meanings weave the major strands of a moral career. It is not a causal analysis of how meanings per se develop, nor a prediction of conditions that give rise to them. Neither is this a study of memory recall nor accuracy of "what really happened." It is, in part, a study of how the past is accounted for in the present. It also involves the interrelations between interpretations of past, present, and future as they are aligned to form a coherent, useful view (even if temporary) of experiences. This study reports and analyzes the wives' perspectives of their experiences living with an alcoholic husband. These accounts are constructions of a segment of their biographies—that segment that I am calling the "moral career of becoming and being the wife of an alcoholic."

In this retrospective-prospective study of the careers of wives of alcoholics, the career is viewed as largely a definitional and moral enterprise consisting of continuous negotiation and definition of situations, interactions, and selves. Primary attention is directed to (1) the wife's process of defining alcoholism in her husband, (2) the wife's process of self-imagery and construction of a life-style for herself, and (3) the possible career contingencies that may influence this ongoing definitional process.

Face-to-face, taped, semistructured, open-question interviews were conducted with fifty-two wives of men diagnosed and treated for alcoholism. All fifty-two women in the study were residents of a seven-county midwestern metropolitan area, were married (including those separated and/or with divorce pending), and had entered one of three area rehabilitative programs for the families of alcoholics.

The number of women refusing to participate in the study was so few (four) that statistical comparisons of sociodemographic characteristics were not practical. These four cases approximated the study sample averages for age, number of years married, education, and number of children. The reasons for their choosing not to be interviewed were not readily apparent.

The social beginnings of the moral career of the women in this sample were fixed retrospectively in terms of the time period in which they first began thinking that their husbands had a problem with alcohol. The segment of this career investigated terminated at about eighteen months following the wives' involvement in the family treatment program.

Each woman was interviewed three times (between 1 ¼ and 1 ½ hours each): when she initially entered the family program (Phase I), at seven months following her program participation (Phase II), and finally at sixteen–eighteen months following her program participation (Phase III). The present analysis is of Phase I and Phase III interviews only. During preliminary analysis I found that Phase II interviews overlapped considerably with Phase I and III interviews, depending on the individual pace of the moral career process. Therefore, the results of Phase I and III interviews most sharply outline the moral career of becoming and being the wife of an alcoholic. Interview question areas for these phases are presented in the following sections.

Phase I

This time period was devoted to interviewing the fifty-two women in the study sample. Interviews lasted approximately 1 ¼ hours and were held on either of the first two evenings of the wives' participation in the family programs. The interviews focused on three primary areas: the wife's historical construction of her husband's drinking problem, contingencies in her moral career, and her aspirations for the future.

A. Historical Construction of the Problem
Following Yarrow et al. (1955), this task was broken down into four categories: (1) beginnings of the problem, (2) the wife's initial interpretation of the problem, (3)

the wife's reinterpretation of the problem, and (4) the wife's recognition of alcoholism. Although this part of the interview was minimally structured in order to obtain the wife's own emphasis and organization of the process, seven primary areas were addressed:

1. The attitudes and behavior of the alcoholic husband that the wife defined as problematic

2. The motives and rationales offered by the husband for both his drinking and problematic behavior

3. The motives and rationales used by the wife to explain her husband's drinking and behavior

4. The emotions—for example, guilt, hurt, anger—experienced by the wife during this time

5. The motives and rationales used by the wife to explain her behavior and feelings during this time

6. What pretreatment needs and attitudes the husband communicated to the wife and how the wife, behaviorally and psychologically, acted on these communications

7. How the husband came to be recognized by the wife (and other family members) as needing help for alcoholism

B. Career Contingencies

This part of the interview assessed the events and experiences in the wife's life that might have an impact on her definition and recognition of alcoholism. This was broken down into nine question areas:

1. Familial and community drinking behavior

2. Familial and community attitudes toward drinking

3. Knowledge of alcohol and alcoholism

4. Social affiliative behavior, including friendships, formal support groups, church involvement, and contacts with social agencies

5. Perceived action alternatives and decisions

6. Affective bonds—perceived agreement or disagreement with significant others (family, friends) on matters of importance to the wife

7. Problem-solving perspective, in terms of both source and solution and help-seeking behavior

8. Perception of major life events experienced

9. Personal assessment of overall marital relationship

C. Aspirations for the Future
This part of the interview focused on the wife's ideals and expectations for the future. These were broken down into five question areas:

1. Future expectations for the family
2. Perceptions on conditions for personal happiness
3. Future expectations for the husband
4. Personal short- and long-range goals
5. Overall perceived quality of life

Phase III

Phase III of this study continued the investigation of the definitional enterprise and contingencies that may affect the moral careers of women married to alcoholics. One new component in the experience of the subjects was their potential involvement in Al-Anon or other formal support activities following their husbands' treatment for alcoholism and their own participation in the family program. The subjects in Phase I of this research comprised the sample for Phase III. This final interview lasted approximately 1 ½ hours and was prearranged by appointment and at the subject's convenience. The questions focused on areas similar to those covered in Phase I. Some questions were geared to elicit a more summary or reflective response, looking back over the moral career as a whole. Subjects were asked to reflect on the entire experience with their husbands' drinking and to make comparisons between pretreatment and family program periods, the first seven months following treatment/family program participation, and the last nine to eleven months of the investigation period.

The number of Phase III interviews contributing data for analysis was reduced by ten—from fifty-two to forty-two. This was due either to (1) nonavailability of respondent (for instance, out-of-state move, no forwarding address, or incapacitating physical health), (2) failure to keep scheduled interview appointments (or reappointments) within the temporal parameters of the study design, or (3) mechanical failures in tape recordings.

This investigation is exploratory and qualitative in that the interviews, although keyed to certain topics, were open-ended, and the subjects' own words comprise the data. Analysis of the data produced conceptualization of the ambivalence management process and the various tasks and phases of the moral career. An overlapping of the final interviews of any one phase with the beginning interviews of the next phase of the study allowed for a keen awareness of *process*. The ongoing multitude, variety, and periods of biographies I was exposed to and could juxtapose at any given time enhanced my understanding of this process as a moral career.

In accordance with stipulations for the Rights of Human Research Subjects, the respondents were informed that they could refuse to answer any questions and that they could end the interview process at any time. Confidentiality and anonymity were assured, and prior to Phase I interviews respondents were informed that, through my own participant-observation as a researcher having attended the family program, I was familiar with what they were participating in. This information was conveyed in a letter of introduction given by a program counselor, on the first day of the family program, to all women meeting the sociodemographic criteria of the study. The letter also included a statement of informed consent, which was signed by those participating in the study. Before each interview, I reiterated the purpose of the study and asked the respondent if she had any questions about it.

Notes

Introduction

1. Orford suggests that "alcoholic marriages" share many characteristics of relationships under other kinds of stress. In his argument against specialism he recommends the term *alcoholic-complicated marriage*. See Orford, "Alcoholism and Marriage."

2. For other examples of the process of defining problem behavior see Goffman, *Relations in Public*, and Yarrow et al., "The Psychological Meaning of Mental Illness in the Family."

3. *Codependent* is a widely used term for the spouse or significant other who is in a close relationship with an alcoholic. Not all women married to alcoholics necessarily embark on a moral career of becoming [being defined as] a codependent, but all of the women in this study participated in specialized programs that operate as a contingency toward such a moral career in that they emphasize the concept of codependency or coalcoholism.

4. Interestingly, our desire to define is such that when we cannot readily make sense of a situation we may conclude that its "nonsensibility" *is* the meaning of the situation. See Hilbert, "Approaching Reason's Edge."

5. Gregory P. Stone has suggested that a "meaning-response" relation is more complex than Mead would have it, noting that there can be response and imagined response, an individual's response to self, and others' response to self (informal conversations/lectures).

Chapter 4

1. For an illuminating presentation of the many facets of secrecy see Simmel, "The Sociology of Secrecy and of Secret Societies." In the present text, secrecy relates to

acts that seem to stave off embarrassment or acts that give the appearance of normalcy. In both instances, the secrecy represents a wife's view that her marriage or her husband is different and that her problems are unique.

2. *Deficient negotiated-self* is a concept of interaction, not an inherent part of self. Thus, it is the performance of self in interaction that is being subjectively appraised. There may be a relation between this and a more individualistic "impoverished self," but here I neither claim nor reject this, and I certainly think it is worthy of further research. I can imagine situations wherein a woman might be successful in negotiating a certain positive view of self or outcome by exiting a dehumanizing relationship but still operate out of an impoverished-self framework in other and future relationships, thereby re-creating a deficient negotiated-self in ongoing interactions.

3. Guilt often emerged along with retrospective reinterpretations of experiences, aided by participation in Al-Anon or the family program. Even though some of the women blamed themselves in the problem amplification phase as the cause of problems, definitions of culpability remained ambivalent. The difference, in part, can be viewed as feelings of being at fault for problematic behaviors and being at fault in character through a moral inventory of character assets and liabilities, variously called defects and flaws.

Chapter 7

1. This study sample was drawn from wives attending family treatment programs; thus, the moral career indicated here necessarily includes a treatment phase. We cannot conclude from this study whether wives not attending such programs follow a similar moral career. In her study, "An Alternative Role for the Wife of an Alcoholic in Finland," Wiseman indicates that experiences akin to problem amplification and ambivalence limiting, as presented here, did occur for a majority of the women in her sample. For a substantial minority of her subjects the latter types of experiences were related to more satisfactory, independent new directions for self through a variety of strategies, including (but not necessarily) treatment programs.

2. A situation that characterizes a husband's personal decision to enter treatment was described this way: "He really got smashed . . . ended up over at my brother's . . . 25 degrees below . . . in the car . . . passed out . . . my brother . . . brought him in, and before he fell asleep on the couch there, he asked my brother to call me and call AA. . . . So I called AA, and they told me to let him be. If he wants to help himself, let him take care of it. . . . The next morning everything just went one, two, three, and all of a sudden he was going."

3. A case illustrating this type of situation follows: "I went to get the newspaper and put the coffee on, not planning [on a treatment crisis], not nothing, and I took a look into the living room and I saw plates and food and silverware and glasses— things that had been thrown—and something just went [off] in my head. That was it. I went downstairs and I told him to get up and get out of bed, and I said, 'And I mean right now. . . . This is it. You don't have a choice. You are going, or they are coming for you. What is it going to be? I want an answer right now. Either you go on your own or they are coming for you. I'm calling right now.'"

4. A case that best represents medical concerns and intervention was described in this way: "He'd had these dizzy spells on and off for about ten years. It used to be like maybe once a year and then twice a year, and it just [happened more often], but he would always recover from them in two or three days. I could always see that it was when he had moved off a plateau of drinking and gone into an excessive period. . . . This last time his best friend who is a very heavy drinker came for ten days and then one of his brothers who was a heavy drinker for another ten days, and by the end of that time he was flat in bed with this dizziness which lasted for about two weeks. And I called and made an appointment for him . . . first he was saying no, no, no, but then he said yes he would go. . . . The doctor took blood tests and things and said . . . 'I'd like to put you in the hospital . . . and run some tests on you next week.' So then he had to decide whether he really was gonna go into the hospital or not, because he knew what it meant. And he did decide to do that. . . . Of course, the detoxification took place the next two days, and he had a tough time with that. . . . The doctor found that his liver was three times the size it should be and in very serious condition, and he said that he absolutely had had his last drink."

5. The following case illustrates how involvement with the legal-justice system becomes a path to entering alcoholism treatment: "He got one [a DWI citation] in October, went into the court system, and they told him, 'Okay, you got a fine and we will give you time, but if you go into an out-patient treatment center then you won't have to do the time.' So he . . . was in the process of doing that, but he didn't quit [drinking] while he was going to out-patient like he was supposed to be and then he got another DWI while he was doing that. So he was straight with them at out-patient and . . . told his probation officer that he got one, and then they said, 'Well, you should really go into in-patient.'"

6. The following interview excerpt illustrates attending the family program for education: "I came for two reasons. One, to find out about myself and how this alcoholism has affected myself and also my children, who are grown up, and also to show him I was in support of what he was doing and willing to learn."

7. The comments that follow illustrate attending the family program for psycho-

logical-emotional well-being: "[I came] mostly for myself, because my husband had been drinking. We had been through treatment together three times already, and I just felt each time that I needed it as badly as he did."

8. Marital relationship concerns are represented by the following comments: "Basically, I have been contemplating getting a divorce for a long time. I have been carrying a lot of responsibility and a lot of guilt because of it. So I guess my main reason [for entering the family program] was to work through [it]—I felt I had already made my decision and I wanted to work it out where I felt at peace with it. Make peace with my decision because of the guilt I've been carrying or laying on myself, I guess."

9. This response typifies outside influence or pressure as a reason for attending the family program: "[I came] because my husband is in here, and they [someone from the program staff] had called me and asked me if I could participate in this. And even though we had just recently been through two other programs, I thought, well, it can't hurt."

Bibliography

Anderson, Margaret L. 1988. *Thinking about Women: Sociological Perspectives on Sex and Gender.* 2d ed. New York: Macmillan.

Asher, Ramona M. 1985. "The Social Reconstruction of Reality and the Role of Al-Anon Ideology." Unpublished manuscript.

Asher, Ramona M., and Dennis Brissett. 1988. "Codependency: A View from Women Married to Alcoholics." *International Journal of the Addictions* 23:331–50.

Bacon, Seldon D. 1973. "The Process of Addiction to Alcohol." *Quarterly Journal of Studies on Alcohol* 34:1–27.

Bateson, Gregory. 1972. *Steps to an Ecology of Mind.* San Francisco: Chandler.

Becker, Howard S. 1960. "Notes on the Concept of Commitment." *American Journal of Sociology* 66:32–40.

———. (1963) *Outsiders.* New York: The Free Press.

Bepko, Claudia, and Jo-Ann Krestan. 1990. *Too Good for Her Own Good: Breaking Free from the Burden of Female Responsibility.* New York: Harper and Row.

Berger, Peter L., and Thomas Luckmann. 1967. *The Social Construction of Reality.* Garden City, N.Y.: Anchor Books.

Blumer, Herbert. 1962. "Society as Symbolic Interaction." In *Human Behavior and Social Processes,* edited by Arnold Rose, pp. 179–92. Boston: Houghton Mifflin.

———. 1966. "Sociological Implications of the Thought of George Herbert Mead." *American Journal of Sociology* 71:535–44.

———. 1969. *Symbolic Interactionism: Perspective and Method.* Englewood Cliffs, N.J.: Prentice-Hall.

Camus, Albert. 1965. *The Myth of Sisyphus and Other Essays.* Translated by Justin O'Brien. London: H. Hamilton.

Chodorow, Nancy. 1978. *The Reproduction of Mothering.* Berkeley: University of California Press.

Conrad, Peter, and Joseph W. Schneider. 1980. *Deviance and Medicalization*. St. Louis: C. V. Mosby.

Cooley, Charles Horton. 1902. *Human Nature and the Social Order*. New York: Scribner's Sons.

Coser, Rose Laub. 1966. "Role Distance, Sociological Ambivalence, and Transitional Status Systems." *American Journal of Sociology* 72:173–87.

Denzin, Norman K. 1984. *On Understanding Emotion*. San Francisco: Jossey-Bass.

Emerson, Robert M., and Sheldon Messinger. 1977. "The Micro-Politics of Trouble." *Social Problems* 25:121–34.

Erickson, Kai T. 1962. "Notes on the Sociology of Deviance." *Social Problems* 9:307–14.

Francis, Roy G. 1963. "The Anti-Model as a Theoretical Concept." *Sociological Quarterly* 4:197–205.

Gierymski, T., and Terrance Williams. 1986. "Codependency." *Journal of Psychoactive Drugs* 9:7–13.

Gilligan, Carol. 1982. *In a Different Voice: Psychological Theory and Women's Development*. Cambridge: Harvard University Press.

Glaser, Barney G., and Anselm, Strauss. 1967. "Awareness Contexts and Social Interactions." *American Sociological Review* 29:669–79.

Goffman, Erving. 1956. "Embarrassment and Social Organization." *American Journal of Sociology* 2:264–75.

———. 1959. *The Presentation of Self in Everyday Life*. Garden City, N.Y.: Anchor Books.

———. 1962. *Asylums*. Chicago: Aldine.

———. 1967. *Interaction Ritual*. Garden City, N.Y.: Anchor Books.

———. 1971. *Relations in Public*. New York: Basic Books.

Gross, Edward, and Gregory P. Stone. 1964. "Embarrassment and the Analysis of Role Requirements." *American Journal of Sociology* 70:1–15.

Haaken, Janice. 1990. "A Critical Analysis of the Co-dependence Construct." *Psychiatry* 53:396–406.

Hewitt, John P. 1984. *Self and Society: A Symbolic Interactionist Social Psychology*. 3d ed. Boston: Allyn and Bacon.

———. 1988. *Self and Society: A Symbolic Interactionist Social Psychology*. 4th ed. Boston: Allyn and Bacon.

Hewitt, John P., and Randall Stokes. 1975. "Disclaimers." *American Sociological Review* 40:1–11.

Hilbert, Richard A. 1977. "Approaching Reason's Edge: 'Nonsense' as the Final Solution to the Problem of Meaning." *Sociological Inquiry* 47:25–31.

Hill, Rueben. 1949. *Families under Stress*. New York: Harper.

Hochschild, Arlie. 1979. "Emotion Work, Feeling Rules, and Social Structure." *American Journal of Sociology* 85:551–75.

———. 1983. *The Managed Heart: Commercialization of Human Feeling*. Berkeley: University of California Press.

Jackson, Joan K. 1954. "The Adjustment of the Family to the Crisis of Alcoholism." *Quarterly Journal of Studies on Alcohol* 15:564–86.

Karp, David A., and William C. Yoels. 1979. *Symbols, Selves and Society: Understanding Interaction*. New York: J. B. Lippincott.

Katz, Stan J., and Aimee E. Liu. 1991. *The Codependency Conspiracy: How to Break the Recovery Habit*. New York: Warner.

Kemper, Theodore D. 1981. "Social Constructionist and Positivist Approaches to the Sociology of Emotions." *American Journal of Sociology* 87:336–61.

Kitsuse, John I. 1962. "Societal Reactions to Deviant Behavior." *Social Problems* 9:247–56.

Lasch, Christopher. 1984. *The Minimal Self: Psychic Survival in Troubled Times*. New York: W. W. Norton.

Lemert, Edwin M. 1951. *Social Pathology*. New York: McGraw-Hill.

———. 1960. "The Occurrence and Sequence of Events in the Adjustment of Families to Alcoholism." *Quarterly Journal of Studies on Alcohol* 21:679–97.

Leonard, Linda Schierse. 1983. *The Wounded Woman: Healing the Father-Daughter Relationship*. Boulder, Colo.: Shambala.

Lofland, John. 1969. *Deviance and Identity*. Englewood Cliffs, N.J.: Prentice-Hall.

McCall, George, and J. L. Simmons. 1966. *Identities and Interactions*. New York: The Free Press.

Mannheim, Karl. 1936. *Ideology and Utopia*. London: Routledge and Kegan Paul.

Matza, David. 1964. *Delinquency and Drift*. New York: Wiley.

Mead, George Herbert. 1934. *Mind, Self and Society*. Chicago: University of Chicago Press.

Meisenhelder, T. 1979. "The Life World." *Sociological Inquiry* 49(1):65–68.

Merton, Robert K. 1976. *Sociological Ambivalence*. New York: The Free Press.

Mills, C. Wright. 1940. "Situated Actions and Vocabularies of Motive." *American Sociological Review* 5:904–13.

———. 1959. *The Sociological Imagination*. New York: Oxford.

One Day at a Time in Al-Anon. 1979. New York: Al-Anon Family Group Headquarters, Inc.

Orford, James. 1975. "Alcoholism and Marriage: The Argument against Specialism." *Journal of Studies on Alcohol* 36:1537–59.

Roman, Paul M., and H. M. Trice. 1968. "The Sick Role, Labeling Theory, and the Deviant Drinker." *International Journal of Psychiatry* 14:254–61.

Rubin, Lillian B. 1983. *Intimate Strangers: Men and Women Together*. New York: Harper and Row.

Rubington, E. 1973. *Alcohol Problems and Social Control*. Columbus, Ohio: Charles E. Merrill Publishing.

Schaaf, Anne Wilson. 1981. *Women's Reality: An Emerging Female System in the White Male Society*. Minneapolis: Winston Press.

Scheff, Thomas J. 1979. *Catharsis in Healing, Ritual, and Drama*. Berkeley: University of California Press.

Schneider, Joseph W. 1978. "Deviant Drinking as Disease: Alcoholism as a Social Accomplishment." *Social Problems* 25:361–72.

Schreiber, D. 1983. "Why Women Should Be Cautious about CD Treatment." *Viewpoints*. Minneapolis: Minnesota Chemical Health Association.

Schur, Edwin M. 1971. *Labeling Deviant Behavior: Its Sociological Consequences*. New York: Harper and Row.

———. 1976. *The Awareness Trap*. New York: McGraw-Hill

———. 1984. *Labeling Women Deviant: Gender, Stigma, and Social Control*. New York: Random House.

Schwartz, Charlotte Green. 1976. "Perspectives on Psychiatric Trouble in a College Setting." Ph.D. dissertation, Brandeis University.

Scott, Marvin B., and Stanford M. Lyman. 1968. "Accounts." *American Sociological Review* 33:46–62.

Simmel, Georg. 1906. "The Sociology of Secrecy and of Secret Societies." *American Journal of Sociology* 11:441–98.

Stebbins, Robert A. 1967. "A Note on the Concept of Role Distance." *American Journal of Sociology* 73:247–50.

Stokes, Randall, and John P. Hewitt. 1976. "Aligning Actions." *American Sociological Review* 41:838–49.

Stone, Gregory P. 1962. "Appearance and the Self." In *Human Behavior and Social Processes*, edited by Arnold Rose, pp. 86–118. Boston: Houghton Mifflin.

———. 1970. "The Circumstance and Situation of Social Status." In *Social Psychology through Symbolic Interaction*, edited by Gregory P. Stone and Harvey A. Farberman, pp. 250–59. Waltham, Mass.: Ginn-Blaisdell.

Straus, Murray A., Richard J. Gelles, and Suzanne K. Steinmetz. 1981. *Behind Closed Doors: Violence in the American Family*. Garden City, N.Y.: Anchor Books.

Sundgren, Ann A. 1978. "Sex Differences in Adjustment to an Alcoholic Spouse." Ph.D. dissertation, University of Seattle.

Sykes, Gresham G., and David Matza. 1957. "Techniques of Neutralization." *American Sociological Review* 22:664–70.

Tawney, R. H. 1931. *Equality*. London: Allen and Unwin.

Thomas, William I. 1937. *Primitive Behavior*. New York: McGraw-Hill.

Thomas, William I., and Dorothy Swain Thomas. 1928. *The Child in America*. New York: Alfred A. Knopf.

Waring, Marilyn. 1988. *If Women Counted: A New Feminist Economics*. San Francisco: Harper.

Weinstein, Eugene A., and Deutschberger, Paul. 1963. "Some Dimensions of Altercasting." *Sociometry* 26:454–66.

Weiting, Steven G. 1982. *The Family System: An Independent Study Text*. Evanston, Ill.: The Committee on Institutional Cooperation.

Whitfield, Charles. 1984. "Co-Alcoholism: Recognizing a Treatable Illness." *Family Community Health* 7:16–28.

Wiseman, Jacqueline P. 1975. "An Alternative Role for the Wife of an Alcoholic in Finland." *Journal of Marriage and the Family* 37:172–79.

———. 1980. "The 'Home Treatment': The First Steps in Trying to Cope with an Alcoholic Husband." *Family Relations* 29:541–49.

———. 1981. "Sober Comportment." *Journal of Studies on Alcohol* 42:106–26.

Yarrow, Marion Radke, Charlotte Green Schwartz, Harriet S. Murphy, and Leila Calhoun Deasy. 1955. "The Psychological Meaning of Mental Illness in the Family." *Journal of Social Issues* 11:12–24.

Index

Accounts. *See* Motive talk

Addictive/compulsive behaviors, 187

Al-Anon. *See* Rehabilitation programs; Twelve-step groups

Alcohol consumption by wives, 121–24

Alcoholic-complicated marriage, 1, 4, 85, 97, 116–17, 124, 127, 181, 184, 188, 192, 201

Alcoholics Anonymous. *See* Rehabilitation programs; Twelve-step groups

Alcoholism: designation of, 29, 33–35, 44, 89, 112, 143–44, 152, 160; information on, 38, 51; multiple/repeated treatments of, 107, 165; disease conception of, 112, 148, 152; universality of, 148–50, 152, 188. *See also* Definition of the situation; Deviance; Problems

Alcoholism rehabilitation industry. *See* Rehabilitation programs

Aligning actions, 39, 125–26. *See also* Motive talk; Remedial interchanges

Ambivalence, 6, 187

Ambivalence of definition. *See* Definitional ambivalence

Androgyny theory, 200

Apologies, 125–29. *See also* Social interactional strategies/stances

Aura of uniqueness, 86–87, 90, 108, 112, 121, 149

Awareness contexts, 88

Awareness trap, 191–92

Coalcoholism. *See* Codependency

Codependency, x, 4, 13, 28, 143, 150–51, 154, 157, 159–60, 183, 188–92, 195–201. *See also* Deviance; Wives of alcoholics

Collective ignorance, 149

Communication, 99

Communities of commiseration, 193. *See also* Rehabilitation programs; Twelve-step groups

Conflict: general marital, 22–23, 63, 70, 80; low-key overt, 63; substantial verbalized, 63; subjective appraisals of, 64; conflict-talk episodes, 69; no-win situations, 69, 71, 138; interpretation/ negotiation of, 74, 78; issues of, 74–78; and role, 78

Controlling, 117, 189. *See also* Rehabilitation programs

Curvilinear pattern of confrontation-resistance, 110

Deficient negotiated-self, 98–103, 188
Definitional ambivalence: meaning and intricacies of, 5–7, 19–21, 23, 27, 56, 71, 74, 80, 85, 179, 187–88; routine, 6; disruptive, 6, 28, 169; management of, 7, 51, 85, 88, 148, 166, 169–70, 173; about husband, 9–10; about marriage, 9–10, 27; about self, 9–10, 27, 62, 106, 138, 163–64, 189; recognizing, 19, 22, 24, 27; sorting, 27, 29, 36, 40, 45–46, 52, 83, 97, 124, 130; acknowledging, 27, 29, 42, 45, 78, 124; valuating, 27, 46, 53–55, 58–59, 62, 78, 80, 84, 106, 124; personalizing, 27, 46, 85–87, 103, 108, 112, 114, 119–21, 124, 148; heightened, 39, 44, 63, 66, 110, 112, 124, 131, 154, 173; cultural level/factors of, 78, 113, 117, 125, 133, 141, 144; interactional level/factors of, 78, 113, 117, 125, 133, 141, 144; maintenance of, 89, 124–25, 129–30; limiting/diminishing of, 89, 133, 137–41, 143, 145, 147, 152, 154; depersonalizing, 148–51, 155, 157; routinization of, 169; transforming, 169–82; reconciling, 170, 172–73, 175; philosophizing, 170, 176–79; unresolved, 170–71. See also Ambivalence; Definitional ambivalence; Definition of the situation; Moral career; Sociological ambivalence
Definition of the situation, 5, 12; challenges to, 7, 12, 55, 66, 74, 95, 97, 132; plausibility of, 9, 35–36, 83, 89, 130, 141; cultural resources for, 9, 78; shifts in, 43, 46–47, 66, 78, 95, 150,

179; negotiation of, 44; filtering/funneling of, 141, 151. See also Alcoholism; Definitional ambivalence; Problems; Self
Detachment, 170–72, 188, 198. See also Rehabilitation programs
Deviance: medicalization of, 13, 161, 188–89; primary, 44; secondary, 44; sanctions on, 45; stigma of, 187–88; labeling/designation of, 188–90; implication of, 189, 191. See also Alcoholism; Medicalization
Dichotomous introspection, 194
Disease, as metaphor, 191
Dramaturgical team, 93

Emotions: jealousy, 23; emotionality, 59–60, 91–95, 107, 124, 156, 165, 170, 172; anger, 59–60, 94–95, 103, 154; catch-22, 60, 63; embarrassment, 91–94, 103, 112, 156; management of, 95; resentment, 96, 154, 173; justification of, 99–101; stress, 103; rejection, 103–4; fear, 103–5, 156; guilt, 104, 154–55; intimidation, 109, 156; release of, 118. See also Face/facework; Self
Enabler, 150. See also Codependency; Rehabilitation programs
Expressions: given, 40; given-off, 40

Face/facework, 92, 132. See also Role performance
Family: with history of alcoholism, 50; organization, 97; problematic, 97; forbearance of members, 127–28, 138
Family program. See Rehabilitation programs

Feminist scholarship, 14
Forbearance. *See* Family

Generalized other, 12, 40, 44, 79

Home treatments, 185

Imagination, impact of, 114–16
Interaction. *See* Social interaction; Social interactional strategies/stances
Interaction-based model, 185

Labeling. *See* Deviance
Latent function, 196

Marginalization, 195–96
Medicalization: trend, 13, 188–89; social consequences of, 191
Moral career: definition of, ix–x, 4–6, 63, 184, 188, 200; challenges of, 5, 12, 51, 85, 95, 97, 103, 112, 124, 132, 155–57, 160, 162, 176, 181–82, 199; cumulative effects, 7; phases of, 7–8, 15; as process, 8, 14, 54, 67–68, 108, 138; public dimensions, 9, 13, 35, 45, 116, 121, 201; personal dimensions, 9, 13, 35, 116, 121, 201; contingencies, 13, 15, 66, 83, 94, 98, 125, 143, 149, 185; and gender, 15, 197–200; early (problem) phase, 19, 22, 24, 27–28, 33, 110; problem amplification phase, 24, 27, 29, 37–38, 52, 80, 84, 100, 108, 110, 124, 130, 137–38, 148, 154, 157, 170, 175; character of, 27, 63, 98, 200–201; negative case of, 68, 199; proximal treatment phase, 137–38, 143, 154, 163, 165, 170; post-treatment phase, 166, 169–70, 172,

175; transitioning out of, 180. *See also* Self
Motive talk: accounts, 10, 81; offerings, 19, 66, 78, 82, 185; vocabularies of, 79–81; definitional ambivalence in, 80; breakdown of, 80, 83; negotiability of, 80–81; shifts in, 80–81; excuse accounts, 81; justification accounts, 81; techniques of neutralization, 81; acceptability of, 82; disclaimer, 84

No-exit model, 193–94
Normalizing problematic behaviors, 20, 30, 38, 94
Norms of interaction or performance/ Normative expectations. *See* Social interaction

Paradox of freedom and constraint, 114–16
Problems: designation of, 8–9, 24, 27–29, 31–32, 36, 38, 40, 44, 52, 78, 139, 141, 185; perceived sources of, 10, 30–31, 62, 78, 89–91, 137, 141, 150, 154, 158, 178, 190, 197; gradual buildup of, 31; resulting from drinking, 34, 80, 137, 148, 178; duration of, 37; negation of, 42, 94; deception about, 44; continuation of, 61; validation of, 100; management of, 120; recasting of, 139, 158, 160; and self-involvement, 199–200. *See also* Alcoholism; Definition of the situation

Reality testing, 28, 37–50
Rehabilitation programs: family, 13, 28, 34, 58, 111, 145–47, 149, 151, 154, 156–57, 159–63, 170–71, 174–75, 181–82, 188–

92, 196, 198; Al-Anon, 15, 34, 55, 111–
12, 137, 148–51, 163, 170, 174–75, 181–
82, 189, 190–92, 194–96, 198; Alcoholics Anonymous, 15, 55, 194; husbands' reasons for entering, 143–44;
treatment for alcoholism, 143–44,
146–47, 181; wives' reasons for entering, 144–46; resocialization in, 148,
169, 171; jargon of, 150, 159–61, 163,
170–71; working the program, 152,
163, 194; recovery in, 157, 191–94
Reification, 115
Remedial interchanges, 39, 125. *See also*
Aligning actions; Apologies
Resocialization. *See* Rehabilitation programs
Retrospective reinterpretations, 73
Rhetorical participation, 193–94
Role performance, 20–22, 44, 53, 56,
73–74, 79, 89, 92
Role-taking, 12, 40, 69, 79, 141, 149

Secrecy. *See* Social interactional strat-
egies/stances
Self: as process, 11, 110; imagery/ definition of, 14, 39, 40–41, 58–63, 66–68,
70, 74, 86, 88–90, 95, 97–98, 101–3,
107–8, 111, 116, 118, 124, 128, 130, 143–
44, 148, 154–56, 165, 169, 172–73, 180–
82, 190, 195, 197, 200; changing views
of, 41, 44–49, 54, 56, 58–62, 64–65,
76, 147, 149–50, 159, 162–63, 165, 174;
self-esteem, 58, 61, 76, 90, 107, 120;
self-blaming, 61–62, 80, 90, 141, 149,
161, 185, 190; looking-glass, 62, 69, 90,
162; and violence, 66; validation of,
83; performances of, 93, 99, 110, 121,
129, 137, 141, 170, 181; disavowal of,

94–95, 101; self-awareness, 95; emotionally divided, 95; impoverished/
eroded, 97; survival of, 97, 116, 138,
186; self-doubt, 137–38; refocus
on/reinforcement of, 138, 140–43,
147, 162; dissociation from husband,
148, 157, 160; responsibility of/for,
159–60; reconstruction of, 162, 188,
201; vindication of, 173; anti-model
of, 180; essence of, 194–95; crisis of,
196. *See also* Deficient negotiated-self;
Definitional ambivalence; Definition
of the situation; Moral career; Role
performance; Struggling self; Stultifying interaction context; Violence
Sensitizing concepts, 98, 103. *See also*
Deficient negotiated-self; Stultifying
interaction context
Sober comportment, 48
Social construction of reality, 36, 115,
190
Social interaction: line of action, 22;
norms of, 22, 44–45, 79–80, 114, 116,
127–28, 132; order in, 39; factors of, 51,
79, 102, 113, 117, 155, 162; organizing
principle of, 83; disorganization in,
127; factors beyond one's control, 137;
factors within one's control, 138. *See
also* Social interactional strategies/
stances; Stultifying interaction context
Social interactional strategies/stances:
withdrawal, 70; sidetracking, 70, 84;
verbal comeback, 70, 84; turnaround,
71, 84; no-talk, 72; interpersonal
level, 73; structural level, 73; verbal
confrontation, 73, 109–11; knowing
as, 74; *at* another or *with* another, 76;

altercasting, 84; individualism, 87; isolation, 87, 90, 93, 112–13, 116–17; secrecy, 87–90, 93; start-up and halt, 101; placation, 109; ignoring, 118; hoping, 125–32; bargaining, 125–32, 138; as choice or creation, 138. *See also* Apologies; Definitional ambivalence

Social invisibility, 198

Social object, 12, 115, 121, 165

Social power, 114, 138, 144, 197, 199–200

Social solidarity, 195–96

Social stigma. *See* Deviance

Sociodemographic characteristics of study sample, 1–2

Sociological ambivalence, 6, 23, 187, 201. *See also* Definitional ambivalence

Sociological imagination, 116, 201

Sociology of knowledge, 14

Stages of adjustment, 185

Struggling self, 194–95, 201

Study sample, sociodemographic characteristics of, 1–2

Stultifying interaction context, 98–103, 181, 188

Symbolic interaction: theoretical framework, 11–14, 68, 115, 187

Taking the role of others. *See* Role-taking

Transcenders, 193–94

Treadmillers, 193–94

Trouble: normal, 36; special, 36. *See also* Definitional ambivalence; Problems

Twelve-step groups: philosophy/ideology of, 15, 194–95. *See also* Rehabilitation programs

Uniqueness. *See* Aura of uniqueness

Violence: construction of, 63; paradoxical, 63; perpetrator of, 63; victim of, 63; lack of, 63–64; anticipated, 65; battering, 65; rejector of, 66; tolerator of, 66; episodes of, 66, 68; emotional activity toward, 69

Wives of alcoholics, 149–50, 169, 184–85. *See also* Codependency